I am not referring to a
(though yes, that is a big ele

I am talking about the price you **extract** from

your audience, your witnesses, your co-conspirators,

the eternal exchange of time and attention
for an experience that should leave them
irrevocably **changed**.

Welcome to theater that **digs deep**,

spits blood...

demands
answers,

bulldozes *forward* towards the center of

tru

Theater that does not ask for permission.
Theater that provokes and inspires you to
get off up the couch.

Open a door.

Tear   down

the   walls.

Plays that don't just cause ripples,

but ones that cause *seismic shifts,*

**that change how we talk
about the land in front of us
and the people around us.**

Welcome to theater that dreams big

and indeed does believe it can change the world because what other reason do we have to tell stories? With the measuring sand of our lives spilling o u t f r o m under- n e a t h us, merely telling a story is not enough in today's climate. Theater is a platform, a space that is only so useful as it incites. That it makes the fleeting impermanence of the medium permanent in some unexpected way.

We live in dark times. That is true. But recall:
the world has always been dark and fearful.
Since the earliest days, we have always in some
way lived on the precipice of what could be.
Our world is one of entropy, born out of the
universal tendency for things to fall apart.
But that is not who we are as human beings.
Our tenacity, the fight inside of us is endless.
Our world is one of constant aspiration,
constant striving.

Chaos

is the nature
of the
universe

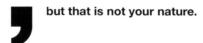 **but that is not your nature.**

It has not been since you were a babe in arms.

We are **makers.**

We are **doers.**

Our sense of injustice and
our wonder for the world
does not allow us to
simply lay dormant.

We follow in the footsteps of our heroes, our teachers, the civilly disobedient that came before us, once as confused and flummoxed as you feel today. Now is not the time to stand down, to wait for another to fight for what you hold so dear, to be anything but defiant. Do not wait for your turn. Find the story within you, what cannot wait until tomorrow.

Stories still have power.
There is nothing more ancient, more powerful, more dangerous than a story, the eternal empathy maker. They are—or should be—the battle cry of every generation, the tool we wield to help the world love what we love, see what we know to be right and true.

Others tell stories to preach to the choir, to get fame, to reiterate, to impress. Do not settle for comfort. Comfort is deceptive, and is unworthy of your time or talents. Embrace the strange, the unfamiliar, the uncanny, the "un-home-like." Respond to the ache in your heart, the wrong you seek to right in the universe. That is your compass.

Harness that power inside of you. Fists raised but hearts open, you are the lighthouses, the truthbringers, the seekers of justice. Run face first into complicated stories of our time with no easy answers, paint me a picture of the world with all ugliness, grace, transcendence, and contrariness.

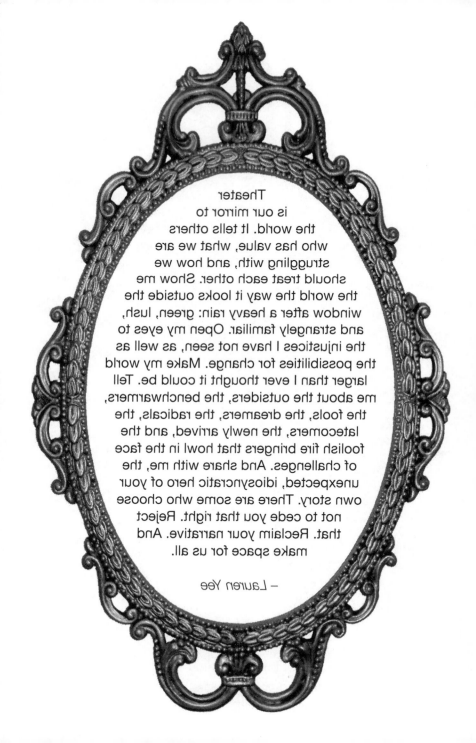

Theater
is our mirror to
the world. It tells others
who has value, what we are
struggling with, and how we
should treat each other. Show me
the world the way it looks outside the
window after a heavy rain: green, lush,
and strangely familiar. Open my eyes to
the injustices I have not seen, as well as
the possibilities for change. Make my world
larger than I ever thought it could be. Tell
me about the outsiders, the benchwarmers,
the fools, the dreamers, the radicals, the
latecomers, the newly arrived, and the
foolish fire bringers that howl in the face
of challenges. And share with me, the
unexpected, idiosyncratic hero of your
own story. There are some who choose
not to cede you that right. Reject
that. Reclaim your narrative. And
make space for us all.

– Lauren Yee

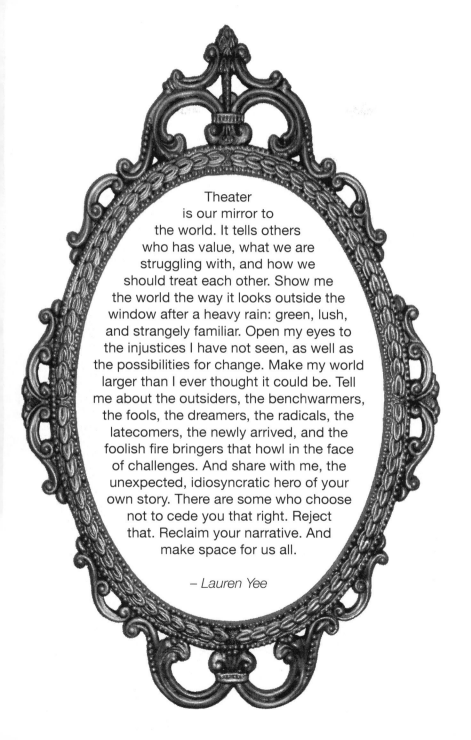

Theater
is our mirror to
the world. It tells others
who has value, what we are
struggling with, and how we
should treat each other. Show me
the world the way it looks outside the
window after a heavy rain: green, lush,
and strangely familiar. Open my eyes to
the injustices I have not seen, as well as
the possibilities for change. Make my world
larger than I ever thought it could be. Tell
me about the outsiders, the benchwarmers,
the fools, the dreamers, the radicals, the
latecomers, the newly arrived, and the
foolish fire bringers that howl in the face
of challenges. And share with me, the
unexpected, idiosyncratic hero of your
own story. There are some who choose
not to cede you that right. Reject
that. Reclaim your narrative. And
make space for us all.

– *Lauren Yee*

man·i·fes·to (man-*uh*-fes-to) A public declaration of principles, policies, or intentions, especially of a political nature.

MANIFESTO series

edited by
Lauren Yee

Volume 5

Benjamin Benne

Keiko Green

Karen Hartman

Elizabeth Heffron

Don X. Nguyen

Seayoung Yim

CONTENTS

ACKNOWLEDGEMENTS

The editors wish to thank the following for their assistance
in compiling this volume.

18th & Union

Pruzan Abode

Rain City Projects is powered by Shunpike.

FOREWARD

In your hands is the fifth book in the Manifesto Series. These are plays born and raised in the Pacific Northwest. Here, we have lots of coffee. We are arguably the center of the tech industry. We have great music. And we do really great theater.

In the 1990s I read somewhere that the quantity of new work produced in the greater Seattle area was second only to New York. Since then, theaters have come and gone, and come and gone again, yet through it all this area has remained a locus for world-class plays, and a feeding ground for the artists that create them.

Rain City Projects started in 1992 to support, encourage, and nourish this community. Over the years we've changed as much as this town has, yet our passion has never waned. This book is an example of our continued excitement. This book is an advertisement for the dynamic and provocative work being produced in this part of the world.

This is not your ordinary, run of the mill anthology. It is the artistic declaration of the playwright Lauren Yee, who in this guise as editor, is a vibrant provocateur with a bold vision to impart. Lauren Yee hand-picked these seven plays with purpose. They are her call to action, her demand to challenge and provoke, and of course to entertain.

These plays are as fresh as morning dew. They don't merely reflect our times, but reach out, grab you by the heart, slap you in the face, and scream with immediacy. These plays will submerge you in disparate and dynamic points of view, make you wrestle with the world, and in the end inspire you to cheer. They are the sound, color, light, space, time, and movement of theater right here, right now.

We want you to embrace these plays. Remember them. Produce them. Preach about them, because that's why this book is being spread to the four corners of the globe in the first place.

Thank you, Lauren Yee, for turning us on to them; thank you for having the vision to see what we are all about to see.

Enjoy.

– K. Brian Neel
Board Member, Rain City Projects
raincityprojects.org

Volume 5

BENJAMIN BENNE is a 2017–18 McKnight Fellow in Playwriting at the Playwrights' Center and was previously a 2016–17 Many Voices Fellow. He is a winner of the Robert Chesley/Victor Bumbalo Playwriting Award, runner-up for the National Latino Playwriting Award, finalist for the Princess Grace Award, finalist for the Ingram New Works Lab, and a semifinalist for the Blue Ink Playwriting Award. His work has been produced by Annex Theatre, Forward Flux Productions, and Pillsbury House Theatre, as well as developed by The Lark's Playwrights' Week, Two River Theater, Seattle Repertory Theatre, A Contemporary Theatre, Umbrella Project, Parley, and The Playwrights' Center, among others. His plays have been finalists for the O'Neill National Playwrights Conference, Bay Area Playwrights Festival, Headwaters New Play Festival, and Austin Playhouse's Festival of New American Plays. He was born and raised in Los Angeles County, considers Seattle his home, and currently resides in Minneapolis, MN.

Benjamin Benne

Terra Incognita

a play about the unknown

For my father,
Jules Lawrence Benne
(January 5, 1954–February 2, 2013)

CHARACTERS:

NADIA   female, black, 20s.

SHEILA   female, white, early 60s. Nadia's social worker.

SIMON   male, black, late 20s (but looks early 20s).
A Job Placement Specialist.

X.   male, black, early 20s. Nadia's ex-lover.

ANGEL   (also appears as **ATTENDANT**, **BARISTA**, and **GUÍA**)
A shape-shifting being that appears at pivotal crossroads.

CASTING NOTES:

Simon and X. are to be played by the same actor.

The actor or actress who plays Angel/Guía should speak Spanish fluidly/fluently.

The audience ought to be able to recognize that the same actor playing Angel is
playing the additional roles of Attendant, Barista, and Guía.

The actress who plays Sheila should speak some Spanish, albeit imperfectly.

TIME AND PLACE:

The present. Winter transitioning to spring in Seattle, WA.

NOTES ON PRODUCTION:

Dialogue in [ ] are implied or included to clarify meaning but not intended to be spoken aloud.

A slash (/) indicates the point of overlap in dialogue.

The setting descriptions and stage directions contained herein are intended to evoke the atmosphere. How they are conveyed through production is left open. I do feel, however, that suggestion is often more effective than literal representation.

It has been suggested that due to the organic/sensual/primal/ethereal sensibility of this play that it would be appropriate to present it outdoors—at a single or various locations. Again, this choice is left open.

In the world premiere production, for staging purposes, the character X. was confined to the bathtub (as if it were his coffin).

An intermission was taken between Parts I and II. This is optional.

PROLOGUE

Otherworldly light. Angel, an androgynous, wooly being dressed in gauzy tatters, appears on high. They bear a machete in a sheath at their side.

Nadia appears in an isolated pool of light.

She stares into a vanity.

She smears moisturizer on her face.

ANGEL: one's domain is the embers of an old flame

the rotten pulp of the past

a slave to the nectar of nostalgia

she clings to the cinders rather than succumb to despair

Sheila appears in an isolated pool of light.

She stares into a vanity.

She counts her white hairs.

ANGEL: the other's domain is the tides of change

the cleansing waves of the future

but she is consumed with the fear of crops to come

or, truly, the fear that crops will not come

Nadia adorns herself with earrings.

Sheila adorns herself with a pearl necklace.

ANGEL: while the roots of change stem from within

they search for someone who knows the flavor of their sorrow

Nadia and Sheila open their umbrellas.

ANGEL: spicy as cayenne
   and for someone who knows the flavor of their ecstasy
   sweet as mango
   a mirror who reflects their Truth
   (*realization*) together . . . transformation!
   the sun spots will lead the way to land unknown . . .
      Nadia and Sheila face opposite directions and walk away.
      Angel performs a militaristic march.
      The sound of thunder and rainfall.
      Lights out.

PART I

Scene I
      The sound of a clock ticking.
      In darkness:
SHEILA: Have you or a member of your family of origin had an addiction to alcohol?

NADIA: Yeah.

SHEILA: Who?

NADIA: You know the answer to that.

SHEILA: I'm sorry?

NADIA: Me.

SHEILA: Right. I'm still required to ask. Have you been treated or are you currently in treatment for that?

NADIA: Yeah, I'm in AA.

SHEILA: Have you or a member of your family of origin had an addiction to drugs?

NADIA: Yeah.
      Lights fade up slowly.
SHEILA: You?

NADIA: No, my momma.

SHEILA: Has she been, or is she currently being, treated for that?

NADIA: She's clean now. Excuse me, but you've been asking me questions since I walked through that door—so how many more of these you got?

SHEILA: We're just about half way through.

NADIA: Shit.

SHEILA: Have you or a member of your family of origin had an addiction to food or eating?

NADIA: No.

SHEILA: Have you or a member of your family of origin had an addiction to caffeine?

NADIA: Are you for real?

Sheila maintains a stern composure.

NADIA: . . . Nah.

SHEILA: Have you or a member of your family of origin had an addiction to sex or pornography?

NADIA: No.

Lights up at full to reveal Nadia and Sheila sitting in an impersonal, clinical, stale, claustrophobic, antiquated room. The white walls feel angular, irregular—they are narrowing, caving, closing in. This is Sheila's office.

Sheila scribbles notes.

SHEILA: Have you ever been physically abused?

A slight beat pregnant with hesitation. A crow caws outside.

NADIA: (*a lie*) No.

Sheila catches whiff of the lie.

SHEILA: Have you ever been emotionally abused?

NADIA: Nah.

SHEILA: Have you ever been sexually abused?

NADIA: Nah.

SHEILA: Have you ever been physically abused?

NADIA: You asked me that already.

SHEILA: Have you?

NADIA: I said, "No."

SHEILA: Did you ever witness any physical violence in your home or elsewhere growing up?

NADIA: I guess . . . yeah. / Not really.

SHEILA: Involving whom?

NADIA: I dunno. Just back in the day. When I was a girl, I always heard yelling next door and then the neighbor would come over with a black eye or whatever.

SHEILA: How old were you at the time of this incident?

NADIA: I dunno. Little . . . You know what? I'm actually not cool with this.

SHEILA: I understand that these are difficult questions. It's alright to feel uncomfortable.

NADIA: My sponsor didn't say I was gonna have to answer a bunch of shitty, fucking questions. He said you was gonna help me.

SHEILA: I am required by law to ask certain questions and document the answers. But this is a safe space. Everything we discuss is confidential.

NADIA: You know what? Fuck you and fuck your questions.

SHEILA: Nadia, wait. .

NADIA: I don't gotta be here.

SHEILA: Nadia.

NADIA: / I'm out.

SHEILA: Please, wait. What brought you here today?

NADIA: I dunno.

SHEILA: Well, simply, why are you here?

NADIA: 'Cause.

SHEILA: Because?

NADIA: Look, I been sober for twelve days, three months, and one year now. Right?

Sheila brushes her fingertips lightly over her strand of pearls.

NADIA: Things was fucking dark as shit for me for a while, aiight? And then they was getting better. But now, I don't got no job and my sponsor's being an asshole and I feel alone and everything's going to shit, again, so—fuck this. / For real, fuck this.

SHEILA: Nadia. Please wait. I know that this is difficult. Really, I do. But . . .

Sheila abandons her note taking.

SHEILA: (*warmer*) Would you be willing to try something for me, please?

NADIA: Depends.

SHEILA: Would you just sit for a moment, please?

Nadia complies.

SHEILA: Can we just breathe for a moment?

NADIA: I am breathing.

SHEILA: Yes. But many times when we breathe, we keep a lot of old, stale air in our lungs.

NADIA: So?

SHEILA: So, about 20% of the air in your lungs is old. You've been carrying it around with you for maybe an hour or a day, a week, a month or—

NADIA: Twelve days, three months, and one year.

SHEILA: Or even longer. And carrying old things can weigh us down. They can make us feel heavy or inadequate or afraid to move forward.

NADIA: K, I got you.

SHEILA: So, you'll try this with me?

NADIA: Yeah.

SHEILA: We're going to break this down into a few steps.

NADIA: Better not be twelve.

SHEILA: Four. Think you can handle that?

NADIA: Aiight.

SHEILA: First step: inhale. Second step: hold it. Third step: exhale. Fourth step: keep exhaling.And then—

NADIA: Repeat.

SHEILA: There. You got it. And we're going to breathe and just LET GO— let go of everything.

NADIA: K.

SHEILA: Inhale.

> *They do.*

SHEILA: Hold.

> *They do.*

SHEILA: Exhale.

> *They do.*

SHEILA: Keep exhaling . . .

> *They do.*

SHEILA: Repeat.

> *They do.*

SHEILA: How are we?

NADIA: Cool.

SHEILA: May I continue?

> *A crow caws outside. Nadia looks out the window.*

SHEILA: Nadia? Are you alright?

NADIA: Yeah, fine.

SHEILA: Shall we continue?

> *Nadia nods. A crow caw.*
>
> *Lights shift to denote the passage of time.*

Scene 2

> *Sheila's office. One week later. A clock ticking. Nadia enters.*

NADIA: Hey.

SHEILA: Welcome back. It's good to see you.

NADIA: You really mean that?

SHEILA: I do. Can I get you anything?

NADIA: You got some soda?

SHEILA: Sorry?

NADIA: I'm thirsty.

SHEILA: Oh, no I don't.

NADIA: Then, why'd you ask if I need anything?

SHEILA: Sorry, it's a polite formality—nobody ever takes me up on it. Would some water suffice?

NADIA: Nah, it's cool.

SHEILA: You sure?

NADIA: Look, you shouldn't offer if you can't deliver.

SHEILA: Point taken. So . . . Did anything happen that held meaning for you this week?

NADIA: Uh, what do you mean by that exactly?

SHEILA: Did anything happen that felt new or significant?

NADIA: New? Like new "new"?

Sheila nods.

NADIA: I dunno—I bought a new kind of soap this week.

SHEILA: A change?

NADIA: Yeah.

SHEILA: What kind was it?

NADIA: It smells like peach. I like it.

SHEILA: That sounds like a gentle, self-loving gesture. Bravo.

NADIA: It was just soap.

SHEILA: Anything else?

NADIA: Um . . . I got a crow following me.

SHEILA: What do you mean by "following"?

NADIA: I just see this crow everywhere I go.

SHEILA: And when did that start?

NADIA: Last week. First time I came to see you. He was outside after.

SHEILA: Uh-huh. So what do you think that means?

NADIA: I dunno. But it seemed important, so I said it.

SHEILA: Why did that seem important?

NADIA: Seriously? I answered a shit ton of questions for you last week. Is it just gonna be more of the same week after week?

SHEILA: Very well. Nadia, would you be willing to try something different this week?

NADIA: What?

SHEILA: An experiment.

NADIA: I'm listening.

SHEILA: I would like to open this up into a dialogue.

NADIA: How's that gonna work?

SHEILA: Well, I might ask a question. Then you might ask a question. I might say something or you might. We can just—talk. Do you think we can do that?

NADIA: Aiight.

A beat pregnant with hesitation.

NADIA: You gonna ask a question first or what?

SHEILA: Alright. What did you do today before you came here?

NADIA: Nothing.

SHEILA: Maybe there was some small thing that you enjoyed?

NADIA: I dunno.

SHEILA: Is there a part of your daily morning routine that you enjoy?

NADIA: . . . I like putting my earrings on.

SHEILA: Why's that?

NADIA: I dunno. I just do. K, my turn. You like wearing them things?

SHEILA: What these [pearls]?

NADIA: Yeah.

SHEILA: I do actually.

NADIA: Don't you think they look kinda . . . old?

SHEILA: Well, they belonged to my grandmother. So they are very old.

NADIA: You like wearing old shit?

SHEILA: (*pointed*) Honey, have you looked at me? (*removing her glasses*) Take a real good, long look at me. THIS is what age looks like. There was a time I looked like you.

NADIA: You was never black.

SHEILA: I meant young and firm. But, one day, you'll wake up with a web of these splashed across your face too.

NADIA: Not me, I moisturize. So what did you do this morning?

SHEILA: I counted my white hairs.

NADIA: All of those?

SHEILA: Not the silver ones—just the white ones.

NADIA: Still, you like doing that?

SHEILA: (*a lie*) I do.

Nadia catches whiff of the lie.

NADIA: Huh. Don't that make you sad?

SHEILA: Why would that make a person sad?

NADIA: Means you're getting old. That you're gonna die . . . soon. Unless you wanna die.

SHEILA: Now, why would a person want to die?

NADIA: I dunno, some do.

SHEILA: Do you identify as one of those people?

NADIA: Do you?

SHEILA: Personally, I don't, no.

NADIA: So you think you can fix me?

SHEILA: What is it that you think needs to be "fixed"?

NADIA: I dunno . . . it's hard to put some of this into words . . . but . . . um . . . I think I'm broken.

SHEILA: I don't use the word "broken."

NADIA: But I don't got a job. I don't got people—I don't got anything.

SHEILA: You don't have any family or friends close by?

NADIA: My momma.

SHEILA: And how would you describe your relationship to her?

NADIA: We don't talk any more.

SHEILA: And why is that?

NADIA: 'Cause she don't wanna talk to me.

SHEILA: But you would like to talk to her.

NADIA: I dunno. When I went to do the "amends," she slammed the door in my face—BAM. Made my nose even flatter.

SHEILA: Nadia, look in the mirror.

Nadia crosses to the mirror.

SHEILA: What do you see when you look at yourself?

NADIA: I dunno any more. I used to have a fire inside of me—(*indicates chest/stomach*) it was right here. But I can't feel it any more—so where did it go?

SHEILA: That fire inside of you. Who's seen it? Your mother?

NADIA: When my momma see me, all she sees is an alcoholic.

SHEILA: Then who's seen it?

NADIA: I dunno.

SHEILA: Who really knows you?

NADIA: Look, my sponsor didn't say anything about this psychiatry bullshit.

SHEILA: / It's not—

NADIA: I just need a job real bad. Can we just deal with that?

SHEILA: Nadia, what line of work do you have an interest in pursuing?

NADIA: I don't care.

SHEILA: But what about your ideal—what might that look like?

NADIA: I dunno.

SHEILA: If you could do anything—what would you want to do?

NADIA: I. Don't. Know.

SHEILA: Come on. Dream a little for me.

NADIA: I can't do *anything*, you know? Everybody's got limits.

SHEILA: OK. So what are yours?

A crow caws as the lights shift.

Scene 3

Sheila's office. One week later. A clock ticking. Nadia enters.

NADIA: Hey.

SHEILA: You're here.

NADIA: Yeah.

SHEILA: I didn't think you were going to show. Your session is almost up.

NADIA: I know . . . sorry. Look, can we just get to it?

SHEILA: Very well. So did anything happen that held meaning for you this week?

Nadia stares out the window, distracted.

SHEILA: Are you alright?

NADIA: Yeah, it's just . . .

SHEILA: What is it?

NADIA: You know how I said that there's a crow following me?

SHEILA: That rings a bell.

NADIA: Well, that motherfucker is still following me—like a shadow. He's out there right now.

SHEILA: Crows all look basically the same. How do you know it's the same one?

NADIA: I just know.

SHEILA: And?

NADIA: And he just watches me. Stares at me. Creeps me the fuck out.

Nadia stares out the window.

SHEILA: Nadia?

NADIA: Nevermind.

SHEILA: If you want to talk about it.

NADIA: I said, "Nevermind." Let's talk work.

SHEILA: Fine. Have you thought more about your ideal?

NADIA: Yeah. (*animated, dreaming*) So I'd really like to do something futuristic—with like, I dunno, computers or robots or something. Fuck the past, right?

SHEILA: Do you have experience with computers?

NADIA: No, but you said to dream, right? And I'm a hard worker.

SHEILA: Do you have a resume?

NADIA: Nah.

SHEILA: Well, let's start there. First, we need an objective. This is where having that ideal comes in handy.

NADIA: Look, I'll do whatever. But I kinda fucking hate people.

SHEILA: Well, let's say, "Seeking a position that will allow me to develop and apply my interpersonal skills."

NADIA: Did you just come up with that right now?

SHEILA: I've been doing this a long time.

    Sheila writes.

NADIA: Hey, so you know how you asked me last week about who really knows me?

    Sheila nods.

NADIA: (*self-conscious*) Sorry, this is kinda weird but . . . what if the person who knows you best is gone?

SHEILA: Pardon me?

NADIA: What if they're dead?

SHEILA: Well, how did this person make you feel about yourself?

NADIA: He made me feel . . . sexy.

SHEILA: Would you care to elaborate?

NADIA: Just like . . . I dunno . . .

    For the first time in the play, Nadia's body becomes truly animated, liquid, serpentine.

    We see the embers of her old flame. X.'s silhouette appears.

NADIA: *Ssssexxxy.* Powerful. Like every part of me is beautiful—even my ears. Like every part of me is fire.

    A smile slips away from Sheila. X.'s silhouette vanishes.

NADIA: What? You laughing at me?

SHEILA: No.

NADIA: I don't think you laughing at me is very professional.

SHEILA: I wasn't laughing at you. You just seem . . . brighter. Invigorated. Do you feel that?

NADIA: (*a lie*) Nah, not really.

SHEILA: What was his name?

NADIA: X.

SHEILA: X as in . . . ?

NADIA: Just "X."

A beat. A crow caw is heard outside.

SHEILA: We're just about at time, so how about we pick up with this next week?

NADIA: But it's 11:50.

SHEILA: Yes, lunch time.

NADIA: But don't I get an hour?

SHEILA: You were tardy.

NADIA: Right, but why don't I get 'til twelve?

SHEILA: Well, a session is only fifty minutes actually.

NADIA: So, question for you: why do you say a session's a hour when it's only fifty minutes "actually"?

SHEILA: We just do.

A moment in which they both consider the absurdity of this.

NADIA: Yeah, that don't seem right.

SHEILA: Very well then, Nadia, I'd like to make a proposition.

NADIA: Shoot.

SHEILA: Next week, we're going to have a session that won't take place in the office.

NADIA: K, so where we gonna go?

SHEILA: It'll be a surprise.

Lights shift to denote the passage of time. A soundscape of birds.

Scene 4

One week later. A Ferris wheel with a view of the sea. It feels magical, otherworldly.

NADIA: You sure this thing's safe?

SHEILA: It may feel intimidating initially, but trust that everything will be fine.

Angel appears as an Attendant.

ATTENDANT: (*to Nadia, authentically*) Watch your step. Watch your head.

(*to Sheila, deadpan*) Watch your step. Watch your head.

Sheila and Nadia situate themselves in the gondola.

ATTENDANT: The Ferris wheel ride is three revolutions. Should you need to get off at any time, you can hit this [centrally located] button right here [above your heads] and we'll stop the ride and let you off. Alright? (*to Nadia*) Enjoy.

Attendant seals them inside and vanishes. It appears as though Nadia and Sheila are floating through space.

SHEILA: Are you feeling anxious?

NADIA: I'm just breathing.

SHEILA: Would you like to breathe together?

NADIA: Nah, it's cool. When's this thing gonna get going?

SHEILA: Looks like they're still loading passengers.

NADIA: Well, they better hurry it up or I'm gonna have to hit that button.

SHEILA: (*distracting her*) Here.

Sheila gives Nadia a card.

NADIA: What's this?

SHEILA: This is a Job Placement Specialist.

NADIA: This guy's gonna get me a job?

SHEILA: I've written the appointment details on the back.

The Ferris wheel begins its first revolution. A whirl of colors.

SHEILA: Oh, here we go.

NADIA: Fuuuck. I think I'm gonna press the button.

SHEILA: What?

NADIA: I'm gonna press the button.

SHEILA: Is it really that bad?

NADIA: I'm gonna be sick.

SHEILA: Nadia, you're going to be fine. / Just breathe.

NADIA: I'm gonna press it. You gonna stop me? Look at me—

SHEILA: / Nadia?

NADIA: I'm gonna press it. / I'm gonna do it.

SHEILA: Nadia?

Nadia reaches a finger and withdraws it.

NADIA: Uh—

She reaches again and withdraws it.

NADIA: Uh—

Nadia laughs uproariously.

NADIA: I'm just fucking with you! You shoulda seen your face. Oh shit . . . WHEW! Sorry.

SHEILA: Don't waste your apologies on me. You're the one who's missing out.

NADIA: What's that supposed to mean?

SHEILA: Look.

Sheila motions to the world without. Nadia, now aware, absorbs the sight.

NADIA: (*in awe*) Whoa.

SHEILA: My grandma and I would ride on a Ferris wheel when she was alive . . . and I used to take my kids . . . when they were young. Their eyes would get all big and bugged out too.

NADIA: What's that supposed to mean?

SHEILA: Like this!

Sheila playfully bugs out her eyes to tease Nadia.

NADIA: Oh, I see how it is.

SHEILA: With eyes like yours, I'm sure you do.

NADIA: Ey! You know something?

SHEILA: What?

NADIA: You aiight.

SHEILA: So what do you see?

NADIA: Oh . . . shit.

SHEILA: What do you see?

NADIA: Nah, for real, there's bird shit all over that fucking roof.

SHEILA: A-ha. And I see the culprits. Gargoyle sea gulls.

NADIA: Fucking birds. I hate birds.

SHEILA: Me too.

NADIA: So how many kids you got?

SHEILA: Two girls, one boy.

NADIA: Where they at?

SHEILA: Oh, all over. Faraway.

NADIA: You go to see them or do they come to you?

SHEILA: I haven't traveled in a long time.

NADIA: Yeah? Me neither. Actually, I've never been on a plane, ever.

SHEILA: Really?

NADIA: Never, not ever. I've never been anywhere but here.

SHEILA: No one ever gets to go every place they wish or desire. But you know what?

NADIA: What?

SHEILA: I hate airplanes.

NADIA: For real?

SHEILA: I've never particularly enjoyed traveling.

NADIA: Yeah? Why not?

SHEILA: I could never shake that feeling of being a tourist.

NADIA: You saying you never feel like you fit in?

Sheila nods.

NADIA: I got you. I don't think this world got a place for me either.

SHEILA: But there has to be. Even in the cities where people live stacked on top of each other a hundred stories high, everyone manages to find a space.

NADIA: But I don't just want some *space*—I need a *place*, you know what I mean? A place that's like, "We want you. We. Want. You." But I don't know any places like that.

Sheila takes this in. Nadia gazes out of the gondola.

NADIA: So if you could go anywhere—where would you go?

SHEILA: The Mayan Ruins in Tikal.

NADIA: Yeah? Why?

SHEILA: Sometimes, I dream about them. In my dreams, there's this dazzling light and fabulous heat and exotic flavors unlike anything I've tasted . . . (*stopping herself*) So I guess I'd like to see if the way I imagine them measures up to the reality.

NADIA: Huh. Didn't the Mayans sacrifice people?

SHEILA: Captives from other tribes, yes.

NADIA: So just 'cause they from another tribe they get taken captive and killed? Now, that's fucked up.

SHEILA: They did it as an offering to the gods.

NADIA: Yeah, well, God can be a mean motherfucker.

Sheila nods in agreement. Nadia stares back out of the gondola.

SHEILA: Have you been with anyone since X.?

NADIA: Nah.

SHEILA: Is that something you can visualize happening for yourself in the future?

NADIA: Nah.

SHEILA: Why is that?

NADIA: I shoulda died with him.

SHEILA: What makes you say that?

Nadia shrugs.

SHEILA: How did it happen?

NADIA: Car accident. Spun off the freeway into a ditch. It was dark. He was drunk.

SHEILA: And you were with him?

NADIA: We was driving home from the desert. I just got banged up real good but he . . . He never wanted to put his seat belt on. But that's not what killed him. It was the airbag. That's what killed him. Funny, isn't it? The thing that's supposed to save him—killed him? That's some shit right there. Fucking bananas.

Sheila places a hand on Nadia's knee (or shoulder) to comfort her. Nadia allows it.

SHEILA: I'm sorry.

NADIA: There was no flowers or preacher-man or nothing like that. 'Cause it was just gonna be me. But the people at the place kept on asking a bunch of stupid questions like, "You wanna pay extra to put his name in cursive on the headstone? How do you feel about mahogany for the casket? Do you want satin lining?" So I say to them, "Can ya'll just put his body in a plain-fucking-wood box and stick it in the fucking ground—you think you can handle that?!" They said they'd call me when they did it. But those fucking assholes didn't even bother to call me—just forgot about me—'cause I'm not important enough to remember. They shoulda just buried me too.

SHEILA: Nadia, how long has it been?

NADIA: Two days, four months, and one year.

A beat.

NADIA: You know from down there—everything just looks so big and in-your-face. But from up here, it don't look so bad.

SHEILA: Isn't it amazing what some distance and perspective can do? Things can go from massive and daunting to small to smaller and smaller until they're just specks below.

A beat.

SHEILA: You know, it's like trying to hold water in the palms of your hands—you can't hold on forever.

NADIA: But you can try.

SHEILA: You can try.

NADIA: I wanna hold a piece of the wave.

SHEILA: But wouldn't you rather let it go so that you could build a sandcastle?

NADIA: Some waves are just too big to—(*snaps her fingers*) forget just like that.

SHEILA: I'm not talking about forgetting—I'm talking about opening yourself up to allow new waves to come in. Do you see what I mean?

NADIA: Huh.

SHEILA: Well?

NADIA: Yeah, maybe.

A beat. A flash of glittery light.

NADIA: You see all them beautiful places that looks like glitter or sequins or something—way out there?

SHEILA: The sunspots?

NADIA: Yeah. See all them sailboats trying to chase after them?

SHEILA: All headed for the distant light.

NADIA: Shoot. If I had a sailboat, that's where I'd be going. You know, most people are afraid to look you in the eye—they just kinda look in your general direction—but they don't really see you. Or you know how they say that thing about eyes and windows and souls? That's how it should be. Eye to eye, you know? Window to window. Soul to soul. I feel like you're actually looking at me and see me. I appreciate that.

Nadia is spent (giving compliments takes an unusual amount of effort for her).

SHEILA: That's what I'm here for. Anytime.

Lights shift.

Scene 5

A few days later. A café.

Nadia enters.

She sees Simon, who is seated.

He looks like X.

Nadia stares at him in disbelief.

Simon waves at her.

Nadia looks around, confused.

SIMON: Hello, you wouldn't happen to be Nadia?

NADIA: Yeah.

SIMON: Hi, I'm Simon.

NADIA: (*a realization*) You're Simon?

SIMON: That's me.

Nadia stares at him.

SIMON: Do I have something on my face?

NADIA: Nice to meet you.

SIMON: Likewise. Sheila told me that I'd recognize you by your earrings.

NADIA: My earrings? She didn't say, "Look for the black girl."

SIMON: No.

NADIA: She's a little devil.

SIMON: Excuse me?

NADIA: You don't see what she's doing—(*motioning to the two of them*) here?

SIMON: I'm sorry, I don't know what you mean.

NADIA: You know what? Never mind, cutie. (*flirtatious*) It smells kinda spicy in here, huh?

SIMON: Yeah, they actually make a hot chocolate with cayenne pepper here.

NADIA: No shit. Is it good?

SIMON: I don't know but I'm about to find out.

Nadia sits, she gets a little too comfortable and flirtatious.

Simon opens a folder and consults some pages.

SIMON: So how are you doing?

NADIA: (*groans*) Well, lemme tell you: I am having a HELL of a day.

SIMON: I'm sorry to hear that.

NADIA: See, the thing is, I got a stalker following me.

SIMON: I'm sorry, what?

NADIA: It's a crow—you know, one of them blackbirds. (*a little too loud*) Scary little motherfuckers!

Simon glances around uncomfortably.

SIMON: Huh.

NADIA: See, I was walking over here, right?

BARISTA: 12 oz hot chocolate special for Simon!

SIMON: Excuse me for a minute, that's my drink. Were you going to get a coffee or anything?

NADIA: You think they'd spike it for me?

SIMON: Um, I don't / think so.

NADIA: Kidding!

SIMON: / Ah.

NADIA: I'm just messing with you!

SIMON: / Right.

NADIA: But, seriously, I don't drink that caffeine stuff. But maybe I'll try one of them hot chocolates.

BARISTA: / Simon!

SIMON: Excuse me.

Simon gets his drink and reorients himself. Simon returns and consults his papers.

SIMON: So . . .

NADIA: So I'm walking down the street, right?

SIMON: / Let's see here—

NADIA: And I was just minding my own damn business—but I hear something coming behind me like—I dunno what—just whoooosh like trying to chop my fucking head off.

SIMON: This was the crow?

NADIA: Yeah, man—and that motherfucking bird makes this sound—and I thought I was gonna die—or have a heart attack or some shit!

SIMON: Really?

NADIA: Yeah. Here, lemme just show you.

SIMON: / Show me what?

NADIA: Just sit there and pretend you're me—minding my own damn business, right?

SIMON: . . . Okay.

> *Nadia goes behind Simon. She waits. Then maneuvers herself, undetected, right next to his ear.*

NADIA: (*mimicking the crow screech*) BLLLAHAHHHAH!!!

> *Simon jumps with a squeal. Nadia laughs at his reaction. Simon composes himself.*

NADIA: It's fucked up, right?

SIMON: Yeah.

NADIA: See? That's what I'm telling you.

SIMON: And this happened to you on your way here?

NADIA: Yeah and I bet it's still out there just waiting for me. I swear—if I ever get my hands on that little motherfucker—I'm gonna pick off every last one of his feathers and then I'm gonna—(*wringing her hands*)—twist his skinny, naked neck until it goes CRUNCH . . . So that's how my day's been. How 'bout you?

SIMON: Not nearly so exciting, I'm afraid.

NADIA: See, but you don't gotta be afraid 'cause you don't got a stupid crow all up in your business.

SIMON: You know, crows are actually really intelligent. Their brains are very similar to humans' brains.

NADIA: Oh yeah?

SIMON: They can recognize faces. Human faces.

NADIA: You making fun of me?

SIMON: No. Seriously. / They've done studies.

NADIA: You're fucking with me.

SIMON: They can even communicate that information to one another.

NADIA: They can talk to each other?

SIMON: And they have regional dialects.

NADIA: Get out of here. Get out of here! That's fucking bananas.

SIMON: (*trying to one up himself*) And they mate for life.

NADIA: Say what?

SIMON: You know they only have one partner / that they—

NADIA: Yeah, no, I got it. Just kind of a weird thing to say.

SIMON: Oh. Sorry.

NADIA: What's your name again?

SIMON: Simon.

NADIA: That's right—Simon. You cool. So you gonna help me find a job?

SIMON: That's what I'm supposed to be doing, / yes.

NADIA: That's something about them crows, man.

SIMON: Yeah, uh, trippy. (*back to business*) / So let's see here.

NADIA: Trippy, yeah. Exactly.

SIMON: According to your resume, you're looking for a position that will allow you to apply your interpersonal skills?

NADIA: Yeah.

SIMON: You enjoy working with people?

NADIA: Yeah, I love it. You sure you just don't wanna give me your job?

Nadia laughs at her own joke with gusto. Simon forces a chuckle.

NADIA: I'm just messing with you.

SIMON: / Yeah.

NADIA: How long you been doing this?

SIMON: For a little while / now.

NADIA: Yeah? You kinda new at it?

SIMON: I guess you could say that.

NADIA: You don't think it's kinda funny that Sheila set us up?

SIMON: No, why?

NADIA: She didn't tell me you were a brotha.

SIMON: (*back to business*) So you have sales experience?

NADIA: Yeah, I'm real good with people. And I love helping people. But you know what I hate?

SIMON: What?

NADIA: Self-checkout. At the store. You know what I'm saying?

SIMON: Yeah, I know what / self-checkout is—

NADIA: I mean, the one time that a white boy gotta do something for a black woman. And they take it away. And now I gotta do it by myself? The fuck is that bullshit, huh? Make me self-checkout, ring up all my own stuff and then bag it too—fuck that mess.

SIMON: I'm sorry, I don't follow [what you're saying].

NADIA: It's, like, the one thing we get and now they're trying to take it away. You know what I'm saying?

SIMON: I guess [not really].

NADIA: I mean, I don't gotta tell you—you know what *they* do to *us*. Shoot.

SIMON: "They"?

NADIA: (*a little too loudly*) You know, white people.

> Simon glances around uncomfortably.

SIMON: I mean, I've heard that things like that can happen. (*back to business*) Would you describe yourself as detail-oriented?

NADIA: What do you mean you "heard"? Are you saying nothing like that's ever happen to you?

SIMON: (*a lie*) No.

NADIA: Seriously? Never?

SIMON: Well . . . not really. No.

NADIA: For real? Either you're lying or you the luckiest son-of-a-bitch I ever met. You're rich, huh?

SIMON: No. (*back to business*) Would working as a customer service representative interest you?

NADIA: What's a "representative" do exactly?

SIMON: Sales on the floor of a retail store, if that's what you want.

NADIA: Yeah, sure. I can do that.

SIMON: Great.

> Simon scribbles notes.

NADIA: How old are you?

SIMON: Older than I look.

NADIA: Yeah, but how old?

SIMON: That's personal.

NADIA: You don't think it's funny that Sheila set me up with you?

SIMON: No. This isn't a "set-up."

NADIA: You sure about that?

SIMON: Positive.

NADIA: You're not wearing a ring.

SIMON: / No.

NADIA: You single?

SIMON: No.

NADIA: You a homo?

SIMON: / What?

NADIA: It's cool if you are—I'm just asking.

SIMON: Unbelievable.

NADIA: I'm just asking.

SIMON: You know, I don't have to wear a ring or be married to be in a meaningful relationship.

NADIA: / Yeah, I know that.

SIMON: And a ring is just a symbol. Nothing more.

NADIA: / I know.

SIMON: So don't make assumptions about me or my personal life.

NADIA: I was just asking some questions!

SIMON: (*putting his foot down*) I'm not asking questions about your personal life, so don't ask me about mine. This conversation is strictly business.

An unforeseen wave washes over Nadia. She cries.

SIMON: What . . .? I . . . I didn't . . . I'm sorry. I . . .

Nadia wipes her nose on her hand. Angel appears as Barista. They bring Nadia a tissue.

BARISTA: Here you go, sweetie.

Nadia blows her nose loudly.

BARISTA: Can I get you anything?

NADIA: Nah, I'm cool. Thanks.

BARISTA: You lemme know, OK?

Barista glares at Simon and walks away.

SIMON: Nadia?

NADIA: Yeah?

SIMON: I'm sorry.

NADIA: Nah, it's cool. It's not you. It's me. You just remind me of someone I know—or knew—or whatever.

SIMON: Nadia, can we get something straight? You are not interviewing me. I am interviewing you. I ask the questions. That's the *extent* of this relationship. You got me?

NADIA: Yeah, I got you.

SIMON: Great. Now, I can certainly vouch for the fact that you are very . . . confident in your approach to interacting with people. Do you feel confident in your ability to approach potential customers in a manner that would make them feel comfortable making purchases from you?

NADIA: Yeah.

SIMON: Show me.

NADIA: You mean like, (*putting on a "professional" demeanor complete with sparkle and pizzazz*) Hi. How you doing today? Good? My name is Nadia.

Is there some way I can assist you today? Any questions I can answer for you? Just lemme know. I'd be happy to help. (*dropping the act*) Aiight?

A smile sneaks away from Simon (though he tries to hide it). He scribbles notes.

NADIA: Is that what you wanted?

SIMON: Yeah, you got it. Alright, thank you. I will be in touch.

Simon shakes Nadia's hand.

SIMON: It's been a pleasure.

NADIA: You're not gonna finish your drink?

SIMON: The cayenne is too spicy for my taste. You have a good day. Oh, and don't antagonize the crows because you'll regret it.

NADIA: Hey, Simon!

NADIA: Is your boyfriend white?

Simon nods and exits.

NADIA: Yeah, it figures.

Nadia takes a sip of Simon's hot chocolate. She digs it. Lights fade out.

Scene 6

The following morning. Back in Sheila's office, claustrophobic. Sheila watches the clock and runs her fingers over the pearls dangling from her neck. Nadia enters, dripping wet, with an umbrella that is in shambles.

NADIA: Yo.

SHEILA: You're tardy again.

NADIA: / Uh—excuse me but—

SHEILA: Your session's almost up.

NADIA: Do you not see this?

SHEILA: What happened?

NADIA: You know what? Fuck it—you wouldn't believe me anyway.

SHEILA: Try me.

NADIA: K, you know that crow that's been following me?

SHEILA: You have my attention.

NADIA: That motherfucker just attacked me.

SHEILA: Attacked you?

NADIA: That's what I just said.

SHEILA: Would you care to elaborate?

NADIA: K, I was leaving my place with my umbrella and the rain's coming down real hard, right? And I see him up in this tree. His eyes to my eyes.

He goes "CAW." I just pull my umbrella down over my eyes and walk real fast, right? I hear "CAW" behind me then it gets real quiet. Then that motherfucker comes at me from behind and screeches right in my ear like a little bitch! He did that exact thing to me yesterday when I was meeting with Simon—so this time I was ready for him—I swing my fucking umbrella to get him, but then the wind comes—gives me a big ol' sucker punch—and fucks up my umbrella. Then that fucking crow comes at me again—he grabs my hair— and I'm screaming and trying to whack him—but he starts pulling and pulling at my hair until he takes out a big chunk and he flies back up into a tree going "CAW CAW CAW HA HA HA"—laughing at me. So now, here I am and my hair's gonna be fucked up all day. Motherfucker.

SHEILA: You keep referring to this crow as a "he."

NADIA: So?

SHEILA: Why do you think that is?

NADIA: Why's everything gotta mean something, huh? How about you just say, "Wow, that's really fucked up." And just leave it at that?

SHEILA: Very well. "That's fucked up." So you had your meeting with Simon yesterday. How did that go?

NADIA: (scoffing) I dunno. Why don't you tell me.

SHEILA: I'm sorry, we seem to have gotten off on the wrong foot here.

NADIA: What the fuck do you want from me, huh?

    A beat.

SHEILA: Have you been drinking?

NADIA: I wish! But, nah, I tried this hot chocolate with cayenne pepper. Real fucking good shit. So I had another and then another and another until I wasn't counting anymore—I didn't sleep a wink—what with all that sugar. Shoot . . . What?

    A beat.

SHEILA: Nadia, is this about the abuse?

NADIA: Excuse me?

SHEILA: (re: the crow) "He."

NADIA: What are you talking about?

SHEILA: I feel like you want to talk about this . . . you just don't know how.

    A beat.

NADIA: Are you fucking serious, right now?

SHEILA: Acknowledging is the first step toward healing our wounds. If you keep slapping on band-aids to hide and avoid confronting the infection, it will only get worse. I'm doing you a favor by starting the conversation. So, how often did he hurt you?

No response.

SHEILA: Was there a pattern, a trigger? Was it the alcohol?

NADIA: (*deflecting*) "Did anything happen this week that held meaning for you?"

SHEILA: Nadia, I'm asking / the questions right now.

NADIA: Did you find a shit ton of new white hairs and wrinkles in the mirror this morning?

SHEILA: We are not having a dialogue / right now.

NADIA: Oh yeah? When did that change?

SHEILA: Right now.

NADIA: I knew it—because you never really wanted to have a fucking "dialogue," / huh?

SHEILA: / That's not true.

NADIA: You really just wanna question me, school me, attack me.

SHEILA: You said that X. made you feel special. What you haven't acknowledged is how he also hurt you.

NADIA: (*an ultimatum*) Really? We're gonna go there? Right now, huh?

A beat.

NADIA: Oh, I get it. You just want me to say that I'm mad and that he was a bad man, right?

SHEILA: You and X. were clearly enmeshed / in a way that was unhealthy

NADIA: Yeah, that's what you wanna hear. Easy peasy. Black and white, right? But you don't know how he's been *in* me—how he *is* in me— / and how I still wear him *on* me.

SHEILA: Nadia, you're allowing him to hinder you from exploring the possibility of finding love elsewhere. Would he want that for you?

NADIA: Duh! He wouldn't want me to be with nobody else obviously.

SHEILA: But is that what you want for yourself?

NADIA: I loved him—all of him.

SHEILA: Why do you think he wouldn't want you to be with another person?

NADIA: 'Cause he's the crazy jealous kind.

SHEILA: Did you like that he was jealous?

NADIA: No, obviously.

SHEILA: So you're saying there is at least one thing about him you didn't love—do you see the contradiction you're making there?

NADIA: You're just twisting my words!

SHEILA: I'm only the mirror.

NADIA: You're not my mirror!

SHEILA: There's a practice called "de-membering" where you remove individuals from your life, who are hindering you from making progress.

NADIA: You know what? You really don't get me. That guy Simon—he's black—but he don't get me. My momma—she don't get me. The only one who got me was X. Have you ever even been with somebody—like really been with them?

SHEILA: Yes, I have.

NADIA: But you're divorced now, huh?

SHEILA: Yes.

NADIA: So you don't really know what it's like to have a real flame. A flame so fucking beautiful that you would follow that light right down into the grave. Sometimes, I can still taste his tongue.

SHEILA: Excuse me?

NADIA: Sometimes—at the gas station pump—when I shove the nose of the gas-thingy into my car, I swear, I can taste and feel his tongue in my mouth. Slimy and spicy. Sweet and strong.

Sheila reacts with horror, and bizarre recognition.

NADIA: He's not gone. No one's ever totally, completely gone. Why are you making that face at me?

SHEILA: What? . . . I'm not.

NADIA: I see your face—can you see your face?

SHEILA: No.

NADIA: So don't tell me what I do or do not see, aiight?

SHEILA: Nadia. / I . . . [I'm sorry.]

NADIA: You see this?

Nadia reveals a tattoo on her arm. The cursive letters bleed from one to the next. The only decipherable character is the first one: "X"

NADIA: We didn't have a wedding—no mister-minister or flowers or any of that other bullshit. This was our vow. His name on me. My name on him. This means I belong to me and I belong to him. I'm his property and he's my property. You know how they take that hot metal with the letters and stick it in the cow's leg?

SHEILA: Branding?

NADIA: Yeah, that. That's exactly what this is. Some people get a ring in gold or platinum with diamonds—or whatever bullshit—and they decide that means something. But, you know what? They can take that ring off whenever. And they do, right? They take it off, give it back, keep it locked away, decide it means everything one day and it means nothing to them days, months, years later. But this isn't that kinda promise. This isn't just some fucking ring that can just slide on or off. He's still wearing this six feet under—and always will.

SHEILA: You don't think that's a little . . . [unrealistic.]

NADIA: What? *Primitive?*

SHEILA: That's not what I was going to say.

NADIA: But it's what you wanted to say, huh?

SHEILA: I wasn't / going to say that—

NADIA: And so what if it is? Lady, we're all just animals anyway—eating, shitting, and fucking. You see them people—out there—they got no problem putting a collar on their fucking dog, right? And, you know what else? They got no problem putting a ring on their fucking bitch's finger, either. And every-body is owned by some-other-body.

SHEILA: I don't believe that.

NADIA: Don't matter if you believe it—it's true.

SHEILA: We're all as free as we want to be.

NADIA: No, we're all slaves to some body: your Boss. Your Lover. God. Whoever. We're never at the top of the food chain—we all just the branded cows waiting to get slaughtered by whoever owns us. But they don't slaughter us until they drain every last drop of milk out of us. Am I right?

Sheila sits in silence. They look at the clock, ticking.

NADIA: Oh, right—look's like my time's up.

SHEILA: / No, wait—

NADIA: Sheila, we all got a fucked up history. Even you. You got a fucked up history, too, right?

No response.

NADIA: Yeah, that's what I thought.

SHEILA: / Nadia, wait—

NADIA: Some people just got their fucked up history down in ink.

Nadia exits.

SHEILA: Nadia!

Blackout.

INTERLUDE

Scene 7

A few days later. Sheila is on an abandoned pier enveloped on all sides by snow-capped mountains, a glistening cityscape, glittery ocean, and the Ferris wheel. She holds her umbrella. Angel appears and watches.

SHEILA: Hm, a familiar place can be like family.

Sheila clutches the strand of pearls.

SHEILA: You know, every time I look at a Ferris wheel—or the ocean for that matter—I think about you, nana [pronunciation: naw-naw] . . .

She isolates and runs her fingers over each pearl on the strand. This is her rosary.

SHEILA: But I must confess, I still dream about jungles. About heat and light and flavors that I've never actually tasted. Last night was no exception. Except that I dreamed a client was there in the jungle with me. Strangest thing. I haven't dreamed about a client in over a decade . . .

Nadia appears in Sheila's imagination, conjured by the Angel.

SHEILA: She says she can still taste his tongue. But his tongue lies in the grave. And the strangest scrap of it all is . . . I know exactly what she means. To taste a ghost tongue. But those ghosts breed bitterness and are best extinguished. And every drop, every fiber, every mote of my existence wants to give her a good, firm shake and say—

Sheila goes to Nadia and takes her by the shoulders. Nadia is surprised by the gesture.

SHEILA: Wake up! Don't you see that you're free? You're free! So what are you going to do with your freedom?

NADIA: I dunno.

SHEILA: Well, look around you—what do you see? Look!

NADIA: (*in awe*) A city.

SHEILA: Yes! A city full of glowing windows and open doors—what else?

They pivot.

NADIA: The ocean.

SHEILA: Yes! An ocean of infinite waves—and what else?

They pivot.

NADIA: The mountains.

SHEILA: Miles of mountainous incline—and then?

They pivot once more.

NADIA: The Ferris wheel . . .

SHEILA: Yes, remember the Ferris wheel?

Nadia nods.

SHEILA: Go climb a mountain until you reach the snowy peak! Conquer a new, glistening city! Sail across the glittery ocean! You're free! Embrace it.

NADIA: But—

SHEILA: What?

NADIA: You're free too. So, why are you here? Why don't you do any of that?

SHEILA: I don't know. (*wholly to herself*) Why don't I do it?

NADIA: It's because you just love to hear yourself talk. You just talk, talk, talk—but you don't walk the walk. You don't do nothing and you don't go nowhere. Why don't you go to your ruins?

SHEILA: Well, maybe we're not as free as we'd like to believe.

NADIA: Yeah, that's what I figured. Look at your reflection in that puddle. You're just getting older every minute, every second.

Sheila looks at her reflection in a puddle. Nadia vanishes.

SHEILA: Where did she go? That fearless woman with iron will and steel resolve . . . and a fire inside? Where did that Sheila go?

She strokes the reflection of her face with the umbrella.

SHEILA: Look at those wrinkles and white hairs. I look like you, nana. And I don't have forever either. So what's it going be?

She stomps in the puddle, rending her reflection.

A sudden otherworldly beam of tropical light shoots through the clouds landing on Sheila.

Oh! I can taste it! Just now, I tasted it! It sounds insane but . . . I tasted Mango & Cayenne. I'm not quite sure what that would really even taste like but . . . I woke up with this flavor on my tongue. Oh, there it is again, I can taste it now . . . right now . . .

She closes her eyes, fully succumbing to the flavor, as the tropical beam of light absorbs her. Sheila vanishes.

Scene 7.5

At the same time as Scene 7 but in a different place. Grey cloaks the sky over a cemetery, Nadia enters with her umbrella, searching. Angel appears and watches. Nadia stops at a grave marker and speaks.

NADIA: (*to the stone*) There you are. Hey. Been a while, huh? I'm sorry . . .

She traces the letters on the marker with her umbrella.

NADIA: Guess what? I got a job! I mean, I work with a bunch of geeky white boys that say they're the same age as me—but they act like little babies and they still live with their vanilla mommas. It's work though, ya know?

She touches her dangling earrings (they perform a dance).

NADIA: Remember these? Don't you wish you could see me wearing them one more time? Wearing *only* them? I wish you could, too. *(flirtatious)* You still my bad boy? Yeah, you'll always be my bad, bad boy. I miss your rough tongue against mine. Slimy and spicy. Sweet and strong. Like Mango & Cayenne. Did you know that we hold old air in our lungs? I think I'm still holding your breath inside me.

A crow caw. The crow casts a shadow onto the stone.

NADIA: *(to the crow)* Oh shit. Not you. You know what? You can just FUCK OFF, aiight? Shoo! I'm not in the fucking mood. So I dare you to come at me. Seriously, try me. *(holding up the umbrella threateningly)* No? Ok, then. *(back to the stone)* So, I started seeing this lady—this counselor—

The crow caws.

NADIA: —and the other day she asked about you and—

The crow caws.

NADIA: *(to the crow)* Hey!

The crow continues to caw.

NADIA: I told you to shut the fuck up!

Nadia swings the umbrella in the direction of the crow. The crow screeches.

NADIA: *(to the crow)* I'm trying to have an important conversation here, aiight!? Fuck.

Nadia runs her fingers through her hair, breaking the icy-gel crust. It slowly evolves into a feral mane.

NADIA: *(to the stone)* This lady—Sheila. More like She-Devil. Yeah, she don't get me. She don't know me. She wanna hear me say my life's wrong, that our love's wrong. But she don't know how you been *in* me—how you *is* in me—and how I still wear you *on* me. And she don't moisturize.

She touches the cursive, ink letters on her arm.

NADIA: It's starting to fade. And my momma told me to laser you off.

Sheila appears in Nadia's imagination, conjured by the Angel.

NADIA: But, fuck it, I'm thinking about getting it redone. My momma always called you—

SHEILA: A pig.

NADIA: And whenever this white lady opens her mouth, I hear my momma's voice come out—

SHEILA: He's a pig.

NADIA: It just makes me wanna scream!

SHEILA: Why do you let that animal turn you all black and blue?

NADIA: (*to Sheila*) Lady, you dunno nothing—especially nothing about being black and blue. You never been black. And you never been blue. And you never will be. And you wanna know what else? You're not even vanilla. You plain—just plain yogurt—that's what you are. Just plain and white. White and plain. So don't try and get me to say stuff you don't know nothing about. I always been black and blue! I've been black and blue on the inside—always—way before I even met him. My momma and papa made me black. My momma and papa made me blue—just as much as they made me black. And he just made me wear the blue with the black on the outside. Scrawled it all over my skin.

Nadia wipes away tears with her fingers. She traces the outline of the cursive, ink letters on her arm.

NADIA: Maybe he was a pig—but he was my pig and I loved his stink. And maybe my life's a pigsty—but it's my mess. It's mine—all mine. This is all I've got!

SHEILA: No, it's not.

NADIA: He's all I got.

SHEILA: You can let him go. You can pursue something new.

NADIA: Don't you think if I could cut him out of me by the roots, I WOULD? But I CAN'T . . .

SHEILA: You want to. And you can.

Sheila vanishes.

NADIA: (*to the stone*) No . . . I didn't mean that. I dunno what I was saying. It just came out. I didn't mean that.

Nadia takes off her earrings and lays them on the stone. The crow's shadow reappears.

NADIA: Hey. I love you.

She begins to walk away. The crow caws. Nadia crumbles.

NADIA: (*condemning the crow*) Bad boy. You're a bad boy.

She pounds the earth in the rhythm of a heart beat as the crow's caws crescendo, enveloping her.

NADIA: (*to the stone*) You're nothing but a bad, bad boy.

X. silhouette appears. His hand stretches out toward Nadia, reaching up and out of the grave (unseen by Nadia).

NADIA: You bad, bad, bad, bad, bad, bad boy . . .

The shadows absorb Nadia. Blackout.

PART II

Scene 8

A couple hours later. Nadia's bathroom.

Nadia stares into a vanity.

She tries on a pair of earrings. She is dissatisfied. She slams them on the counter.

She tries on another pair of earrings. She is displeased. She flings them on the floor.

She tries on another pair of earrings. She is disgusted. She hurls them at the mirror.

A silhouette appears behind her, it's X. with mud smeared all over him.

X.: Hey. You wanna try these?

X. holds up the pair of purple earrings that Nadia left on his grave marker.

Nadia stares at him in the mirror. Is she hallucinating? Dreaming?

She turns and stares at him, vis-à-vis. Her breath becomes audible.

NADIA: No, it can't be.

X.: What?

NADIA: (*to herself*) Wake up.

X.: Not happy to see me?

Nadia splashes water on her face.

NADIA: Wake up. Wake up.

Nadia looks at X.

X.: Still here.

NADIA: What the fuck is happening?

X.: Come here.

NADIA: Stay away!

X.: Come on. Put them [the earrings] on. And strip.

NADIA: Where'd you get those?

X. smirks.

X.: Hey, what'd you do to your hair?

NADIA: Nothing. Just trying something new.

X.: Something new, huh?

NADIA: Your hair—it's longer. You actually got hair again.

X.: And look at this . . .

He displays his fingernails.

X.: So long they're disgusting, right? I need the clippers and soap.

NADIA: I just—I just gotta [feel you] . . .

Nadia reaches out her fingers. She hesitates.

NADIA: Lemme just . . .

Nadia touches X. with the tips of her fingers. She gasps loudly.

X.: Shhhhhhhh.

X. covers her mouth with his hand.

X.: You act like you've seen a ghost.

He seizes her.

X.: So . . . do I still feel the same?

NADIA: You're so cold. Freezing.

X.: You traced my name.

It made my ink tickle.

Like a whisper or a feather.

Then I heard your voice.

You was saying some words.

You wanna say them to my face?

NADIA: I didn't say nothing.

X.: You did.

NADIA: I was just talking about some white bitch / and work and—

X.: Nah, that wasn't it.

You was saying some words and then the ink on my arm starts to boil.
Hot.

It's all gone now.

But you left your earrings.

He washes his hands. She wipes the mud from her mouth.

X.: The body loses water under the earth, did you know that?

Look at me.

My skin's all shriveled.

So now my nails are longer . . . and, yeah, now I've got hair again.

Gotta shave that kinky shit off, right?

(*smelling his hands*) What the fuck kind of soap is this?

NADIA: I dunno. Peach or something.

X.: I don't like it.

NADIA: Well, it's not for you.

X.: Oh, not for me? Right. All done with me now, are you?

Washed your hands of me and got rid of the soap I like and replaced it
with this shit!

He swipes the soap clear from the counter. He breathes audibly.

X.: You wanna cut me out of you, huh?

NADIA: I didn't mean that.

X.: But that's what you said, right?

NADIA: Everybody says shit they don't mean—all the time.

X.: Repeat what you said.

NADIA: I dunno what I said—/ why are you doing this, huh?

X.: Something like, "bad man." Ring any bells?

NADIA: Nah.

X.: Nah?

Ohhh!

"Bad boy"—that was it, right? "Bad boy."

You used to say that really playful.

But this last time you said it and it didn't sound so nice.

Hmmm.

It's not nice to say things like that about the deceased.

. . .

So what do you know about Hell?

NADIA: There's fire.

X.: Nah.

NADIA: The Devil.

X.: Nope.

NADIA: Sinners.

X.: That's what they say, right?

They say, "You're gonna ride a party bus to Hell with all your best friends.

And when you get there, it's a big ol' bonfire with a Dancing Devil and pitchforks and toasty marshmallows."

But some others say, "Hell's a lake of fire with weeping and wailing and gnashing of teeth."

But I've been in Hell.

And it's none of those things.

NADIA: Then what's it like?

X.: Hell is consciousness in a oak box, cold-cold-dirt, and a still-silence that eats at you.

Dirt is my eternal prison.

And your words.

You left me with poison words like acid rain coming down and burning me slow.

You wanna kick me while I'm buried deep down?

He buries his head between her legs. She closes her eyes, throws back her head, and moans softly.

NADIA: I swear I can still feel your arm around me when I sleep. A strong squeeze. I can't breathe, I wake up and there's no one. It's just me in our bed all alone.

She excavates the mud to discover his face.

NADIA: Where'd that weight come from? Where did it go? I felt it—it was there—you was there.

She caresses him, banishing mud from his visage.

NADIA: I wanted your fire.

X.: I want yours.

Their bodies undulate, igniting heat and friction between them. They glide into a trance.

NADIA: We was twin flames—burning into each other—melting into each other until we couldn't feel the pain no more.

X.: You coulda drove. You was more sober than I was.

NADIA: Says you.

X.: And then you whacked the steering wheel.

NADIA: I didn't.

X.: You hit it on purpose.

NADIA: / You grabbed me—

X.: You feel bad. Don't you?

NADIA: You wasn't supposed to leave me. You was supposed to stay and feed me barrels of pomegranates—kernel by kernel—seed by seed. I gave up everything for you.

Nadia obliterates the trance.

NADIA: What am I supposed to do now, huh?

X.: Put them [the earrings] on. And strip.

NADIA: Put them on me.

X. slips the earrings on Nadia.

X.: Strip nice and slow.

NADIA: Fuck.

Off.

X.: So, you don't want none of this no more, huh?

Nadia delivers a pat, a smack, a slap on his cheek.

NADIA: You like that?

X.: I know what you like.

He slowly slides his tongue out.

X.: You want some of this? This muscle?

He wags his tongue, tempting her.

X.: Huh?

She moves in to taste his tongue, he shoves her away.

X.: Come at me, come at me.

She tries again, he shoves her away more violently.

X.: There we go. Come on!

She tries again, he shoves her away with even greater force.

X.: Come on! You wanna taste it? Don't you?

She lunges, he grabs and shoves her against the wall. Nadia turns into a puddle.

NADIA: (*she means, "I wish I didn't love you"*) I hate you. I hate you. I hate you.

He scoops her up and pours her into the bathtub.

X.: Why do you got your hair like this?

He runs his fingers through her hair.

X.: You should slick it back. Want me to get the gel? Huh?

She spits at him.

X.: (*laughing*) Don't you got any respect for the dead?

NADIA: (*seductive*) Fuck you.

X.: Do you remember our last night—that hot night in the desert?

NADIA: You was drawing me pictures in the stars with your thick, cactus fingers?

X.: You remember.

NADIA: We was cruising through the stars on the way home—I've never seen so many in my whole, damn life. But then you unzipped your fly and put your prickly fingers at the back of my neck—and I was trying to keep my eyes on all them stars but then you pull on my hair real hard and that's when I hit the wheel . . .

X.: But, remember, there was that one rattler—it was about to give you a poisonous bite?

But I had the shotgun in my hand.

Double barrel, steady hand, one shot.

X. AND NADIA: BOOM.

NADIA: And the rattler's head just disappeared.

X.: So we ate what was left of that sweet fucker–

NADIA: —roasted with the fire made by your rough hands.

X.: You still got the tail—the rattle?

NADIA: I keep it in a drawer—with the lingerie.

He grips her face and slides his thumb into the corner of her mouth.

X.: See, I made a mistake, right?

    I thought you was a bird.

    I thought your . . . scales was feathers.

    Man oh man, was I wrong.

    You're no pretty little bird.

    You're a snake—a sexy snake.

    You temptress.

    So where are them [nail] clippers at?

NADIA: None of your fucking business anymore.

X.: I ought to stick a fork in it. I'm gonna give you a forked tongue so everyone knows you're a devil—my devil. I'm your pig and you're my devil, right?

NADIA: I'm your devil and you're my fucking pig.

X.: Prove it.

NADIA: How?

X.: Take a blade to your pretty little wrist.

    Angel appears on high and with a machete. Nadia considers it.

NADIA: You gotta kiss me, first.

X.: Come on. Hell will be less lonely with two.

NADIA: Purple eyelids.

    She circles her fingers around his eyes.

NADIA: Black eyes. Purple lips.

    She kisses him and bites on his lower lip and pulls, releases.

X.: This how a ghost tastes?

    She kisses him again, tasting his tongue deeply.

    Angel descends into the bathtub.

X.: So? How was that?

NADIA: It's not like I remember . . .

X.: Better?

NADIA: No. It's not . . .

X.: You're lying.

NADIA: Where did that flavor go?

X.: Your tongue is full of poison.

NADIA: And the light . . . (*a realization*) There was a light, wasn't there?

X.: When?

NADIA: In the car . . . right before we spun out . . . there was a blinding light—was it an angel?

X. nods.

NADIA: It came for you. Not for me . . . it took only you. It's not my time.

Angel lifts Nadia to her feet. Nadia removes the earrings. She flushes them down the toilet.

X.: No, wait—

Angel perches on the toilet.

X.: Say my name. Go on, say it.

He licks the ink on her arm that spells his name.

X.: Don't abandon me. Please, don't send me back to Hell.

Angel presents Nadia with the machete. Nadia accepts it.

X.: Deep down, trapped, and so cold and all alone. Forever.

Nadia points the weapon at X.'s throat.

X.: I'll scream. I could scream with all of me. (*a realization*) But can't nobody else hear me.

Nadia is stone.

X.: Can you imagine what that feels like? Huh? Does this mean nothing to you no more?

X. wipes the mud from his arm revealing Nadia's name tattooed on him.

NADIA: I know what it's like to be all alone.

X.: Sometimes I hear the birds laughing at me. You do, too, don't you? They're the only ones who kill the silence. And they're laughing at us in our misery. Don't you forsake me. How could you, when I gave you all of me?

A beat.

NADIA: No. I'm done with you. You hear me? Done.

Nadia takes the machete and shears the ink lettering off her arm.

X. gasps and shrivels, he crawls into the bathtub. Nadia turns on the shower and closes the curtain.

Angel performs a militaristic march and vanishes. Nadia stares back into the vanity.

Lights fade out.

Scene 9

One week after the action of Scene 6. The Mayan Ruins in Tikal. An otherworldly, tropical beam of light reveals Sheila alone.

She runs her fingers over the individual pearls on the strand. Her fascination overwhelms her fear.

SHEILA: Is this what freedom feels like?

To wander in unknown territory and foreign lands?

Right now I should be stepping into my office to begin our session, like every week for the past month.

But instead I stepped onto a plane and came here.

Tikal. "The place of water."

Sheila fidgets with the strand of pearls. Fear and fascination strike her in equal measure.

SHEILA: There they are . . . the ruins! Just like in the dream . . .

But where is the dazzling light?

And that flavor?

The sound of two scarlet macaws, loud and boisterous.

Oh look! Two avian lovers greet us . . . (*correcting herself*) me. Just me.

Look, at their tail feathers that fall in long scarlet cascades that end in spearheads.

Look at how they clamp their white and black beaks together.

Their rough, deep-purple tongues wriggle together.

Are they necking . . . or do you think they're trying to gnaw out their lover's tongue?

Sheila obsesses over the strand of pearls. She coils and twists it. Her fear increasingly begins to outweigh her fascination. She's having difficulty breathing.

SHEILA: The walls of the temple are closing in—or maybe it's just the heat that makes it harder to breathe. Where is the light?

(*distracting herself*) Oh! Look there, carved deep in the stone—portraits of ancient warriors.

Their eyes are looking at us . . . (*correcting herself*) me. Just me. They're watching me.

Angel emerges from the haze. They perform a militaristic march to the sound of drums.

The pearls begin to strangle Sheila. Haze progressively envelops her. Claustrophobic.

SHEILA: There's a drop of blood trickling from the sky.

(*a realization*) I'm being hunted.

I'm the prey.

I'm their captive.

I'm a slave.

I'm the sacrifice.

Angel binds Sheila and places her on a stone slab to sacrifice her.

The two scarlet macaws appear and orbit the Angel. Their shrieks morph into shrill, glass-shattering screeches. (They are the heralds of death.)

SHEILA: Stop. Stop!

This is supposed to be the place of water—the place of life.

So why can I only see the heads that rolled from ritual sacrifice?

Angel unsheathes their machete. They prepare to behead her. Sheila clutches the pearls attempting to free herself from their chokehold.

SHEILA: Everything is turning red—all I can see is red! Sickening, dizzying, ungodly red . . .

Somebody help—help me, please!

Angel raises their sword.

SHEILA: Is this it? Is this the end?

Nadia emerges from the haze. Blood trickles down from where she cut out her tattoo. She is armed with the bloody machete. Nadia's sword machete against Angel's, impeding it. Nadia and Angel engage in a duel. Nadia delivers a terrifying blow. Angel hisses and slinks away vanishing into the mist. The macaws orbit Nadia, swirling around her. They perch on her.

SHEILA: Nadia?

NADIA: Sheila.

SHEILA: Nadia! You're here!

NADIA: You did it. You finally made it to the ruins.

SHEILA: Yes, I did. I made it but . . .

NADIA: What?

SHEILA: It's not . . . I haven't found the [flavor] . . . oh, nevermind.

NADIA: Look, I'm happy for you.

SHEILA: It's so good to see you.

NADIA: Really?

SHEILA: Really.

NADIA: But . . .

SHEILA: What?

NADIA: You left me.

SHEILA: Let me explain—

NADIA: You left me to the birds.

SHEILA: / No.

NADIA: So they could have me.

SHEILA: Nadia, / please—

NADIA: How could you?

Nadia vanishes into the haze.

SHEILA: Nadia? Come back! Please? Nadia!

Sheila's strand of pearls breaks. She goes limp and collapses. The haze vanishes. Clarity.

Guía sits next to Sheila, attending to her.

GUÍA: *¿Señora?*

SHEILA: *¿Sí?*

GUÍA: You OK?

SHEILA: What happened?

GUÍA: You faint.

SHEILA: Oh.

GUÍA: Drink this.

SHEILA: *¿Qué es eso?* [What is it?]

GUÍA: *Agua. Toméla.* [Water. Drink it.]

Guía gives Sheila a canteen. Sheila drinks.

SHEILA: *Gracias.*

GUÍA: Drink more.

Sheila drinks more.

SHEILA: *Muchas gracias.*

GUÍA: You OK?

SHEILA: *No creo que tomé suficiente agua hoy.* [I don't think I drank enough water today.]

GUÍA: Your Spanish is berry good.

SHEILA: *Gracias.*

GUÍA: You're welcome. You know "Tikal" means "Water Place?"

SHEILA: *Yo sé.* [I know.]

GUÍA: *¡Ay, por supuesto!* [Of course you do!] Are you alone?

SHEILA: *Sí.*

GUÍA: *¿No hay nadie contigo?* [There's no one here with you?]

SHEILA: No one could come with me.

GUÍA: *Ay, qué lástima.* [How sad.]

SHEILA: I dreamed someone was here with me . . . but they're not.

GUÍA: *¿Qué?*

SHEILA: *Nada.* [Nothing.] *Pensé que iba a morir.* [I thought I was going to die.]

GUÍA: No. *No diga eso.* [Don't say that.] You no die . . . not yet. You're still berry young.

Sheila laughs.

GUÍA: *En serio.* [Seriously.]

SHEILA: Sweet lies.

GUÍA: *La verdad amarga.* [The bitter truth.]

    Guía offers her the canteen again.

GUÍA: More?

    Sheila drinks more water. Guía begins cutting a mango.

GUÍA: How old are you?

SHEILA: *Más que*—sixty—uh—*sesenta.* [More than sixty.]

GUÍA: *¿Sesenta? Mi abuelita—la mama de mi mamá—¿comó se dice?* [How do you say that?]

SHEILA: Grandmother.

GUÍA: *Sí.* Grandmother . . . *tiene más que cien años.* [My grandmother is more than a hundred years old.] She is one-hundred-two.

SHEILA: *¡Increíble!*

    Guía offers her a piece of mango.

GUÍA: Try?

SHEILA: (*excited*) Is this—Mango?

GUÍA: *Sí. Comélo.* [Yes. Eat it.]

SHEILA: *Nunco lo he probado.* [I've never tried mango before.]

GUÍA: *¿En serio?* [Seriously?]

    Sheila nods.

GUÍA: *¡Andalé, pues!*

    Sheila tries it. She holds it in her mouth, mulling over the flavor and texture.

GUÍA: *¿Bueno?* [Good?]

SHEILA: It doesn't taste like I dreamed it would. None of this is like it's supposed to be.

    Sheila reaches for the strand of pearls . . . she realizes they're broken and gone.

GUÍA: *¿Señora?*

SHEILA: *Nada. Solo hablando a mí mismo.* [Nothing. I'm just talking to myself.]

    Lights fade out.

Scene 10

A couple weeks later. Back on the pier. A sheet of grey masks the sky.

For the first time in the play: Sheila wears earrings . . . but Nadia does not.

SHEILA: I've never seen you wear your hair like that before.

NADIA: Nah.

SHEILA: You look radiant.

Nadia half-smiles on the outside. A full smile on the inside.

NADIA: Nice earrings.

SHEILA: Thank you.

NADIA: So where your pearls at?

SHEILA: Gone.

NADIA: Oh.

They stare out at the ocean.

SHEILA: How's work?

NADIA: It's going—you know?— / but I . . .

SHEILA: Sure.

NADIA: I quit.

SHEILA: You what?

NADIA: I'm exploring new opportunities.

SHEILA: Oh really?

NADIA: Yeah.

SHEILA: And what spawned that decision?

NADIA: Well . . .

SHEILA: Was it not a good fit or—?

NADIA: Nah, it was aiight.

SHEILA: I see.

NADIA: No, I don't think you do. My sales were through the roof—none of them vanilla momma's boys got nothing on me.

SHEILA: I completely believe that. So what was the issue?

NADIA: You know what? I don't gotta explain nothing to you anymore.

SHEILA: No, you don't.

NADIA: So, where'd you go?

SHEILA: Tikal.

NADIA: Really? Your ruins, for real?

SHEILA: Yes, the ruins. I dreamed . . . funny thing . . . I dreamed you were there with me.

NADIA: Uh, what? Whatever. Look, it must be nice to be able to just up and leave like nothing. Just decide you're done and go someplace tropical.

SHEILA: / Nadia—

NADIA: Some of us don't got the option to just drop everything and go someplace tropical. We gotta stay in our shit—in our sty. So why'd you give up on me?

SHEILA: I didn't give up on you.

NADIA: You ditched me—left me with some bitch named Jessica.

SHEILA: I decided not to retain any of my clients. But I didn't forget you— I couldn't forget you.

NADIA: Then why'd you leave? Be straight with me—because it seems like a really crazy coincidence that you up and *retire* when you did. Why'd you do that?

SHEILA: Because . . .

NADIA: That's what momma use to say, / "Because. Period."

SHEILA: I wasn't finished. / Because . . .

NADIA: 'Cause let's get one thing straight: I don't need you. The crow's gone now.

SHEILA: He is?

NADIA: Yeah, so be real with me. Why'd you call me?

SHEILA: The thing you said about the tongue. / I can't stop thinking about it.

NADIA: What are you talking about?

SHEILA: It's the tongue.

NADIA: What did I say about some tongue?

SHEILA: That you could taste *his* tongue. Don't you remember that?

A beat.

NADIA: He'd hurt me, aiight? Even when it wasn't cool with me. There, I said it. You happy now?

SHEILA: No. / That doesn't make me happy.

NADIA: And what do you know about it?

SHEILA: More than I wish I did.

NADIA: You know what? You ask a lot of questions, you talk a lot of fancy talk—really pretty, really eloquent talk. But I need you to actually say something real. Something ugly, dirty, and real. Go on. Do it.

A beat.

SHEILA: Nadia, we're not . . . I know it's not the same—not exactly—but it's similar . . .

NADIA: What are you talking about?

SHEILA: My ex-ex-ex-husband—I can't put enough X's through his name or his eyes—he'd hurt me, too . . . so I left him. But he always stayed inside of me—poisoning me. One summer day, I was filling a water balloon. And as the water from the hose jets into the balloon, growing in my hand, I swear I could taste his tongue.

NADIA: You making fun of me?

SHEILA: No.

NADIA: So what did it taste like then?

SHEILA: Slimy and spicy. Sweet and strong.

NADIA: You never got back with him?

SHEILA: No. Never. You remember what I said about "de-membering"?

NADIA: I loved him—not all of him—but he was all I had. You understand? So now who do I got left, huh? No one wants me. Who do I got? Tell me.

Gull guffaws.

NADIA: Why're they laughing at me?

SHEILA: No one's laughing.

NADIA: Yeah, they are. Feels like everywhere I go, the birds laugh at me. I fucking hate birds. They're God's spies—always watching and flying stories up to God. And God laughs with them. They're the only ones that see me . . . and they're laughing at me.

Sheila moves to comfort her.

NADIA: Don't touch me. The only ones not laughing are the Angels. Angels don't laugh.

SHEILA: How do you know that?

NADIA: I think I've seen one.

SHEILA: Really?

NADIA: Well, my nana saw one for sure. She saw the Blinding Light at The End. It was an Angel. A solider. A killer. When God decides it's your time—he sends an Angel to cut off your head and take your life. It's a trip, right? How a thing that can be a savior can be a killer, too? I mean, lucky for nana, she had a machete in her hand when it came—so she lived to tell the tale. But then another Angel came and . . . she didn't have the machete with her that time.

Sheila is overcome with the memory of being alone in Tikal, she weeps.

NADIA: You aiight?

No response. Nadia holds Sheila.

NADIA: Sheila, you aiiight?

SHEILA: I will be in a second. Thank you.

NADIA: Don't mention it.

SHEILA: You know, I usually come here to be alone. But today, I feel like the world is going to swallow me.

NADIA: Gimme your hand. Let's breathe. Together, aiight?

They close their eyes and inhale, hold, exhale . . .

NADIA: Keep exhaling. And—

They inhale, hold, exhale in unison.

SHEILA: Thank you. That was lovely.

NADIA: Yeah? You think I could do your job?

They smile together.

NADIA: So who'd you go to the ruins with?

SHEILA: I went by myself.

NADIA: Why'd you go all by yourself?

SHEILA: I went in search of this flavor that I tasted in a dream.

NADIA: Yeah, you told me about your dream.

SHEILA: You remember that?

Nadia nods.

SHEILA: Well, I imagined this flavor that would be there—but I didn't taste anything like what I dreamed. And now the flavor's gone. I can't even remember it anymore.

Sheila removes her earrings.

SHEILA: I bought these [earrings] in Tikal—to make it feel more real. These [earrings] are evidence. But they're not working. They just feel out of place on me.

NADIA: You couldn't get one of your kids to go with you?

SHEILA: I can't even remember the last time one of them called me. I've spent most of my life looking for places. Places to belong. But it's not about finding the places—it's about finding the people. I'm not going to "fix" you. I can't heal you. I can't save you. But I can offer you my support.

Sheila gives Nadia the earrings.

SHEILA: Here, I want you to have them.

NADIA: Really?

SHEILA: Please, take them.

Nadia slips them on and tosses her head. The earrings perform a dance. Nadia's countenance lightens.

SHEILA: They suit you far better than they do me.

A beat.

NADIA: Why'd you ask me to meet you here?

SHEILA: I'm . . . I'm trying to apologize.

NADIA: Is that what this is?

SHEILA: I'm trying.

NADIA: You're not doing so hot.

SHEILA: I'm not used to giving apologies.

NADIA: (*playful*) No duh.

> *A beat.*

SHEILA: Nadia, look around you.

> *They pivot their bodies slowly in a circle, absorbing the world around them. A whirl of colors. They inhabit and embrace the present, together.*

SHEILA: Look. The mountains. The ocean. The Ferris wheel. The city. They all make me think thoughts that I love.

NADIA: Yeah? Like what?

SHEILA: The mountains. What will they be adorned with today? Snow? Green jewels? Fog?

> *They pivot. A flash of glittery light.*

SHEILA: The ocean. I think about all the fish—layers upon layers of fish swimming in perpetual lanes—disturbed by prismatic light, supple kelp, and fickle currents. You know they say our body is two-thirds water?

NADIA: Yeah, I know that.

SHEILA: And the earth is 70% water. Two fabulous, terrestrial bodies that have comparable amounts of water.

NADIA: The ocean always looked like a dress to me—all covered with sequins. It's like a dress I wanna wear. Aw, I wish I could wear it!

> *They pivot.*

SHEILA: Then there's the Ferris wheel . . . children, parents, grand-parents . . .

NADIA: You think anyone's died or had a baby while riding it?

SHEILA: I think they typically discourage riders that would be liable to die or give birth.

NADIA: There's always someone somewhere breaking some rule.

> *They pivot. And people watch.*

SHEILA: Ah, the city. I think about every person in every window of every building and every car—what colors are their fingernails? Natural? Aqua? Neon pink?

NADIA: Black today, purple tomorrow. And next week: whore-red. To match they ho-lipstick.

SHEILA: What are they eating for dinner?

> *For each of the following images, they pick out a specific member of the audience as if they are a person passing by. It's a fun game.*

NADIA: Ham. Chicken. Liver.

SHEILA: Kidney beans. String beans. Lentils.

NADIA: When's the last time they kissed somebody?

SHEILA: A week ago.

NADIA: Like four-ish days.

SHEILA: Twelve minutes.

NADIA: Aw, 37 seconds.

SHEILA: Yesterday.

NADIA: Last night.

SHEILA: This morning.

NADIA: (*sadly*) Never.

> *A beat. The game ends.*

NADIA: So it's gone.

SHEILA: What?

> *Nadia shows Sheila her arm, sans XAVIER's name. One letter remains.*

NADIA: I woke up one morning and it had faded away. All except the—

SHEILA: X.

NADIA: It's like a—whatchamacallit?

SHEILA: A memento.

> *A beat.*

SHEILA: Do you . . . ?

NADIA: What?

SHEILA: Do you smell that?

NADIA: Smell what?

SHEILA: Never mind. It's nothing.

NADIA: What do you smell?

SHEILA: I can almost taste it . . . it's the flavor of a tropical fruit.

NADIA: And chili pepper?

SHEILA: Yes. Cayenne.

NADIA: & Mango.

> *A moment in which they succumb to the flavor, together.*
>
> *Sunlight percolates through the marine layer. Sunlight reflects off the ocean, the snow on the mountains, the cityscape, and the Ferris wheel . . . it becomes blinding.*
>
> *END OF PLAY.*

KEIKO GREEN is a playwright and performer based in Seattle. She received her BFA in Experimental Theater from New York University's Tisch School of the Arts. Her play, *Nadeshiko*, produced by Sound Theatre Company, was an Honorable Mention on the 2017 Kilroys List and received Outstanding New Play at the 2017 Gregory Awards in Seattle. At Annex Theatre, she wrote the book and lyrics for the musical *Bunnies*, as well as the Comic Con show *Puny Humans*, co-written with Bret Fetzer. She was a member of the 2015-2017 Seattle Repertory Theatre Writers Group. As a performer, she was a member of ACT Theatre's 2016 Core Acting Company. She has performed at the Seattle Repertory Theatre, ACT Theatre, and Seattle Shakespeare Company among others.

Keiko Green

Nadeshiko

CHARACTERS:

RISA	Female, Late-20's, Asian-American.
WHITE HAIRED MAN	Male, 40-50, white.
NADESHIKO	Female, 70, Japanese.
SUE	Female, 21, Asian-American. Risa's cousin. A goth-punk student. *Also plays* **SHOKO**, Female, 15, Japanese. A young Nadeshiko in 1945.
TOSHIO	Male, 19, Japanese. A tokko pilot in 1945. *May also play* **MAN IN SHADOW**, Male, age unknown. A mysterious man in a chat room. (This role may be cut and instead be projected text.)

SETTING:

Various locations in Seattle.
A small theatre outside of Tokyo, Japan. 2016.

NOTES FROM THE PLAYWRIGHT:

A slash (/) indicates the next line begins with some overlapping. A double dash (--) indicates an interruption, sometimes by one's own thoughts.

An incomplete line indicates the thought completely stops, unfinished

The Nadeshiko should have a Japanese accent when speaking English. Everyone in Japan (Toshio, Shoko) are speaking Japanese. They should speak in standard American accents during their scenes.

Casting of the White Haired Man: Despite his character name, white hair is not necessary.

Act I

Scene I

Lights up on a pristine and very expensive-looking apartment. Art. Lots of art. All-white furniture, walls, rugs.

The White Haired Man is at the door with a young, Asian-American woman. This is Risa.

RISA: Hi, I'm looking for

I'm Monica, are you --

WHITE HAIRED MAN: Come in come in. Oh, would you mind taking off your shoes? Thank you. Can I take your jacket or bag or

RISA: No not yet thanks.

WHITE HAIRED MAN: Sure. Make yourself at home.

The MAN opens the door wide and stands to the side. Risa enters shoeless, checking out the apartment.

RISA: Wow, white rug. This is a nice place. You live here alone?

WHITE HAIRED MAN: I do. I do now, yes.

RISA: Cool. It's nice. Very clean.

WHITE HAIRED MAN: Yes it's easier for me if I keep it clean.

RISA: Sterile.

WHITE HAIRED MAN: Pardon?

RISA: Nothing. So do you mind if we skip right ahead to the business of it?

WHITE HAIRED MAN: The business of the -- yes, yes! Of course. Let me just -- Pardon me for just a moment.

The MAN exits into his bedroom, Risa notices a painting. The MAN re-enters with his wallet.

WHITE HAIRED MAN: We agreed on three hundred?

RISA: I've seen this. Haven't I seen this? In a gallery downtown?

WHITE HAIRED MAN: Very possible. I buy local.

RISA: Oh.

You know, my *boyfriend* -- he's an artist. Yeah. He's waiting at the Starbucks next door, actually. So.

WHITE HAIRED MAN: Is he? . . . That's kind of him.

RISA: Yeah. So.

I've never known anyone who actually does that. Just buys -- Just goes and buys the paintings in the galleries.

WHITE HAIRED MAN: I don't know many people who go to galleries at all.

Beat.

WHITE HAIRED MAN: So, three hundred.

RISA: Yeah.

WHITE HAIRED MAN: (*handing cash to her*) Here you are.
I won't be offended if you count it.

RISA: Ha, thanks I -- I probably should, actually.
*Risa quickly counts the money. She holds the cash in her hand for the rest of
the scene.*

RISA: All here. Great. Thanks.

WHITE HAIRED MAN: So shall we get / started

RISA: Can I have something to drink?

WHITE HAIRED MAN: Oh sure, of course. What do you
Just some water? I have a sparkling as well, somewhere in

RISA: No, like whiskey
Or wine. Wine would be good too.

WHITE HAIRED MAN: Oh
Let's see, I have a very nice single-malt scotch, as well as a bourbon --
though I'm not quite sure of the quality of that one. It was a gift from
a former student, actually -Sometimes they try to impress you post-
graduation, show you how well they're doing. I've / also got

RISA: You a teacher?

WHITE HAIRED MAN: Former teacher.

RISA: Oh, I see. Huh.

WHITE HAIRED MAN: There's a brandy as well -- been in there a little while.
I don't drink much, so

RISA: Wow brandy
That's so weird.

WHITE HAIRED MAN: I'm sorry weird, how?

RISA: Just -- I mean -- it's fictional.
The only people who drink brandy are characters in mystery novels.
Some lady passes out at the sight of a dead body, right?
And like all these dudes are like
"Quick, the brandy! Bring the brandy!"
And they like guzzle booze down the windpipe of this passed out lady,
you know?
(*terrible English accent*) "The color is back in her cheeks, good good!"
Meanwhile the lady is like waking up on the floor, brandy in her mouth,
and this huge group of men surrounding her, like forcing it down her
throat. It's so weird.

WHITE HAIRED MAN: Hm. I've never considered that. / So

RISA: Yeah, I'll have the brandy.

WHITE HAIRED MAN: (*terrible British accent*) "Good good."

> *A small beat, as the MAN waits for Risa to acknowledge his joke. She doesn't.*

WHITE HAIRED MAN: Let me get that for you.

> *The MAN moves to the bar area. He, of course, has the correct glass for every bottle of liquor he owns.*
>
> *Risa sets her bag down and sits.*
>
> *The MAN pours brandy.*

WHITE HAIRED MAN: A little early isn't it?

RISA: Huh?

WHITE HAIRED MAN: (*Re: Brandy*) For . . .

RISA: Well I don't exactly do this everyday, now do I?

WHITE HAIRED MAN: I apologize, I didn't mean

RISA: No, it's fine. Sorry, I'm just

Liquid courage, you know?

> *He hands her a glass.*

RISA: Thank you. Can we just

Would it be okay if we just wait a minute here?

WHITE HAIRED MAN: Of course.

I understand that it's a strange request. This whole

RISA: Job.

WHITE HAIRED MAN: Pardon?

RISA: Job. "Request." -- I don't like that. It makes it sound like I'm a volunteer or something. Like this is what I do in my free time. No, this is a job. This is me fulfilling a task for the exchange of money.

> *Beat.*

WHITE HAIRED MAN: Perhaps I'll have one with you.

> *The MAN fixes another brandy.*

RISA: Not too early?

WHITE HAIRED MAN: It's not that early.

RISA: . . .

So, do you do this often?

WHITE HAIRED MAN: Well that's

I don't really know what constitutes the term "often" in this case.

RISA: Regularly?

WHITE HAIRED MAN: It's such a subjective term

RISA: But you've done it before.

WHITE HAIRED MAN: Yes, I've done it before.

RISA: More than once.

WHITE HAIRED MAN: More than once.

> *They sip brandy.*

WHITE HAIRED MAN: How do you like it? The the brandy

RISA: Oh (*considers*)

> Yeah, it might wake me up from a good faint.
>
> God, I wonder if I would. Like if I was in that position.

WHITE HAIRED MAN: You mean wake up or

RISA: No, like if I saw a dead body, if I would faint. I wonder how many people do, in real life. Would you?

WHITE HAIRED MAN: I never have.

RISA: Oh shit, I'm sorry.

WHITE HAIRED MAN: It's fine.

RISA: Shit, you're like a widower aren't you?

WHITE HAIRED MAN: What? No, why do you

RISA: I don't know. You looked so sad just now. Plus! Earlier when I asked if you live alone, you said "Now, I do" which means that you didn't before, right? There was someone else here. I Sherlock-ed you.

WHITE HAIRED MAN: I could have had a roommate

RISA: No way.

WHITE HAIRED MAN: Or a divorce.

RISA: Did you?

WHITE HAIRED MAN: I'm not a widower.

RISA: (*disappointed*) Oh. Okay.

WHITE HAIRED MAN: Your boyfriend doesn't mind you doing this?

RISA: My -- boyfriend *does* mind me doing this, of course. But he knows I'm broke, so. He knows I'm kind of desperate right now, so. I mean, I don't want you to think that I'm

> Like I had a job until recently, okay? Like a *real* job.

WHITE HAIRED MAN: What happened?

RISA: Just -- I guess they lost a bunch of clients or something, so. It was a small office, so.

WHITE HAIRED MAN: So they let you go.

RISA: You don't work, huh? You're rich for a teacher. Former teacher.

WHITE HAIRED MAN: I've had other jobs.

RISA: Is there more of this?

> *Risa holds out her now empty glass.*

WHITE HAIRED MAN: You know what? Why don't we have another glass after the session?

RISA: Oh. Right. Sure. Right. Of course, we have to -- So where do you want to

WHITE HAIRED MAN: Over here.

The MAN pulls a stool out and sets it in the empty space in front of him.

WHITE HAIRED MAN: You brought something with you, like I requested?

RISA: Yeah. It's umm. In my bag. Let me just.

Risa retrieves a book from her bag.

RISA: Frannie and Zooey. You read it?

WHITE HAIRED MAN: Oh, yes. Years ago.

RISA: Sorry, does that -- is that a problem or

I don't really know how this works.

WHITE HAIRED MAN: I'd love to hear it again.

RISA: Okay. Okay, so I guess I'll just

WHITE HAIRED MAN: Whenever you're ready.

RISA: Right here?

WHITE HAIRED MAN: There's a restroom you can use to get ready if you prefer, but

RISA: But it doesn't really matter, does it?

WHITE HAIRED MAN: If it would make you more comfortable, that would matter.

RISA: But then I'd just come out here.

WHITE HAIRED MAN: Yes.

Risa still has the cash in her hand, which she clenches and holds close to her chest.

RISA: Fuck. Fuck I don't know if I

Sorry, I don't know why this is so much harder than I thought it would / be

WHITE HAIRED MAN: If you're having second thoughts, I understand. Of course, I'll be disappointed -- but if you've changed your mind

RISA: God, I feel bad. Which is ridiculous. I mean, you're -- no offense, but you're basically a pervert.

WHITE HAIRED MAN: I realize it's a peculiar request.

RISA: I mean, if you had like garbage bags laid down or something, I could just be like "No, he's fucking American Psycho," and like jet out of here, but you're not. You're

Why do I feel bad? I don't know why I feel bad. Maybe because you looked sad earlier and you're a widower and

WHITE HAIRED MAN: No one's forcing you to stay.

RISA: Fuck. Right, I just. I just have to give this back, right? Then

WHITE HAIRED MAN: Well. Yes. I can't give you the money, if you don't do the job.

RISA: I guess not.

WHITE HAIRED MAN: So

RISA: Hold on. I just --

Risa paces around the room, cash still in her hand.

WHITE HAIRED MAN: Is something bothering you?

RISA: I think I'm going to be sick.

WHITE HAIRED MAN: What?

RISA: You know, I think I'm coming down with something actually. I'm sorry, I'm not feeling well I

WHITE HAIRED MAN: Can I get you a glass of water? Was it the brandy? Why don't you sit down and

Risa quickly gathers her things.

RISA: I have to go I have to get out of here I have to I'm sorry I just can't right now it's not

No offense

Sorry I'm so sorry

She exits down the hall.

WHITE HAIRED MAN: Wait a fucking -- Hey (*out the door*) Hey! You took the

He picks up a phone on the wall and dials.

WHITE HAIRED MAN: Hey there, Jerry. The young woman you let up a few minutes ago -- she's about to rush past you. Could you

(*pause*) Actually, just let her go. Nothing. Just let her go. Thank you, Jerry.

He hangs up the phone and sips at his brandy.

Scene 2

The Nadeshiko, an elderly Japanese woman, appears onstage. She seems surprised to be there, collecting herself -- looks around nervously for a moment.

NADESHIKO: *A-re? Doko --?*

The Nadeshiko clocks the audience, the stage.

NADESHIKO: *Gaijin?*

Oh my ga-! So sorry, so sorry!

I do not know *how* I . . . So embarrassing!

She sits in the audience, or in the aisle, or wanders around the house. She asks the audience, "What are we watching?" If she sees a program, she takes it with a "May I see?" Eventually she finds out the play is called Nadeshiko.

NADESHIKO: Nadeshiko, you say? Oh.

Oh my ga-! Me, it is me!

She rushes back on stage.

NADESHIKO: So, so sorry! No one told me I was telling a story. I was at home, I drinking some tea and go to sleep and --

Maybe this is a dream. I am feeling much more *genki*. Lots of energy and (*she studies her hands*) Oh my ga-! Do you have a mirror I can borrow? Anyone?

She finds a mirror hidden on set.

NADESHIKO: You know, I look good. Very good. Many years younger. Skin is *pichi-pichi*! Yes, this definitely a dream! I hope it is not a nightmare. I had one where all my teeth fall out and they have swords and chase me all around!

I go to my dentist, but he say nothing wrong.

Ok, but if dream --

The Nadeshiko pinches herself.

NADESHIKO: *Itta*! No, not dream. Hmm.

(*starting to panic*) I -- I should really get going.

The Nadeshiko tries to exit, but she can't find the door or the door is stuck or she gets caught in a curtain or something else that keeps her on the stage.

NADESHIKO: Oh my ga-. I am stuck here.

Why?

Why cannot leave? Why?

Come, Shoko. Think, think, think.

(*to the audience*) Oh! You are here for a story! For the *Nadeshiko* story. Correct?

(*Maybe someone answers*) So then maybe.

Maybe I tell the story, then. Then you let me go. Poof. Go.

Okay.

Okay!

You are American?

This is my first time in America! My daughters, they move to America – but . . . it was too far. Too far and long for me.

Look at all of you! Many -- uh -- "dye job?" No judging, no judging! My english not so bad, no? I learn it to talk to my grandchildren, but it has been a long time.

Okay.

The Nadeshiko.

Maybe some accompanying music starts up, but the Nadeshiko cuts them off.

NADESHIKO: Just let me tell the story, ok?

It starts in 1945 and -- I have never told anyone about this before.

A shameful part of Japanese history -- removed from textbooks sometimes. For Japanese cannot live with the shame.

We were much younger than all of you. 14, 15.

We harvest potatoes, we dig bunkers, we cook and clean, put on our uniform for the pilots and -- and we wave goodbye.

She waves.

Her hand falls. She looks at the palm.

NADESHIKO: So much power in a hand -- in an arm. It holds so much power and I cannot bear the weight sometimes. My right arm is heavy. It hangs so heavy on my body. Oh! I am not having a stroke, do not worry!

(laugh) Sorry so sorry to scare you.

They call us the "Nadeshiko Unit."

Do you know what that means? "Nadeshiko?" No? Shame, shame! It comes from the term "Yamato Nadeshiko:" the essence and beauty -- the purity of an ideal Japanese woman.

Feminine. Delicate. And shy -- like me! *(laugh)*

Taken from the Nadeshiko flower -- graceful pink, purple fringed petals, thin and fragile.

Leaves edible, nectar sweet, roots filled with medicine. It is a tough, wild, helpful flower.

But named and noticed purely for its beauty. And so were we.

Noticed for what we were -- pretty, young, Japanese.

And then.

When the war ended, the women were left to live on, with nothing but boring old stories.

That's it. The end. Bye bye. Poof.

Beat.

NADESHIKO: Poof!

She waits for something to happen.

NADESHIKO: Poof?

Hmm. Something is not right.

Let me sit down.

Think, Shoko, think.

She sits in the house. Or on the stage in the corner. Her presence is felt,
though she does not interact in the following scene.

Scene 3

Risa and Sue, Risa's cousin, a young, goth-punk, Asian-American woman,
complete with multiple facial piercings, enter through a door to a large bed
with pillows. They are barefoot.

SUE: Shit, I haven't seen you in ages. You look good. A little dark and
broody, but good. Sit down. You want anything?

RISA: On the --

SUE: Yeah

RISA: But is this

(*whispering*) Is this is where you do it?

SUE: Yes! Jesus. Just sit down. Stop being so weird.

RISA: Is it clean?

SUE: Oh fuck off.

RISA: But seriously I mean how does it all actually you know

SUE: What?

RISA: Work.

SUE: Doing some research, are you?

RISA: I mean kinda.

SUE: Wait. Really?

RISA: I don't know. Yeah. I don't know.

I've been looking at some things on Craigslist lately.

SUE: No. That's so sketchy.

RISA: Sure, but -- I mean.

There's a listing, it just says "WATCH ME."

Like what's the story there, you know? You just show up and watch
someone jerk off in their window or whatever or what, you know? Don't
you wonder?

SUE: Yeah, I wonder who the hell would call them up.

RISA: Well, you know I -- might have contacted someone like that.

I mean not *that* that but someone *like* that.

. . .

What?

I didn't do it! I couldn't . . . follow through.

SUE: What do you mean?

RISA: I ran away. It's humiliating. I don't want to talk about it.

Sue gives her a look.

RISA: What!?

SUE: Nothing. I'm surprised, that's all. Can't I be surprised?

RISA: Of course you can . . .

SUE: Mom talks about you all the time.

RISA: Aunt Yoko? Why?

SUE: She says you're on track.

RISA: Track? What track?

SUE: You know, the track. The right track, whatever.

RISA: I still am. I'm on track.

SUE: My mom's been pointing at you as an example since forever.

RISA: Just a different track. In a different direction.

SUE: Smart and respectful and

RISA: Stop sounding so disappointed. Can you just . . . help?

SUE: You want like pointers and shit?

RISA: Yeah. Yes.

SUE: You say that

And then you're gonna get all weird. Everyone thinks they're so fucking liberated and then they get all weird

RISA: No, it's not like that. (*off her look*) It's not! No disrespect, no assumptions. Genuine curiosity.

SUE: Well it's pretty straightforward, Ris.

RISA: You just do it right here?

SUE: Yeah. My office. Behold.

RISA: I mean it's so convenient.

SUE: Okay

RISA: Right above your parents' restaurant?

SUE: Well *technically* I live above the laundromat next door.

RISA: Uh-huh.

SUE: Shut up, it's embarrassing. Living above my parents place.

RISA: Why aren't you at the restaurant anymore?

SUE: I'm on my own now. I'm an adult.

You didn't like working there either! You cried on your first day. That lunch rush? All that snot coming out of your nose, all "I can't I just can't do this!"

Fucking flower fucking delicate flower

RISA: Okay.

SUE: So sensitive.

RISA: Okay!

SUE: Wait, how did you even know I

Shit they told me they wouldn't put me in the ads. Did you see me in a pop-up or some shit?

RISA: No I

SUE: Then how did you

RISA: Well

Auntie mentioned it to / me but

SUE: Oh god. She's telling people?

RISA: What exactly does she think you're doing? I mean she said "cam girl" so casually, like

SUE: She thinks I'm a host at some internet lounge or something or

RISA: Internet lounge? What even is that?

SUE: Yeah, I don't know, like this ridiculous thing came out of my mouth and she believed it. But then -- God. One of her customers recognized me, and ugh fucking nightmare. You'd think that of all the millions of anonymous creeps, you could live a relatively small, normal life without someone recognizing you, but some guy comes in for lunch, right? A round of Kamikazes for the table!

Not even one of my customers.

Mom heard him say to his friend, "Oh shit I've seen that girl online!" They're all, "Which one?" "That one." And he's like pointing at me, I guess. "Tight body, badass tattoos."

RISA: Oh shit

SUE: Yeah, next thing I know, Mom pulls me into the bathroom, pulls my shirt over my head, and sees the one I've been working on --

Sue pulls up her shirt to show off a big tattoo on her rib cage.

SUE: I still want to add some more color here and here.

RISA: Yeah, no wonder you're in trouble.

SUE: I know. What's the big deal, anyway? She doesn't give a shit about piercings, but get some art on your ribs and it's World War 3.

RISA: It's a Japanese thing. Yakuza thing. Still connected, I guess, and Auntie's so traditional.

SUE: Fucking yakuza -- they have to ruin tattoos for like every generation after them. Assholes.

RISA: Right. *That's* why the Yakuza are assholes.

SUE: Whatever. I don't regret it. So good for business, my dudes love these.

RISA: So what, you get more money with tattoos, or . . . ?

SUE: . . .

This is so weird.

RISA: You think this isn't weird for me? Help me, Cuz. Help. (*mock begging*) Please? Pretty please? You're so smart and pretty and and funny and . . . pretty and

SUE: Ugh fine whatever

RISA: Seriously?

SUE: Quickly! Quickly before I change my mind.

RISA: Okay! Okay, so how long have you been

SUE: Three years.

RISA: THREE YEARS? And you didn't think to mention it to me *one* time?
Risa hits her with a pillow.

SUE: Ow! It's not like I'm always doing it full-time. Like when school starts back up, I'll cut down, you know? It's not a big deal, Ris. It's just like a side thing.

RISA: So you like it.

SUE: I don't know, I guess. People like you and I -- we're guaranteed a certain amount of customers because we offer something alternative, you know?

RISA: Yeah sure

And is it financially -- I don't know -- viable?

SUE: A good week, I take home a full grand. A bad night can look like a hundred. Depends on the time of day, if you can build up regulars -- it's like serving. Kind of. So you'd be terrible at it.

RISA: Fuck, a hundred? That's not quite

SUE: Beats the phone sex girls -- those bitches work for minimum wage, you know that?

RISA: That is so disappointing.

SUE: And like a lot of these guys don't even want

RISA: Sex?

SUE: Dude some of these guys don't even want your clothes off

RISA: You know I've heard that but I just assumed that was really rare

SUE: My friend Kate only does non-nude -- she made eleven grand last month.

RISA: ELEVEN FUCK WHAT

SUE: Yeah, there's all kinds of fetish clients, you know? And know that no matter what you look like, no matter what you do -- someone wants to see it.

RISA: Fetish?

What does that

What does that entail

SUE: Fetish clients. You know, fetish clients.

RISA: Like foot stuff?

SUE: Sure, yeah, that too -- but like

I'm a fetish.

RISA: What do you mean?

SUE: This whole thing? This whole situation here?

Fetish.

RISA: Right.

So no foot stuff.

SUE: Don't insult me. I know the basics.

Like -- Hold on

Sue takes out a tiny little camera.

RISA: (*surprise and awe*) . . . Oh my god, is that it?

SUE: Okay, calm down. It's not baby Jesus, it's just a fucking camera.

And you just like clip it onto your laptop, right?

She does.

RISA: That's it? You don't have a tripod or something or

SUE: Bitch, what century are you living in? Just get something HD, it's all in the lighting.

Ok so first you just show them all these different angles like

Sue leans back and poses her feet in different angles in front of the camera.

RISA: Oh they're like framing your / crotch

SUE: I know

Then something like

Sue grabs a sock from the floor and slowly puts it on.

RISA: Oh, I get it! LET ME TRY

Risa pushes Sue off the bed. Sue helps Risa's feet out into the right position, until Risa loses her balance.

RISA: No. No. NO.

(*falling over*) Ow!

SUE: Dude you have to do some yoga or pilates or some shit before you try that stuff out. You'll pull something.

Then there's that classic dominatrix and humiliation stuff, you know (*to camera*) "You're pathetic! You're a worthless piece of shit! You're embarrassing!"

It comes pretty naturally to me. I love yelling at men.

RISA: I don't think I could do that.

SUE: Well no one's forcing you. No one's even politely asking you.

RISA: True.

Sue laughs.

RISA: What?

SUE: (*laughing*) Your face. You're so fucking serious about this. Jesus. Don't look so scared. You're making me feel gross, like a predator or some shit. You don't want to do it? Don't do it. Easy.

Really I should be charging you for this comprehensive tutorial.

RISA: Sorry I'm just thinking through

SUE: How far are you willing to go?

RISA: Oh. I'm not sure. I think not very far. Maybe. There *are* guys that just want to talk, right? That's a real thing?

SUE: Yeah, some guys.

. . .

You doing ok?

RISA: What? Yeah.

SUE: Okay, it's just

Risa -- your Mom -- your Mom is worried about you and

RISA: What the fuck do you know what my Mom thinks?

SUE: She wrote me a letter.

RISA: From Japan?

SUE: Yeah, from Japan. Check it out.

Sue takes out an envelope -- pulling out some old photos from it -- maybe an old newspaper clipping.

Risa grabs at it.

RISA: Holy shit. Is this --

SUE: Grandma Shoko. Auntie K found it when she was cleaning out the place in Japan, I guess.

RISA: Damn. She -- she looks

She looked just like you.

SUE: Yeah. I know.

When was the last time you saw her?

RISA: God, like 10 years ago?

SUE: I met her a couple times when I was a little kid, I guess. Mom flew us out there.

. . .

Kinda shitty, isn't it?

RISA: Well, yeah.

SUE: Yeah.

Yeah. Well, look -- if you need help with other shit --

RISA: I'm fine

SUE: I know it's been awhile since your Dad -- you know.

RISA: Died. You can say it.

SUE: But your mom is grieving too and if you need to talk to someone then --

RISA: -- That's not it. That has nothing to do with it. I just -- I can't see her, okay? Not right now.

SUE: Did she like *do* something to you? Because if it is something like *that*, then --

RISA: No, no. It's nothing like that.

SUE: If you're struggling, you'll let me know, right?

RISA: Yes. Thank you. Yes.

SUE: Okay.

Okay, I'll set you up with my site, if you're interested, ok?

RISA: Seriously?

SUE: I'll send you a link, watch a group show, and see if you're into it.

RISA: Watch your "show" like

Won't that be weird?

SUE: Just don't talk to me about the specifics. If you give me pointers, I'll fucking kill you.

RISA: Ok ok

SUE: Now, let's go. I'm starving.

And you know you're going to spill about all the weird shit you've been up to.

RISA: . . .Okay.

They exit.

The Nadeshiko has gotten up, following the girls a bit as they exit. Looking after her granddaughters.

She turns to us.

NADESHIKO: So I *am* dead. Ghost.

Wow.

Give me one little minute.

She wanders off.

Scene 4

Risa sets out her laptop and rearranges the lights slightly. A sound.

She waits.

She drinks some of a beer on the table. She dials from her cell phone with the other hand.

RISA: Yo, Sue. Like what the hell do I do now? Yeah I'm logged on but like How do people even know I'm here

A log-on sound.

RISA: Oh wait I think someone -- Yeah, there's a "1" down there on the What??

Risa covers her face.

RISA: Sue? Go away, Sue! Go away! I'm fucking shy that's why -- can't you give me a little privacy for my first

A log-off sound.

RISA: Thank you! But what the fuck do I do in the meantime? Just sit here and wait for like the perfect algorithm to send some dude to my What if I know them? I feel like I'm going to spend the rest of my life wondering if everyone fucking knows.

She chugs some of her beer.

A log-on sound.

RISA: I have a visitor!

A log-off sound.

RISA: Fuck they left already. This is terrible for my self-confidence.

Two log-on sounds. A Man In Shadow appears elsewhere onstage, just a silhouette.

Man In Shadow can also be a purely online presence, so we see his text projected, which is all Risa would actually see.

RISA: Shit I have to go bye.

She hangs up. She turns seductively over her shoulder and looks at the camera.

RISA: *(attempting sexy)* Hello, there.

A log-off sound.

RISA: GODDAMMIT.

She sits down, drinks her beer, blows over the top of the beer bottle.

MAN IN SHADOW: Wanna chat privately?

RISA: *(startled)* OH! Jesus. I didn't -- sorry, I didn't know you were still here. This is my first time doing this and

MAN IN SHADOW: Wanna chat privately?

RISA: Private?

Oh, I don't

I'm not really sure how that works, how do I

A sound effect. Risa looks at her screen.

RISA: Oh my god -- money! You just sent me money! Holy shit! Ok so umm

MAN IN SHADOW: Private show?

RISA: Ok look, I'm new to this and I don't know how much I really want to -- This is my first time and

MAN IN SHADOW: Oh yeah?

RISA: Umm yeah. That's not. I wasn't being sexy there, I was just telling you umm

I'm supposed to be upfront with you about how far I'm willing to go.

I read that on the Frequently Asked Questions, when I was signing up. So I should probably preface this with: I'm not interested in any kind of

MAN IN SHADOW: Hey, I just want to talk.

RISA: Wait, seriously?

MAN IN SHADOW: I just want to talk.

RISA: Fuck, I thought that was like really rare, I was just telling

Yeah, definitely. Yeah! Let's do it. Let's talk! Ok -- so I just click here I think and

Another sound effect.

RISA: Here we go. Hi.

MAN IN SHADOW: Hey there.

RISA: . . .

So how does this

MAN IN SHADOW: What's your name.

RISA: Oh uh my name is Starla.

MAN IN SHADOW: Sounds like a stripper name.

RISA: Does it? I was trying to pick something normal yet you know, exuding confidence.

MAN IN SHADOW: You're supposed to pretend it's your real name.

RISA: Shit. You're right. Umm, so no, my real name is Monica

MAN IN SHADOW: Monica?

RISA: Yeah.

MAN IN SHADOW: You know, you don't look like a Monica.

RISA: Well, ok that's probably racist.

MAN IN SHADOW: Isn't that a Jewish name?

RISA: Can you please just let this go? I'm Monica. My name is Monica.

MAN IN SHADOW: Okay, whatever you say, Monica.

RISA: So umm

How is your week going?

MAN IN SHADOW: Just fine, Mom. Thanks.

RISA: Ok ok why don't you just tell me something or ask me something or Where do you live?

MAN IN SHADOW: I'm outside Boston now.

RISA: Cool I'm in umm

Oh, I think I'm not supposed to tell you like personal information about myself but -- Boston! Boston sounds . . . *sexy*.

MAN IN SHADOW: Boston's not really a sexy town.

RISA: It's not?

MAN IN SHADOW: It's like a theme park.

RISA: Theme park?

MAN IN SHADOW: Locals dressed in costumes, giving tours. Everything roped off or behind glass.

Fucking closed on weekends.

RISA: That sounds fun!

MAN IN SHADOW: And the coffee sucks.

RISA: Well maybe you're just not a city person.

MAN IN SHADOW: Maybe.

RISA: One of my cousins -- we grew up in the city and he was just getting into all this trouble, and my uncle sent him to this uh boarding school down in North Carolina.

He totally mellowed out.

MAN IN SHADOW: No way! I did too! North Carolina!

RISA: You did!? What was it called? Not Wolf Creek --

MAN IN SHADOW: Wolf Creek! That's it!

RISA: You're lying.

MAN IN SHADOW: I'm not! Small world.

They really have you howl at the moon, you know? Everyone did it.

RISA: You howled at the -- ? I never heard that. I went to visit once for his graduation

There was a lake on the property too, right? Covered in -- what are they called

MAN IN SHADOW: Tip of my tongue

RISA: Azaleas! I think. Pink little flowers everywhere, so pretty.

MAN IN SHADOW: Azaleas! That's right.

RISA: You remember them too?

MAN IN SHADOW: Of course.

RISA: Wow that really is

Fucking small world, Jesus.

MAN IN SHADOW: Sure is. You're cute.

RISA: Oh

Oh thanks

MAN IN SHADOW: Adorable.

RISA: Thank you

MAN IN SHADOW: I think we have a connection.

RISA: I guess.

MAN IN SHADOW: Let's go further. I like you.

Another sound effect.

RISA: Oh, you gave me -- more money. Umm, look I don't know

MAN IN SHADOW: Take your shirt off.

RISA: Take my -- ? No.

MAN IN SHADOW: Oh come on

What's your real name

RISA: No I don't really

MAN IN SHADOW: I paid you

Take your shirt off

RISA: I'm sorry no

I told you, I'm not interested in that kind of thing.

MAN IN SHADOW: Take your fucking shirt off

RISA: No, I don't want

MAN IN SHADOW: Chink whore

She slams the laptop closed and chugs the rest of her beer.

Scene 5

Eerie sounds fill the theatre.

The Nadeshiko slowly approaches us like a cliche Japanese horror ghost.

Maybe her hair is covering her face.

NADESHIKO: (*ghostly*) OoOOOOOooooooOOOooOOOoooooooh.

OooooOoOOooOoo -- ahahahahaha.

Ghost! I am ghost!

Have you seen that movie with the Japanese girl -- "*Ringu*" -- Scary, right?

Japanese know thing or two about scary. Though, I am much better looking than her.

Sometimes in Japan -- the ghost, they look like fox.

Or sometimes, they have little ghost magic when they raise their hands like --

BAN!

She raises her arm and lightning strikes in the theatre. It surprises even her.

NADESHIKO: Wow. Did you see?

DON!

She makes lightning strike in another area of the theatre. She laughs.

NADESHIKO: Okay, let us try --

The Nadeshiko raises an arm -- it's like a radio. She changes the station with a gesture, until she finally finds something she likes. Some J-pop. (Google "SMAP" for a highly recommended Japanese boy band.) Maybe she dances along for a bit.

NADESHIKO: It is really not so bad here, you know.

Scene 6

Back in the apartment of the White Haired Man, who is in the kitchen with an apron, cooking.

A knock on the door.

The MAN glances at the door and returns to his cooking.

More knocking -- He opens it.

Risa stands in the doorway.

RISA: Hi.

WHITE HAIRED MAN: Hi there. You're

RISA: Monica from the / other

WHITE HAIRED MAN: Monica! Right. How did you get up here? My doorman usually calls before

RISA: I saw an older woman with groceries, so I helped her carry them in. He never even asked.

WHITE HAIRED MAN: Oh. Clever.

RISA: I thought you might not let me in, so.

WHITE HAIRED MAN: I'm not

I wasn't expecting you, correct? Am I forgetting something we had discussed?

RISA: No No I'm so sorry -- I don't know what I'm thinking

Of course you're busy you're

I just wanted to talk to you about the other day and apologize for

WHITE HAIRED MAN: You don't have to apologize for anything, Monica.

RISA: I do, actually.

I'm so sorry, I didn't realize it was still in my hand and

WHITE HAIRED MAN: Okay

RISA: I just wanted to explain, umm . . .

Can I come in? It's just a little awkward to be

WHITE HAIRED MAN: Sure. Yes.

How rude of me

Please come in

Risa takes off her shoes and enters.

RISA: It smells good in here

You cooking or something?

WHITE HAIRED MAN: Yes, I was just making some Agnolotti Piemontesi.

RISA: Fancy. Pasta?

WHITE HAIRED MAN: Pasta.

RISA: Wow I just totally interrupted like your whole evening flow

This is so embarrassing

WHITE HAIRED MAN: No no, you startled me of course but

RISA: I texted you before coming.

He checks his cell phone.

WHITE HAIRED MAN: Ah. So you did. I forgot you had my number.

I should probably be more careful about giving that out.

Risa bursts into laughter.

WHITE HAIRED MAN: What? What is it?

RISA: (*laughing*) I thought for a second that

I thought for a second that I had been texting a landline or something and

It's not funny it's not funny at all but

Risa laughs harder.

WHITE HAIRED MAN: Whoa. Whoa there, what's going on?

RISA: Oh my god!

She is uncontrollable.

WHITE HAIRED MAN: Hold -- hold on.

He pours her a drink.

WHITE HAIRED MAN: Not quite a faint but they pour stiff drinks when
women are being hysterical too, you know? No offense to you.

RISA: None taken. Thank you.

WHITE HAIRED MAN: Or they'd slap her. Quite hard.

In those old books, I mean. I'm afraid that didn't come out how I
intended.

. . .

Are you hungry?

RISA: What?

WHITE HAIRED MAN: Would you like to join me?

RISA: No. No, I couldn't possibly just interfere with your whole

WHITE HAIRED MAN: Please. There's more than enough. I always make
extra in case I want to spoil myself with seconds

My doctor tells me I should be taking it easy on carbohydrates, so really
you'd be doing me a tremendous favor.

RISA: Seriously?

WHITE HAIRED MAN: Very much so.

RISA: Fine

Sure, yes. Sure! Bring it on. Fucking carbo-load, I guess. Maybe I'll run a
marathon tomorrow.

WHITE HAIRED MAN: Wonderful. Make yourself at / home

RISA: Why didn't you call the police?

WHITE HAIRED MAN: Pardon?

RISA: I stole your money and you didn't call the police.

WHITE HAIRED MAN: I thought it was an accident.

RISA: It was. It was, but as far as you knew -- I mean, you didn't. Know.

WHITE HAIRED MAN: Maybe I thought you'd be back.

RISA: That would be a weird assumption.

WHITE HAIRED MAN: Maybe I thought it would be awkward.

RISA: Oh. I guess.

The MAN hands Risa a glass of wine.

Risa takes her wine and looks at the painting from before.

RISA: I think I get your whole design thing. Your whole place.

WHITE HAIRED MAN: Oh yeah?

RISA: If everything is white -- if everything is blank

All that's left is the painting, and it becomes everything.

WHITE HAIRED MAN: That's an interesting theory.

RISA: Is it true?

WHITE HAIRED MAN: I'm very sensitive to dirt. Filth. This way, I know when something needs to be cleaned.

RISA: Oh.

The MAN presents a tray complete with bowls of pasta, silverware, and cloth napkins.

RISA: Wow. This looks great. Thank you again.

WHITE HAIRED MAN: I'm sorry, are you allergic to anything? I should have asked before I

RISA: No way, allergies are for white people

No offense

Are you allergic to

WHITE HAIRED MAN: Peanuts and shellfish

RISA: Ah.

They eat.

RISA: How old are you?

WHITE HAIRED MAN: Hold old do you think?

RISA: I dunno.

They eat.

RISA: Do you have kids?

WHITE HAIRED MAN: You ask a lot of questions.

RISA: I'm being polite.

WHITE HAIRED MAN: Ok, I have a question.

RISA: Shoot.

WHITE HAIRED MAN: Do you remember what you called me the other night?

RISA: Huh?

WHITE HAIRED MAN: You called me something the other night. Do you remember what it was?

RISA: Umm no

WHITE HAIRED MAN: You called me a "pervert."

RISA: Did I? I'm so sorry, that was rude

But I mean

You ask

What you ask is kind of

WHITE HAIRED MAN: Do you think what I ask is "perverted?"

RISA: I think it's strange.

WHITE HAIRED MAN: I suppose it must seem that way.

They eat.

RISA: I'm sorry, did I offend you because I didn't

WHITE HAIRED MAN: Not at all I think you're very strange too.

RISA: Oh?

WHITE HAIRED MAN: Absolutely. This kind of thing certainly doesn't come naturally to you. This line of "work."

RISA: Right. I told you I lost my job and

WHITE HAIRED MAN: I remember what you said. So get a new one.

RISA: You say that -- you say that like it's so easy but

WHITE HAIRED MAN: You're a smart girl. Obviously well-educated. You could at least get a crap job. You'd be over-qualified, but that would be an option

RISA: That's embarrassing

WHITE HAIRED MAN: *That's* embarrassing?

RISA: What does that mean?

WHITE HAIRED MAN: I don't know, Monica. Perhaps I'm saying you have an atypical view of what constitutes an "embarrassing" or "not embarrassing" job.

Beat.

WHITE HAIRED MAN: I didn't mean to insult you

RISA: I don't know what I was thinking.

WHITE HAIRED MAN: Or judge you

Risa gets up to leave.

RISA: I never should have come back.

WHITE HAIRED MAN: But the thing is you still have my money.

Beat.

Risa takes the money out of her purse.

RISA: The thing is

The thing is I kinda need it.

WHITE HAIRED MAN: I know.

RISA: I could try again.

WHITE HAIRED MAN: I don't know about that.

RISA: I could bring a different book.

WHITE HAIRED MAN: It's not the book.

RISA: Maybe you have something I could borrow?

WHITE HAIRED MAN: It's not the book.

RISA: I want to earn it.

WHITE HAIRED MAN: Look I'm sorry I stopped you. I wondered about you
Not inappropriately, just -- you're strange, and I didn't want you to leave
like that. If you really need the money, you can keep it.

RISA: I want to earn it.

The MAN clears the plates to the kitchen.

*Risa gets an idea, she waits for him to enter -- sits down on the couch and
sticks her hand down her pants, as if she's mid-orgasm.*

Her arm is pumping and she breathes hard.

WHITE HAIRED MAN: WHAT ARE YOU DOING

RISA: What!? I thought you *wanted* like --

WHITE HAIRED MAN: NO no I don't no

RISA: OH! I wasn't even doing anything, I promise! That was pretty much
my thigh!

WHITE HAIRED MAN: Just keep the money, okay? Let's call it a gift.

RISA: From a?

WHITE HAIRED MAN: From a

Friend

Scene 7

*The Nadeshiko enters with a station she likes. She has a towel around her to
wipe sweat.*

*Perhaps she is doing Japanese Radio Calisthenics -- or she's just dancing to
some music, out of breath.*

NADESHIKO: I have not had this much energy in quite a while!

She dances or exercises for a bit more -- gets a cramp and grabs her side.

NADESHIKO: Ah! Ok, ok. I stop. You are here for story, not *exercise /
dancing.*

Oh, I remember something for you! Toshio, he loved this story and he
showed it to me in a magazine long ago. *Chizome* --

She gestures, and the station cuts out.

Perhaps in the next section, she turns her towel into "the doll."

Nadeshiko: Chizome no ningyo --.

It means (*spooky*) "The blood-stained doll . . ."

Sounds scary, no?

A young girl, Ema, sews this doll and sends it to a very brave and lonely
soldier stationed in China.

The soldier gives it her name: "Ema." The soldier, he carries Ema with
him everywhere.

Ema is his sister and mother and every girl and woman in Japan.

One day this soldier is killed in battle -- and Ema's dress is stained red with blood.

And very far away, after hearing the news, the far away little girl -- Big Ema makes a new dress for Little Ema.

The soldiers -- the man's comrades -- redress her in the new clothes.

Our pilots too. The tokko? They have dolls. So they are not alone, they carry the dolls with them.

The dolls a symbol of the women. And the women a symbol of Japan.

But you know

Being a symbol can be very exhausting.

There you are -- what you call it?

(*American accent*) "Closure."

Okay, okay. Bye bye now. Very serious bye bye now.

   She waves.

NADESHIKO: Bye bye.

   She waves longer and longer.

   She looks up into the sky.

NADESHIKO: Oh, this is some bull shit.

   She wipes her brow with her towel and throws it over her shoulder as she exits.

Scene 8

   White Haired Man's apartment. He is at the door with Risa.

   There are two clean glasses and a bottle of wine out on the table.

   Risa enters, wearing all-black, clawing her shoes off at the door. She's holding a plastic bag.

WHITE HAIRED MAN: Monica.

RISA: I brought you something.

WHITE HAIRED MAN: You should really call before you

RISA: Oh please, like you weren't expecting me. It's Monday. You know how I feel about Mondays.

WHITE HAIRED MAN: That Jerry is an absolute waste.

RISA: (*clocking the extra wine glass*) Is that glass for me?

WHITE HAIRED MAN: You never know when someone might drop by unannounced, so

RISA: Like someone else? Like someone other than me? Do you even *have* other visitors?

WHITE HAIRED MAN: No I just

> *Risa drops the bag and starts looking around -- under the couch, under the coffee table. She's crawling on all-fours.*

WHITE HAIRED MAN: What are you doing? Stop it. Get up

RISA: Hold on.

WHITE HAIRED MAN: Just sit down and have a glass. You're making me nervous. Will you please sit down?

RISA: Fine, it's just -- It's just I've been here so many times and I've never seen any evidence.

WHITE HAIRED MAN: Evidence?

RISA: Of all the people you've murdered.

Cheese plate? It's good stuff. Expensive.

> *Risa opens the bag and presents a Styrofoam box.*

WHITE HAIRED MAN: Where'd you get this? Wine?

RISA: Yes please.

I catered a funeral today.

WHITE HAIRED MAN: Is that right?

RISA: Yeah just some gig online

You look pleased.

WHITE HAIRED MAN: Do I?

And how does this job relate to you bringing me a very expensive cheese plate?

RISA: Oh, you know. There was a bunch of extra food, so they let us take stuff home. Come on, you've worked a service job, right? Like once in your life?

WHITE HAIRED MAN: No, I haven't.

RISA: Seriously? Not even in college or anything?

WHITE HAIRED MAN: Never.

> *The MAN serves her a glass of wine.*

RISA: Huh. I didn't know that was a thing. But you've had shitty jobs, right?

WHITE HAIRED MAN: Of course.

. . .

So you think I'm a murderer.

RISA: Oh yeah.

WHITE HAIRED MAN: Why?

RISA: Because there's no evidence!

WHITE HAIRED MAN: You think I'm a murderer because you don't have any evidence.

RISA: There's no evidence that you even live here -- it's bizarre. Like do you vacuum every hair out of the carpet every day?

WHITE HAIRED MAN: I keep things very clean because of orders from / my doctor

RISA: Uh-huh Nope. Murderer. I figured it out for sure when I was at this funeral today.

WHITE HAIRED MAN: How's that?

RISA: Well this guy was also like most definitely murdered.

WHITE HAIRED MAN: Is that right?

RISA: Oh yeah. I almost called the cops right then. It was his brother.

WHITE HAIRED MAN: How do you know?

RISA: Well you see, there are some mysterious circumstances surrounding his death -- and like heart attack? Please.

WHITE HAIRED MAN: I think you watch too much TV.

RISA: I think you don't watch enough. His brother went up there to speak in front of everyone, and he was forcing himself to cry. He was trying so hard to cry, but it wouldn't come, you know? And he had this vibe about him. It reminded me of you. And that's when I knew -- you both did it. Boom. Mystery solved.

WHITE HAIRED MAN: Well, I can't say I'm flattered.

RISA: Oh come on, I'm kidding.

WHITE HAIRED MAN: Of course.

RISA: But I mean you have to admit -- there's a lot of mystery around here Come on, tell me. What's your deal? Who used to live here with you? Your wife?

WHITE HAIRED MAN: I've never been married.

RISA: A lover? How scandalous. Oh my god, was it a student? Is that why you retired?

WHITE HAIRED MAN: No, nothing so newsworthy as that.

RISA: An Asian girl, right? That's why you ask for Would she read / to you

WHITE HAIRED MAN: Monica, this isn't something I feel comfortable / discussing.

RISA: Stop calling me that.

WHITE HAIRED MAN: What?

RISA: Monica. That's not my name. You know that's not my name.

WHITE HAIRED MAN: So what is it?

RISA: Risa.

WHITE HAIRED MAN: Risa That's a nice name.

> *Beat.*

RISA: Well?

WHITE HAIRED MAN: What?

RISA: What. Is. Your. Name.

WHITE HAIRED MAN: What do you think it is.

RISA: Oh my god, seriously?

> *Risa gets up, looking around.*

WHITE HAIRED MAN: What are you looking for now?

RISA: Well, you've got to have some email lying around here somewhere.

WHITE HAIRED MAN: Just sit down, Risa.

RISA: Come on. You never tell me anything about yourself. It's so one-sided.

WHITE HAIRED MAN: You choose to tell me as much as you do. You enjoy it more than I do.

RISA: Yeah, I guess.

> *Risa drinks wine.*

WHITE HAIRED MAN: You uh

You been to a lot of funerals?

> *Risa glares at him.*

WHITE HAIRED MAN: I've seen my fair share.

RISA: Yeah, me too.

WHITE HAIRED MAN: You're too young to have seen that many.

RISA: Well, I have. So.

WHITE HAIRED MAN: Oh yeah?

RISA: My dad.

WHITE HAIRED MAN: He . . . ?

RISA: Yeah. Few years ago.

WHITE HAIRED MAN: I'm so sorry.

RISA: Oh, it's ok! It's totally ok. He was an asshole. It's fine.

I'm totally fine with it.

Oh god -- it's not. It's not like I have daddy-issues or something -- that's not what this is.

It's just something that happened and I'm fine with it and it has nothing to do with -- I'm over-sharing again, aren't I? I'll shut up.

WHITE HAIRED MAN: . . .

How was the rest of the funeral?

RISA: I mean it was fine, it was just ugh

WHITE HAIRED MAN: What?

RISA: Well it's weird to tell you now.

WHITE HAIRED MAN: I'm a good listener.

RISA: I know, I don't know how, but you get me to tell you everything -- my deepest darkest thoughts and

Ugh fine

So there's something like 150 people there and like and everyone is white I'm literally the only non-white person in the entire building. And the white women are staring at me like always, you know

WHITE HAIRED MAN: Always?

RISA: Yeah, they just do that. But the men are feeling ballsier than usual, I guess? Because it's a funeral? So they're staring at me too. Usually it's out of the corner of their eye, you know? But today, they're straight up staring. And I can't tell if it's because they're like checking me out?

Like they are showing their sexual attraction to me because this is just how they are dealing with their immense grief

Or they are just like "Look at that person there. Look at that person that's different. How strange."

WHITE HAIRED MAN: I won't pretend I know what that feels like.

RISA: Well. Say you're getting on the bus, right?

And like two white guys are sitting near the front, talking about you and laughing. And you can't hear what they're saying, but it's obvious. They're making it obvious.

WHITE HAIRED MAN: Okay.

RISA: Now, you'll probably think like, "Wow, those guys are assholes."

WHITE HAIRED MAN: Maybe not in those exact words, but sure.

RISA: Now imagine you're a black man: You walk on the bus and people are laughing and you're like "Either: 1) those guys are assholes or 2) they're racist." And you just don't know which.

WHITE HAIRED MAN: I see that.

RISA: Or like a white girl, right? "Either 1) those guys are assholes or 2) they're sexist." Now for a non-white woman: 1) They're assholes. 2) They're sexist. 3) They're racist.

It could be any of them.

WHITE HAIRED MAN: But does it matter, at that point? Does it matter? Aren't they just assholes no matter what?

RISA: It matters to me. And as far as the funeral -- Like if I'm going to get paid for that experience, I want us to all be on the same page, you know? Like here I am. We both know you are here to look at me. Or I'm here to look at you "That'll be however much money, please."

If I'm gonna get stared at, why not make some money off it, you know?

. . .

I mean not with you, obviously. I couldn't do it for you, but

WHITE HAIRED MAN: But you think you could for someone else?

RISA: I don't know. Maybe.

WHITE HAIRED MAN: I

I hope you don't mind me being honest with you, Risa.

RISA: Not at all.

WHITE HAIRED MAN: It's something I've been wanting to talk to you about.

I don't think you should pursue this line of work. I don't think you're well-suited for it. I think it's great that you're trying your hand at something else, and this cheese plate is wonderful, and I think other more traditional jobs won't be so awkward in the future if you keep at it. I mean no offense by this, but you're very nice. Some might say naive.

RISA: Okay.

WHITE HAIRED MAN: I mean no offense, of course.

RISA: None taken.

. . .

Huh. Well. I actually have been, so.

WHITE HAIRED MAN: Have been

RISA: I mean not exactly the same but

WHITE HAIRED MAN: Is that right?

RISA: Yeah umm -- my cousin Sue (*realizing she gave Sue's real name*) . . . zan Susan. She hooked me up with this gig, so.

WHITE HAIRED MAN: What kind of a gig?

RISA: Well, I told her about what had happened with you, / and she

WHITE HAIRED MAN: You told her about me?

RISA: What? Well, yeah. I mean -- not the details, just that I couldn't you know do the thing and so she set me up with

Or one of her friends, really. It's good money, really good money And I'm good at it. I just watch.

She got me in touch with this couple, and I watch them have sex.

WHITE HAIRED MAN: I see

RISA: Yeah. I just sit in the corner and watch. I don't have to do anything. And it's via like apps and stuff, so if I get murdered or whatever, there's a record of them sending me money, so there's very little chance of you know -- murder. I could walk away at any point. It's basically on the honor system. Which is kind of cool. It's really safe, And they make sure I feel really safe -- and

I mean

I don't know why I'm like explaining myself to you.

WHITE HAIRED MAN: You don't have to.

RISA: I know. You just seem so pissed, so.

WHITE HAIRED MAN: I'm sorry for getting agitated I

I have bad days too, Risa. Just like everyone else

RISA: I don't know how -- you barely leave this place

Oh my god.

Do you leave this place?

WHITE HAIRED MAN: That's ridiculous

RISA: Do you *ever* leave this place?

WHITE HAIRED MAN: Of course I do.

RISA: Then -- Then what is it? What's the big fucking deal?

What's the thing

Come on, what's your thing

Why do you post the gigs

Why, tell me why.

I just want to know why.

WHITE HAIRED MAN: Risa

RISA: Why?

WHITE HAIRED MAN: Risa, I can't have you talking about me.

RISA: What? Oh, to Susan?

WHITE HAIRED MAN: To anyone. It's not something I feel comfortable with.

RISA: No, that's nothing. It's not a big deal.

WHITE HAIRED MAN: I have a very specific way I like things and

RISA: She's seen like everything there is to / see

WHITE HAIRED MAN: MY PRIVACY IS VERY IMPORTANT TO ME.

Beat.

RISA: Right. Sorry I'm I'm sorry, I should have asked you before I mentioned
it. I didn't know it was such a big deal for you

WHITE HAIRED MAN: I've learned some things are best left private, that's all.

RISA: I'm sorry

WHITE HAIRED MAN: I

. . .

I think you should stop visiting me here.

RISA: Are you kidding me?

WHITE HAIRED MAN: This relationship has gotten confusing for the both of
us and I don't think it's appropriate for it to continue any longer.

RISA: Is that right? You don't think it's *appropriate*.

WHITE HAIRED MAN: Yes.

RISA: So, it's just over -- just like that?

WHITE HAIRED MAN: I'm afraid so.

You ask too many questions, Risa.

> *Beat.*

RISA: Fine. Whatever. I have a gig anyway.

> *Risa exits.*

ACT 2

Scene 1

> *The Nadeshiko centerstage. She is very excited.*

NADESHIKO: Welcome back. Is everyone here?

I hope the line was not too long for the rest room.

Ok ok -- I figure it out! You see, I do it all wrong.

The ghost. They have a a *heaviness*.

Something heavy in them. That stop them from --

> *She gestures flying up into heaven.*

NADESHIKO: There is weight. There is burden. There is regret.

So I

I will confess to you. My story as a Nadeshiko. I have never told. My regret.

And then you must let me go.

Oh! Also --

> *She pulls out a program -- it is dog-eared throughout. She has been studying this.*

NADESHIKO: I was looking through this, and I noticed we have not seen this actor: [NAME OF ACTOR PLAYING TOSHIO]. Handsome. So we will start with --

Oh! Oh no.

Someone was sitting right *there* before. In that seat right there.

Do you know what happened to him?

Maybe he is still in the restroom. Very long line for that man, maybe.

Should we wait for him? I hope he is ok.

It is rude to start without him, I think. We must show respect to others.

Beat.

NADESHIKO: Eh. Perhaps we get started and catch him up later.

1945. A bright spring day.

The lights shine a little too brightly.

NADESHIKO: Maybe not quite so bright.

The lights lower a little.

NADESHIKO: Very nice. Two young Japanese are on the street in Chiran.

1945. Shoko follows Toshio on the street. He is eating an ice pop. He stops -- she stops. He looks back slowly, Shoko looks casually at the sky.

The Nadeshiko takes a seat, watching from the audience/aisle/stage.

Toshio starts walking again. Shoko follows him. Toshio quickly turns and catches her.

Shoko stands frozen, a deer in headlights.

TOSHIO: You've been following me.

SHOKO: I

haven't.

TOSHIO: I was stating a fact, not asking a question.

SHOKO: Well, your fact was wrong.

TOSHIO: Okay. Well, fine then. It was very nice to . . . meet you -- I'll see you / around.

SHOKO: What's your name?

TOSHIO: Sorry?

SHOKO: I was just wondering what your name was.

TOSHIO: I'm Watanabe Toshio.

SHOKO: Oh. Okay.

TOSHIO: Well?

SHOKO: What?

TOSHIO: . . .Your name?

SHOKO: Oh! I'm so sorry. I'm Shoko.

You're

New to town.

TOSHIO: Just recruited. Started training on Tuesday.

SHOKO: There are so many of you here.

TOSHIO: Just one me. I'm an original.

SHOKO: You're just a boy. You're all just boys.

TOSHIO: Can I *help* you with something?

SHOKO: No.

Actually yeah

Umm you forgot your change at the store. I told the owner I'd deliver it to you.

But you were walking really fast, and it was hard to keep up.

Shoko looks at the coin in her hand.

SHOKO: I thought about keeping it.

I could tell all the stores in town I'd deliver all the change left by these absent-minded boys new to Chiran. Gather all this money and travel off to -- I don't know.

Egypt.

TOSHIO: Egypt? With the pyramids? Why Egypt?

SHOKO: I don't know. I think the camels must be cute and

It seems untouched -- by the war.

I'm not sure, but I feel like it might be untouched.

TOSHIO: No way. It's occupied by the West.

You wouldn't last a day.

A little girl like you.

SHOKO: You don't know anything about me.

TOSHIO: I know your name is Shoko and you thought about stealing my money.

SHOKO: Yeah, I did. So what? You can fantasize about whatever you want. It doesn't hurt anyone.

. . .

It's just not fair. I used to get an allowance, but I don't anymore because of the war. My father's off somewhere and my mother is . . . well, she's just been different. -- and I *help*. I'm helping. I'm *working*. -- but I don't get any money because we're "volunteers." That's what the principal at our school told us. We're "volunteers." But I don't remember volunteering for anything.

Beat.

TOSHIO: Just -- you keep it.

SHOKO: What?

TOSHIO: Hold onto it. The money.

Wait, I know I have some more coins somewhere around

Toshio fishes around in his pockets.

SHOKO: Oh, no.

That's okay.

TOSHIO: No, I remember having --

SHOKO: I don't want your money.

That's not what I was saying.

I want to earn it.

Shoko returns the money to Toshio.

TOSHIO: Okay.

See you around.

He turns to leave.

SHOKO: Wait! I'm sorry!

People tell me I talk too much. It's so exciting having you all here, and I -- I didn't mean to be rude -- I was just curious what you're like.

TOSHIO: Why me? You said it yourself. This town is infested with soldiers.

SHOKO: Oh, them? They're always . . . together -- You never see them on their own, really. Spending their money on sake and stupid little things

But I've seen you and you're always alone -- you keep to yourself.

Very mysterious.

TOSHIO: Is that right?

SHOKO: Mm-hmm.

Complete mystery.

TOSHIO: Alright.

Two minutes.

SHOKO: Two minutes for what?

TOSHIO: Let's play a game. You ask, I answer.

SHOKO: Really?

TOSHIO: Yeah. I'm bored. You're entertaining. I can spare you two minutes.

Extra points if you stump me.

SHOKO: Okay, where are you from?

TOSHIO: Yawn. Shizuoka. Is that really the best you can do?

SHOKO: We're starting off easy. What's your family like?

TOSHIO: Well, my parents are old -- and kind. Father is a fisherman. A kind, old fisherman.

I have a little sister. Loud, full of energy, always bothering me with questions: a lot like you.

SHOKO: Do you miss her?

TOSHIO: Of course I do.

Come on. What else?

SHOKO: Will we win?

TOSHIO: Excuse me?

SHOKO: Do you think we'll win the war?

TOSHIO: (*looking around*) What --

What is this? Who told you to --

Of course we will. Why wouldn't we?

SHOKO: Some say we're underestimating them.

TOSHIO: The Americans?

Shoko shrugs.

SHOKO: I don't know.

But maybe *someone's* grandfather was a businessman, who lived in America for years and years and years.

TOSHIO: Someone?

SHOKO: Yeah, *someone*. And when the man came back, he told this *someone's* mother all about his time there, and the man says that the Americans --

They're too strong. They're too organized. There's too many of them. They're smart and *human* and

TOSHIO: They're killers, Shoko. Monsters. It's in their blood.

They will rape you until you scream and scream and wish you were dead -- they will kill you in the most horrible ways.

You think your life is bad now? Just imagine what will happen if they win and they come here.

SHOKO: If we keep up this illusion that they are lesser than us -- we will lose this war. And maybe we already have.

TOSHIO: Do you have any idea what would happen to you if someone heard you saying something like that?

SHOKO: But don't you wonder? What they're like? What they're *really* like? I *know* that you

TOSHIO: Shoko, you don't know anything about me.

SHOKO: Then maybe I just hoped.

TOSHIO: Stop wasting your time with things that don't concern you.

We'll take care of the war. You just -- survive.

SHOKO: Right.

Right, of course.

I'm sorry.

TOSHIO: You know I could report you right now -- have your whole family arrested.

SHOKO: You wouldn't.

TOSHIO: Sure about that?

SHOKO: Yeah, I figured you out.

And I stumped you.

An awkward beat. Toshio gathers himself.

TOSHIO: You didn't.

SHOKO: Mm-hmm.

TOSHIO: You're strange.

SHOKO: They say that.

TOSHIO: Look, the truth is: I don't know much.

I've never seen an American. I pretty much don't know anything about Egypt.

But I *do* know this one thing:

We will win this war. We will win because we have to.

Stay safe, if you care to.

> *Toshio exits.*

NADESHIKO: You understand Japanese now, eh?

OoooooOoOOoooooooh, ghost magics, oooOOOooooooahahahahaah.

Scene 2

> *Shoko sits on a bed in the barracks. She looks at the ground, in thought. Toshio walks in. She doesn't notice him. He watches her for a moment.*
>
> *Toshio makes a sound, making his presence known. Shoko stands up immediately, back to work, changing the sheets on a bed.*

TOSHIO: Hi.

SHOKO: (*not looking at him*) I'm sorry, I'll be out of here in a minute.

TOSHIO: No, no. It's ok. I just came back for a quick nap, but I'll go find some shade outside somewhere.

SHOKO: Okay.

> *Shoko continues changing the sheets.*
>
> *Perhaps Toshio starts physically getting in the way of her work.*

TOSHIO: Do you umm

SHOKO: What is it?

TOSHIO: Do you not remember me? You interrogated me pretty aggressively the other day.

SHOKO: Of course I do.

TOSHIO: Okay, it's just . . .

SHOKO: WHAT.

TOSHIO: I've seen you around here since then, and you don't. You won't even look at me.

SHOKO: We're not supposed to, you know.

TOSHIO: I really don't.

SHOKO: Fraternize. With the soldiers.

TOSHIO: Ah.

I didn't know that you were -- You didn't tell me you were part of the Unit.

SHOKO: That's ok.

TOSHIO: The other day, in town.

SHOKO: You didn't ask.

TOSHIO: I didn't mean to snap at you.

SHOKO: It's fine.

I didn't realize either

TOSHIO: What?

SHOKO: What you all are doing here.

TOSHIO: Yeah. I know.

SHOKO: I must have sounded like an idiot.

"I don't remember volunteering." "I deserve money." "I'm escaping to Egypt!"

TOSHIO: No, it was funny.

SHOKO: Ugh God.

You should have said something.

TOSHIO: It didn't bother me.

SHOKO: You should have said something.

That you're sacrificing yourself. You're basically a human bomb.

TOSHIO: Right. Sorry.

Well, everyone knows now. The whole town.

SHOKO: Yep.

TOSHIO: There was a sortie this morning.

SHOKO: Yes.

TOSHIO: The first one here.

SHOKO: Mm-hmm.

TOSHIO: Were you there?

SHOKO: Mm-hmm.

TOSHIO: Are you . . . okay?

SHOKO: Mm-hmm. It's my job.

TOSHIO: That's not what I asked.

SHOKO: I'm fine.

TOSHIO: It must be hard. If you ask me, I don't think it's right to have you girls here. It should be reserved for men. For soldiers. It's not fair for you

SHOKO: I like that my work is important

TOSHIO: The women in town can wash the sheets -- I mean, hell, maybe we should be washing our own sheets or

SHOKO: That's not the job. You know that's not the job, right?
We're the flowers. It's for morale. It's important.

Beat.

Shoko changes a pillowcase.

SHOKO: **Kimura-san** left today.

TOSHIO: You were in that little "class" he was organizing, weren't you?

SHOKO: He's very smart.

TOSHIO: I know he is. We *all* know he is. Talked endlessly about his schooling and his teaching -- intolerable bastard.

SHOKO: He's gone now, you realize that, right?

TOSHIO: Death doesn't change what someone was.
Personally, I think it's disrespectful to remember them in a false light.
Fact: I didn't like him. But I can still thank Kimura-san for his service, despite the fact that he was an intolerable bastard.

SHOKO: He kind of was.
And that thin little moustache.

TOSHIO: Oh god, that moustache.

They laugh. It dies.

Beat.

SHOKO: His pillow was wet.

TOSHIO: What?

Shoko sits on the bed.

SHOKO: This morning, his pillow was wet.
I umm -- I came in to change the sheets and his pillow was soaking wet. He must have been crying early in the morning, or maybe all night -- I don't know. I pretended like I didn't notice. He's so proud. Always seemed to have it together.
I wish I hadn't seen it.

TOSHIO: Huh.

SHOKO: And I went with the other girls to the sortie, and they told us to bring flowers, so I was holding a branch of cherry blossoms we had just cut down from the tree by the school, and it was so awkward, and he looked so small, and . . .

TOSHIO: . . . And what?

Toshio sits next to her on the bed. They are close. A moment.

Shoko gets up immediately.

SHOKO: Nothing. I'm sorry, I should get back to work.

TOSHIO: Come on, I wasn't trying to

That's not what I want from you. I just want to talk.

SHOKO: No, I didn't think you --

It's fine. I'm fine. You should take a nap in here, so you don't catch a cold. I'll leave. I'm leaving.

TOSHIO: Yeah, whatever you want.

Shoko stops at the door. She doesn't look at him.

SHOKO: He licked his lips.

TOSHIO: What do you mean?

SHOKO: I gave him the flowers and went back to stand with the other girls and he looked at me -- there was something strange in his eyes, and and he looked me right in the eye and he

TOSHIO: Licked his lips.

SHOKO: Yes. And I felt. Dirty.

He didn't say anything, but I knew what his eyes meant. He looked at my legs up to my breasts and up to my face and --

And it was just so much and the blood was draining out of my head and my fingers and I wanted to just throw up or scream or run but

But I remembered his pillow. How it was wet.

And I smiled at him and I took it. And I let him think whatever he wanted because

TOSHIO: Because why?

SHOKO: Because we're supposed to take it.

TOSHIO: Take . . . what?

SHOKO: All of it.

It's my job. Isn't it?

Shoko exits.

Scene 3

Gunfire. Explosion. War outside.

Toshio is in a barracks, Shoko runs in.

TOSHIO: Thank god -- I thought you got killed out there --

SHOKO: I'm ok. I'm ok, I just

I just need to catch my breath.

Gunfire.

SHOKO: They found us.

TOSHIO: What were you doing out there?

SHOKO: I just froze. I saw the planes -- I saw them, I didn't know what to --
I saw the man in the plane. The pilot. I *saw* him. He was so close. I
couldn't move.

TOSHIO: You didn't see him, Shoko. That's impossible.

SHOKO: His eyes were a cold blue or grey maybe. I couldn't see his hair but
I bet it was yellow.

Just like they say. An ugly yellow or that bright orange they have over
there.

TOSHIO: Hey. Hey! Look at me.

SHOKO: What?

TOSHIO: Was anyone else with you?

SHOKO: They . . . they they all ran before me. I think they're all safe. I
just came here. I wasn't paying attention. They're okay, I think. I think
everyone's okay. Where are your --

TOSHIO: They're in town today. I stayed back to write a letter, and
Shit. How did they find us.

Silence. They listen intently.

SHOKO: Do you think they're gone?

TOSHIO: I don't know. Probably not. They like to double-back to find
stragglers. We should hide out here for a little while. Just in case.

SHOKO: Ok.

TOSHIO: You're shaking.

Shoko retreats from him.

TOSHIO: You have every right to be scared. You could have been killed
today.

You have to tell them you won't do this anymore. Your principal, the
general, whoever. Tell them.

SHOKO: Toshio.

TOSHIO: It's not your job! It's like you said: You didn't volunteer for this.

SHOKO: No, Toshio. You were right. They're monsters. I saw them. And
they saw me.

They saw *who* I was and they still -- We have to win. We have to, or --

Gunfire, the planes over the base again. Shoko jumps.

Toshio holds her.

TOSHIO: It's okay. They'll be gone soon.

They'll be gone soon, Shoko.

He squeezes her tighter.

Scene 4

Late at night. Shoko is home alone.

A knock at the door. Shoko panics and goes to the door. Either another part of the stage or offstage:

TOSHIO: (*O.S.*) Can I come in?

SHOKO: (*O.S.*) Are you kidding me? No! You'll wake up my Mother --

TOSHIO: (*O.S.*) Go for a walk with me then. Please?

Just for a little bit -- and I'll leave you alone, I promise.

SHOKO: (*O.S.*) Fine, just

Just for a minute. Okay?

TOSHIO: (*O.S.*) Okay.

We are transported outside. Shoko and Toshio on a walk.

SHOKO: How did you find my house?

TOSHIO: Maybe I followed you. Like you did to me once.

SHOKO: (*laugh*) I thought you were such an ass then.

TOSHIO: That's because I was being an ass to you.

SHOKO: Did you hear the news?

TOSHIO: What news?

SHOKO: I read in the newspaper today: we're winning.

TOSHIO: Is that right?

SHOKO: Mm-hmm. It's all going to be over. Any day now.

TOSHIO: That's great.

SHOKO: What are you going to do? When it's over, I mean. Do you think you might stay here?

TOSHIO: Oh, I don't know. I can't think that far away.

SHOKO: You know, a lot of the families around here already lost their sons. There's gonna be a lot of work to do. If you wanted to stay, I mean.

TOSHIO: Yeah, maybe.

SHOKO: Or not.

It was just an option.

Beat.

SHOKO: Wow, look over there.

Toshio glances over and stops in his tracks.

TOSHIO: Wow.

Fireflies.

SHOKO: So many of them.

He sits on the grass looking down onto the river.

SHOKO: Are you okay?

TOSHIO: Yes. I'm fine. I'm --

Toshio holds his head in his hands.

SHOKO: Toshio.

Are you crying?

TOSHIO: No.

Shoko sits next to him.

SHOKO: Everyone cries. It's normal. It's a scary time.

TOSHIO: It's not that it's --

SHOKO: What?

TOSHIO: My sortie is tomorrow.

SHOKO: Oh God.

TOSHIO: I wanted to tell you because

I just wanted to tell you.

I'm not like you -- I don't usually talk this much, I don't know why I want to talk so much.

SHOKO: Are you scared?

TOSHIO: I don't know.

. . .

They're so bright.

SHOKO: The fireflies?

TOSHIO: (*nodding*) Not another light around. This peaceful little country town, so quiet -- and then a whole city just buzzing down the hill.

SHOKO: Do they have them where you're from?

TOSHIO: I don't remember.

SHOKO: My mother says fireflies are the souls of the people that have passed.

TOSHIO: That's ridiculous.

SHOKO: No. It's not.

TOSHIO: You don't believe that, do you?

He wants to believe it -- Shoko sees this.

SHOKO: I do. Why not?

Why not believe it?

TOSHIO: Ha, no wonder there are so many now.

So much death. Everywhere.

And me too. Just tomorrow. So fast.

That would be nice. For maybe just a night. To fly around. To be a light in the darkness.

SHOKO: That's what I want. To lose my whole weight and just float away. So peaceful.

    Beat.

TOSHIO: You'll be there tomorrow, right?

    Of course you will. It's your job. You have to.

SHOKO: Right.

TOSHIO: Take some of the weight off my shoulders. Make my plane a little lighter.

    Shoko smiles at him.

SHOKO: It's late.

    I have to head home.

TOSHIO: I'll walk you.

SHOKO: No, it's ok! I'll be fine on my own.

TOSHIO: Right. Thanks for humoring me tonight.

    Toshio exits.

Scene 5

    Shoko stands, looking around to see if she is alone. She is.

SHOKO: Dear Tennou-sama,

    Or Grandfather or Grandmother -- whoever is looking down to help when we are stuck -- Thank you for your continued help through these hard times. Mother and I are so thankful.

    I have a favor to ask.

    I know I've asked this before.

    Bring rain. Please.

    Bring a storm, flooding our barracks.

    Bring a wind so strong, our planes cannot lift off.

    A rain so heavy, the whole town shuts down and never sees the light again.

    Let it not relent. Please.

    Find a way.

    Drown the whole world if you must.

    Thank you.

    Shoko finishes the prayer and looks to the heavens.

Scene 6

Next day. Afternoon. A beautiful, sunny day at the airbase.

Toshio stands at attention. He looks around for Shoko, but cannot see her.

TOSHIO: Goodbye, Shoko-chan.

He bows to the unseen crowd and exits into his plane.

Engines start. Propellers spin. The planes take off.

Toshio is gone.

Engines overhead.

NADESHIKO: It's too late Shoko. You missed it.

Shoko runs onstage, seeing the planes flying higher into the sky.

SHOKO: Wait! Toshio, wait!

NADESHIKO: You will carry this with you for your whole life.

You took his weight after all, and he never even knew.

Beat.

Risa enters -- seems to see Shoko. Two worlds existing in one.

Scene 7

RISA: Sue, what the fuck.

SUE: What? I was working.

What!?

It is Sue. Maybe some set pieces are pushed in, so we see we are once again in Sue's bedroom.

RISA: Why are you dressed like that?

SUE: Well, remember that photo of Grandma Shoko I showed you a while ago? It got me thinking, see? There's like this whole other side of Asian fetishism that I haven't even been playing into, you know? Like this whole other market.

RISA: Where did you even find that?

SUE: Ebay.

RISA: Jesus. You're setting us back like 20 years -- you realize that, right?

SUE: Look how fucking cute I look!

RISA: Mm-hmm.

SUE: Oh, big fucking deal. Like I'm the only one doing this -- Since when is it my job to like "fix fetishism." If I don't do it, they'll find some other bitch . . . or turn to porn or whatever. You really want that?

RISA: How is what you do different from porn?

SUE: Seriously, you want to have a discussion about terminology right now? What do you want? I'm busy.

RISA: Can you hook me up with another gig?

SUE: Are you kidding me? You get all judgemental on *my* shit, then you want my help? You need to take a business class or something -- learn how to make a deal.

RISA: That's not what they teach in business school.

SUE: Okay, you know what? I know you're like "finding yourself" or whatever, but slow down. You have been *killing* it with that couple I hooked you up with. They are so happy. They don't want me back. I think your awkward, amateur thing is working for you. Milk it.

RISA: Come on.

SUE: You don't need it. It's not the money.

RISA: I *do* need it, Sue.

SUE: Fine. Be a fucking egg donor.

RISA: What?

SUE: You can make like tens of thousands of dollars by donating. Especially Asian women, man. We can make bank with eggs.

RISA: Sue.

SUE: I'm serious! Like double some other groups. This Korean chick in Salt Lake got like fifty grand because white people assume our babies will be smarter or something

RISA: Whoa, really?

SUE: Suckers. And the higher your SAT score, the more money you get and they pay for the doctors and the hospital stuff and all of that and

RISA: Sue?

SUE: Yeah?

RISA: No.

SUE: I'm just saying! If it's just about the money.

RISA: I can find stuff online, you know. All kinds of stuff.

SUE: What, Mr. "WATCH ME?" Please.

RISA: Yeah. Yeah, sure. Why not? If you won't help me, why the fuck not?

SUE: Why not? Because you don't even know what this dude wants from you. You heard of the Craigslist Killer? Stop being so naive.

RISA: Thanks for the help, truly, but I know what I'm doing. I like making white people pay.

SUE: Ris, you're not made for this.
      You're too . . . soft.

RISA: Soft. You mean weak.

SUE: I didn't say that.

RISA: I'm not weak.

SUE: Look, this is my *job*, ok? It's not some hobby -- just leave it to the professionals.

RISA: You don't know shit about me.

SUE: I'd like to.

Is this about your Dad? Because you never talk about it and it feels like -

RISA: No, it's not about him.

SUE: Are you fucking pregnant or something?

RISA: NO.

SUE: Well, what the fuck, what's wrong with you. You depressed?

RISA: No. I don't know. I don't think so.

SUE: What the fuck is it?

RISA: I DON'T KNOW

I just want to, ok!?

> *Risa starts to leave.*

SUE: DON'T YOU WALK AWAY FROM ME!

> *Sue hits Risa with a pillow -- HARD.*

RISA: THE FUCK IS WRONG WITH YOU

LEAVE ME ALONE

> *Sue hits her again.*

RISA: STOP IT, THAT'S

> *Risa hits Sue with another pillow -- HARD. They hit each other. It's not cute. It's brutal.*

SUE: Ow! Ow, stop it, stop it, okay?

RISA: Omigosh are you okay? I'm so sorry --

> *Sue turns on Risa and shoves her backwards on the bed, straddles her with the pillow raised threateningly.*

SUE: What the fuck is going on with you?

RISA: Leave me alone!

> *Sue smothers Risa. Risa struggles violently and pushes her off.*

RISA: WHAT THE FUCK SUE

SUE: YOU STARTED IT

RISA: WHAT? THAT'S NOT EVEN CLOSE TO

YOU COULD HAVE KILLED ME.

SUE: No way -- it's physically impossible to kill someone with a pillow. It's totally breathable. That whole thing is an urban legend.

RISA: Like SO MANY PEOPLE HAVE BEEN SUFFOCATED WITH
PILLOWS
SUE: AGREE TO DISAGREE
They sit, exhausted.
SUE: I'm worried about you.
RISA: If you're not going to help, I'll figure it out myself.
Risa starts to exit.
SUE: Where the fuck are you going?
RISA: Just mind your business, will you?
SUE: Whatever. Fine.
Beat.
SUE: Be safe.

Scene 8

NADESHIKO: Why am I still here?
My story is over.
Risa enters on the phone, looking up into the sky.
RISA: Hello, Mr. WATCH ME.
NADESHIKO: Risa.
RISA: (*laugh*) That's what I call you. You're a mystery and I love me a
mystery.
Seriously? Yeah, show me. I'm down. What am I gonna see?
(*looking around*) No, no one else is here
Beat.
RISA: Whoa. You look great. No, seriously. Perfect.
You don't believe me?
Well, that's on you because it's true, okay?
It's true.
There is literally no such thing as a perfect person.
I've been thinking about all those women you see, you know -- the ones
with no flaws and everything is perfect?
Even them, they actually have bad breath or cellulite or they're going
blind or
You get the idea.
It's not that everyone is beautiful.
It's that everyone is ugly. So no one is ugly.
So it doesn't matter. You see?

Me? I'm ugly. I'm really ugly.

I've disowned my mother for no reason.

I might be the ugliest.

What? Well, no. Not for

No, I'll tell you. It's okay. We're equal. You share, I share, right?

A little different, I know, but this is *my* naked. I give it to you.

So, my Dad died like what

A little over a year ago?

What? Oh, thanks. Thank you, but -- it's actually fine. It's really fine.

But

my family was like this overly strict, controlling, unreasonable, patronizing fucking stereotype of an Asian family -- unbearable and embarrassing and

That's how it always was, right?

And then my Dad died and like

My mom turned into this different woman.

She's full of life now and like immediately started like dating and

No, that's not what

That's not what bothers me. I don't care about -- what bothers me is

Fuck

What bothers me is

Where the fuck was this woman before? Where the fuck was this fun, lively, loving, happy, supportive woman ever? Ever in my life?

Just this one man this fucking boring-ass, dumb-fuck of a man kept her so hidden from us for so long -- for decades. For our whole lives, and she just let him.

It's pathetic.

It's so weak and sad and it makes me so fucking angry to see

To *know* that my mother is just so embarrassingly weak.

I can't bear to look at her.

Her weakness fills me with fury

I can't I can't even filter it into anything useful, it doesn't make sense. I just.

I can't be happy for her now

You see, I'm ugly.

I'm sorry, I got side-tracked that was

Sometimes it's easier to talk to a stranger, I guess.

You're welcome.

But right now, you -- You are the most perfect person in the world.

(*laugh*) I'm not messing with you, I swear.

I mean it.

I see you. We breathe the same air.

Yeah. Open the window. Breathe in that cold, night air.

Wow there you are, flesh and blood.

Hi.

> *Risa waves.*

RISA: Careful out -- I'm not sure you should come out --

NO.

> *Risa lunges forward.*
>
> *The sound of an ambulance.*

NADESHIKO: So much power in a hand. I cannot bear the weight sometimes.

Scene 9

> Night. *Some knocking in the blackout. Beat. Then endless, fast, scared knocking. Lights up on the White Haired Man, looking through the peephole, panicked.*
>
> *A pair of black boots sits by the door.*

RISA: (*O.S.*) Let me in!

WHITE HAIRED MAN: Risa? I can't

Look, it's not really a good time I

RISA: (*O.S.*) Just let me in! Please. Please! I don't know where else to

WHITE HAIRED MAN: . . .

Okay

Okay hold on

> *The MAN opens the door. Risa stands in the doorway, there's some blood on her jacket --*

WHITE HAIRED MAN: Risa. Jesus come in, I wasn't expecting

Are you okay? What's happened. Are you bleeding?

RISA: No. This isn't my

They brought me here

The

WHITE HAIRED MAN: What? Who

RISA: The police I told them I told them I live here

WHITE HAIRED MAN: Why?

RISA: I'm not sure. Maybe I felt dirty, and I wanted to be somewhere clean.

Risa notices she is still wearing shoes.

RISA: Sorry. Oh my god, I'm sorry I didn't mean to
   She begins to take off her shoes.

WHITE HAIRED MAN: It's okay, Risa.

RISA: No, you keep it so immaculate in
   Risa notices the pair of boots already by the door.

RISA: . . . here.

WHITE HAIRED MAN: I told you this isn't

SUE: (*O.S.*) If you invited a friend, that's way extra.
   Sue enters.

SUE: Ok, where do -- Ris!

RISA: What?

SUE: Yo what the fuck are
   Whoa. Is that blood? Ris, you okay? Are you / bleeding?

RISA: I'm sorry, Sue? What is
   What the fuck is going on here?

WHITE HAIRED MAN: I'm sorry, I'm trying to catch up myself -- do you two
   know each other?

RISA: Yeah, this is my fucking cousin

WHITE HAIRED MAN: Umm Susan?

SUE: Sue. It's Sue.

RISA: But what is she doing here
   What are you doing here

WHITE HAIRED MAN: She

SUE: I answered the ad.

RISA: You answered the ad.

SUE: Yeah, I
   Fuck, you pissed at me? I'm sorry, I'm sorry! I wasn't poaching, I swear I
   wasn't poaching. I looked online, and there was a new listing, and -- I'll
   split it with you. Right down the center, you know? No hard feelings?
   Like what, did he double-book or
   Or shit. Look, I don't do lesbian stuff. Especially with family.

WHITE HAIRED MAN: No. No -- Risa and I don't have that sort of
   relationship

SUE: Ha. Relationship? What do you mean?
   . . .
   Risa, what does he mean? You seeing him? Are you fucking seeing
   this guy?

RISA: No

WHITE HAIRED MAN: No, Risa and I are friends. Isn't that right? Friends.

SUE: Uh-huh, umm. I don't like this. This is
There is something super fucked up going on here. Come on, Ris. You gotta go -- Let's take you to the hospital.

RISA: I'm fine. I'm not hurt, I

SUE: Fine, we'll take you home. Come on. You're coming with me.

RISA: No you go ahead

SUE: RIS COME WITH ME

RISA: SUE GET THE FUCK OUT OF HERE RIGHT NOW

SUE: Risa, whatever this is? Is not okay. This is not how this works. You gotta have boundaries. And this shit is not boundaries. This shit is the opposite of boundaries.

RISA: It's not like that. Please just go away.

SUE: Uh yeah, Ris. It's like that. It's definitely like that.

RISA: Sue, just / go.

SUE: You are not talking me into leaving you here, covered in God knows what in some client's house, okay? I don't care if you're weird fucking "friends" or whatever. You gotta keep this shit separate, Ris.

RISA: Please.

SUE: You get 5 minutes. I'll be downstairs.

RISA: Fine.

> *Sue exiting, stops at the door.*

SUE: (*to the Man*) Aren't you forgetting something?

> *The MAN fetches his wallet. He hands her a wad of cash.*

> *Sue counts it.*

SUE: Five hundred. All here. I'll be downstairs.

> *She exits.*

RISA: Five hundred?

WHITE HAIRED MAN: Your cousin knows how to bargain.

. . .

I'm sorry that was I didn't know I didn't know she was your cousin

RISA: This is disgusting.

WHITE HAIRED MAN: Pardon?

RISA: "Pardon?" Oh my god "Pardon" you're so fucking fake British whatever

WHITE HAIRED MAN: I don't quite know / what you

RISA: We got goddamn Gwyneth Paltrow over here.

You fuck her?

WHITE HAIRED MAN: Is that what you think?

RISA: You fucked her.

WHITE HAIRED MAN: Risa, you know that's not what I seek / out

RISA: Tell me just fucking tell me the truth Please

. . .

You fucked her.

WHITE HAIRED MAN: And what if I did? Frankly, it is none of your business what I do with any other woman. There was a job, I hired you for it, you did not fulfill your role. That is our relationship. That is how this started. Everything else is irrelevant! Did she look upset to you? Did she look humiliated or angry to you?

RISA: But we're just interchangeable to you. It's fucking insulting.

WHITE HAIRED MAN: How is that insulting?

RISA: Sue is my cousin

Sue is my same blood

Sue is different

She's not one of your girls that you can just hire

WHITE HAIRED MAN: Risa, what happened? Who's blood is that?

RISA: OH THIS?

This is just Blood. It's not mine.

WHITE HAIRED MAN: I know.

RISA: It's not mine, I'm fine.

WHITE HAIRED MAN: Just because it's not yours doesn't mean you're fine.

RISA: You didn't even fuck her? Like do you not --

What the fuck is wrong with you?

You're not attracted to women or what?

WHITE HAIRED MAN: I have been very clear from the beginning about what I want and I don't want and

Frankly, this is why I discontinued our friendship. This is why

RISA: Yeah, you're so fucking specific about what you want, aren't you?

WHITE HAIRED MAN: Risa, calm down.

RISA: "Seeking: Asian Female, 20's to 30's."

WHITE HAIRED MAN: Come on. Don't

RISA: Why, because we're friends?

WHITE HAIRED MAN: Yes, I consider you my friend. So please stop

RISA: (*SIMULTANEOUS*) "Come
read to me nude. Literature
provided and chosen by you.
Send a single photo to the e-mail
provided to verify physical
needs. No touching. No sex.

WHITE HAIRED MAN:
(*SIMULTANEOUS*) Stop it. This
isn't what I -- I don't want this,
okay? Not like this. I care, I do.
Just stop this.

WHITE HAIRED MAN: STOP IT.

She freezes. He is holding her wrists.

RISA: You're hurting me.

WHITE HAIRED MAN: I

I apologize.

He releases her. Tries to tidy some things.

WHITE HAIRED MAN: There's a little spot of blood.

RISA: What?

WHITE HAIRED MAN: It's no problem. I'll just

RISA: A spot of

WHITE HAIRED MAN: I have some baking soda -- and an old toothbrush. I
saw this trick on TV

RISA: What the fuck are you talking about right now?

Beat.

RISA: Look, if it's not about sex, then what the fuck is it?

Your whole story -- there's got to be something there, right? You used to
be a teacher and you longed for a student and you threatened her

You made her do this or she wouldn't pass or something, or she
volunteered and and

She was an art student. That's her painting you have hanging on the wall.
Everything else is blank so that's all that exists. The painting is the only
real thing. And your wife found out and she left you or she killed herself,
right? And now you can't leave your apartment because you're stuck
here. You're stuck here emotionally and physically

Your body started deteriorating, and that's why you're

You're allergic to the outside. You haven't been outside in two years. You
used to have a nurse and she would read to you, but she disappeared and
she always kind of gave you a hard-on, so you're living out this fantasy
with other women who might look like her, waiting for the day you
finally find her and when you do

WHITE HAIRED MAN: And when I do?

RISA: Then you'll kill her for leaving.

WHITE HAIRED MAN: I had a wife. We divorced. She lives in California now,
she's happily remarried. We are on good terms.

I say former teacher because I am retired. My career was uneventful. I taught 7th grade English. I have money because I inherited from my Uncle when he passed twelve years ago. I request this one task because it is what I want. I'm not living out a fantasy of a student or a nurse. I find these women beautiful, but I'm not particularly interested in sexual interactions with anyone. And I can afford it. And the painting.

The painting is because

The painting is because I like that painting.

RISA: No.

WHITE HAIRED MAN: What?

RISA: That can't be it -- that can't

That can't be the end of it.

WHITE HAIRED MAN: I am very boring.

RISA: I don't believe you.

WHITE HAIRED MAN: Well, that's what's true, Risa.

RISA: No. No, you --

Why would you hide all that, it makes no sense.

WHITE HAIRED MAN: Risa.

RISA: You told me -- you told me before you weren't divorced.

WHITE HAIRED MAN: Did I?

RISA: I

I know you did! Why are you doing this?

WHITE HAIRED MAN: Risa.

RISA: Why can't you just tell me the truth? Jesus.

WHITE HAIRED MAN: Fine.

RISA: Fine?

WHITE HAIRED MAN: Fine

I taught English in Japan when I was younger. I met a woman there -- she taught art in the middle school I was employed. She was beautiful and intelligent and when she spoke, my world was consumed by her. I taught her English and she painted for me.

She was never a successful painter -- but was a wonderful teacher.

She would sit in my living room and read my books aloud -- and I would listen and at times correct her mistakes. One hot summer night, after too many glasses of wine, she read aloud and I never forgot the sight of her sitting on that stool, as so many did after her.

But I had left behind a fiance in America -- and she was uninterested in being a mistress to me. I never touched her. We never engaged in any sexual activity but when I returned here, it took a single month to realize the terrible mistake I had made. I returned immediately to Japan, but she had already married someone else. She wouldn't see me. I've never seen her since.

All I have left is the memory of the two of us in my living room in Japan. The happiest moment I can never recreate. And this painting.

Beat. Risa takes it all in.

RISA: Is that

Is that the truth?

WHITE HAIRED MAN: No.

RISA: God. You're so ordinary, it's unbearable.

. . .

Why am I here? It's like the dumbest thing.

WHITE HAIRED MAN: Because I needed someone.

Nadeshiko enters through the front door.

Nadeshiko locks eyes with Risa.

NADESHIKO: Risa!

RISA: . . . Are you?

NADESHIKO: My story isn't for them. Look at them. Fuck them.

Risa sees the audience. She is suddenly self-conscious.

NADESHIKO: Pay no attention to them. This story isn't for them, Risa.

There is a flower, Risa. A fragile, pink flower that is stronger than any weed. That's you.

RISA: No, I'm not that.

NADESHIKO: Risa -- you will feel the weight of so many others. As a Nadeshiko, you will carry their weight because they don't know they do this. They don't even realize what they put on you.

But!

You can be free of this burden. Understand?

It is not your weight to carry.

Beat.

RISA: Okay . . .

Okay.

Risa grabs her stuff and heads to the door.

RISA: I don't even know your name.

WHITE HAIRED MAN: I'm

I'm Tim.

RISA: Tim

Tim.

That's a stupid fucking name.

NADESHIKO: Leave it, Risa.

RISA: Good bye, Tim.

TIM: Bye.

Risa waves and exits.

Nadeshiko closes the door. She watches TIM with curiosity.

TIM is in thought. Finally he goes to the phone on the wall, dials a number.

TIM: Jerry. The young woman you let up a few minutes ago -- she'll be passing you in just a moment. Yes. I will no longer be requiring her services. And from now on, I will not be as lenient with guests being allowed up to my unit without my prior knowledge. That won't be necessary. Thank you, Jerry. Good night.

TIM puts the phone down. He sees the Nadeshiko. They stare at each other for a long time.

Beat.

TIM: A firefly -- in the city. How strange.

-- then exits.

The Nadeshiko looks up into the sky. Fireflies cover the stage. Brighter and brighter and brighter, then -She turns to us.

Beat.

She looks at her hand. She raises it -- perhaps to wave?

NADESHIKO: Stop looking at me.

She gesture for the lights to cut out.

Black out.

END OF PLAY

KAREN HARTMAN had four productions of three world premieres during the 2016–2017 season: *Roz and Ray* at Victory Gardens and Seattle Repertory Theater (Edgerton New Play Prize winner), *Book of Joseph* at Chicago Shakespeare Theater, and *Project Dawn* at People's Light in Malvern, PA (NEA Art Works Grant). Her *Goldie, Max, and Milk* premiered at Florida Stage and the Phoenix Theater, and was nominated for the Steinberg and Carbonell Awards. Other works: *Gaza Rehearsal* (Victory Gardens Ignition Festival), *Goliath* (Dorothy Silver New Play Prize), *Gum, Leah's Train, Going Gone* (N.E.A. New Play Grant), *Girl Under Grain* (Best Drama in NY Fringe), *Wild Kate, ALICE: Tales of a Curious Girl* (Music by Gina Leishman, AT&T Onstage Award), *Troy Women*, and *MotherBone*, score by Graham Reynolds (Frederick Loewe Award). New York: Women's Project, National Asian American Theatre Company, P73, Summer Play Festival. Regional: Center Stage, Cincinnati Playhouse, Dallas Theater Center, the Magic, and elsewhere. Publications: Theater Communications Group, Dramatists Play Service, Playscripts, Backstage Books, and NoPassport Press. Honors: McKnight National Residency, New Dramatists, Sustainable Arts, Rockefeller Foundation at Bellagio, the N.E.A., the Helen Merrill Foundation, Daryl Roth "Creative Spirit" Award, Hodder Fellowship, Jerome Fellowship, Fulbright Scholarship. A longtime New Yorker, Ms. Hartman is now Senior Artist in Residence at University of Washington, Seattle. Her prose appears in the New York Times and The Washington Post. www.karenhartman.org

Karen Hartman

Roz and Ray

CHARACTERS:

DR. ROZ KAGAN   plays late 30s through early 50s. Warm and direct.
She usually wears a lab coat. Caucasian. From Ohio.

RAY LEON   plays late 20s through early 40s. Capable of great
love and great rage. Latino, African-American, or
Caucasian. From Texas. If the actor playing Ray
is Latino, his last name is pronounced LÉON.

SETTING:

Medical and home locations in San Diego, California.

TIME:

1976–1987, and a single day in 1991.

The dates and text in **bold** at the top of each scene should be indicated by
projection, voiceover, or signs.

OTHER THOUGHTS:

The scenes flow fluidly, in most cases without transitional music or sound. Therefore
the actors will generally stay in the same clothes. Exceptions are indicated.

It's probably best if people talking on the phone don't use actual phones.

Although Ray and Roz discuss Roz's nicer office and bigger desk in 1987 (also her
office in 1991), it is fine to use the same desk throughout.

Overlapping text is indicated by a slash (/) where the next speech begins.

1976

San Diego Children's Hospital.

Roz sits on a doctor's stool, wearing a lab coat and a clown nose.

Ray sits next to her in a regular chair, wearing nicely kept working class clothes.

Her stool might be higher than his chair.

They face Ray's twin sons, age seven, unseen.

ROZ: Here we go!

I'm going to show you how to inject a magic medicine.

I will use a needle, and soon you will be the needle experts, the needle twins; my goodness you boys will be the needle super heroes!

Look at you boys.

I am so happy to meet you today.

(*One child cries. We don't hear him*)

Oh no.

RAY: (*Stern*) Mikey don't you cry this is fun.

Roz takes off the nose.

ROZ: No clowns. Just me.

Better already? Good for you.

The other child laughs. We don't hear him.

RAY: (*Stern again*) Ray Ray don't you laugh this is serious.

ROZ: It is pretty silly.

(*Roz plays with the clown nose, on and off*)

Clown.

Doctor Roz.

Clown.

Doctor Roz.

Did you know that we can't learn when we're scared? It's true. So if I'm ever explaining something, and you get scared, you tell me, okay? I want you both to understand what's going on, so you can take good care of your bodies.

Ready to learn?

(*Roz demonstrates*)

I clean my hands with antiseptic, and my skin.

I use a disposable needle.

I draw the Factor 8—mine is saline but yours will be genuine Factor 8!

I draw just past the blue line here, then push the syringe so I see a drop of fluid—

(*To Ray*)

This is important. You don't want to waste medication but you need to see that liquid. An air bubble will cause a real problem.

(*Back to the boys*)

I'll stick myself first.

Then you can stick Dad and me.

(*Quick glance at Ray*)

Or just me.

Then you can each stick yourselves.

I find the vein.

(*Patting her arm at the crook of the elbow*)

I have to pat pat pat pat pat pat pat.

Ah, there it is.

I pop the needle right into the vein.

I push the plunger.

Done.

It will take a little longer when you do this because you need to get all that good medicine.

Ready Mikey? Ready Ray Ray?

RAY: Do what the nice nurse says.

ROZ: I'm a doctor.

RAY: Excuse me, Ma'am.

ROZ: Please call me Doctor. Doctor Kagan, or Doctor Roz.

RAY: Pardon me. We never had a doctor take so much time. At Edgemoor we saw a nurse.

ROZ: Oh. Good. I am a different kind of doctor.

RAY: Do what the doctor says.

ROZ: Once they learn the procedure, they can inject the Factor three times a week. They don't need to wait for a bleed. They can self-inject at home.

RAY: What about transfusions?

(*Roz holds up a vial of medicine*)

That's it?

ROZ: We're done with the dark ages. I came to help open a state of the art hematology-oncology unit right here at San Diego Children's.

What do you boys like to do?

RAY: Sports.

ROZ: What's your favorite?

RAY: Ray Ray begs to do Pop Warner but I said no way.

ROZ: Your kids can play football.

RAY: Don't mess with their heads ma'—Doctor.

ROZ: Life expectancy for a hemophiliac boy born today is seventy years.

RAY: Seventy years. That's / normal.

ROZ: Normal.

> (*Roz and Ray look at each other, then back at the boys*)

Are you ready to inject Doctor Roz?

> *They aren't ready.*

RAY: Show respect.

ROZ: You're seven; you decide when you're ready.

Would you like to know a little more about the magic medicine first?

Okay. Do you ever bake cookies? With your / mom?

RAY: No.

ROZ: Well. You need all the ingredients. For cookies, for your body, for any project. Your blood is missing one ingredient, called clotting factor. So in the past, a hospital would pump you full of blood, and cryo, all those transfusions, right? But now:

(*Holds up vial of medicine*)

An advanced laboratory spins hundreds of gallons of blood, bathtubs of blood, a swimming pool of blood, and they separate it with big motors to extract this—

(*The vial*)

Factor 8. All that blood, concentrated. To deliver your missing ingredient so that when you get a cut or a bruise, your body can heal.

This is precious. For you.

(*Other bottle*)

This is saline. For Doc Roz.

Who remembers how to fill the needle?

RAY: Careful, Ray Ray.

> *Roz offers the syringe and vial to the boy.*

ROZ: Go ahead. You won't hurt me.

1991

> *Ray rises straight from his chair.*
>
> *He holds up his sign: "Dr Roz Kagan Killed My Son." Ray yells with all his might.*

RAY: **DR ROZ KAGAN KILLED MY SON.**

DR ROZ KAGAN KILLED MY SON.

DR ROZ KAGAN KILLED MY SON.

DR ROZ KAGAN KILLED MY SON.

DR ROZ KAGAN KILLED MY SON.

DR ROZ KAGAN KILLED MY SON.

DR ROZ KAGAN KILLED MY SON!

Roz in her office. She lets the phone ring. Then:

ROZ: This is Doctor Kagan.

Tom, my old friend. Gina's good? Kids are good? You still—what is it, windsurfing? Old dog new tricks, you old dog.

Yeah I hear him. It would be hard not to—

Sure I remember Ray Leon. I remember all my—

Will I make time to speak with you? When did we start saying that, "make time," did Reagan's people invent that? Even time is something you can just make if you've got the gumption? We'll never see the eighties again, and that's a silver lining.

Tom. Tom tom tom tom tom. You know me. You have seen me. Done feature after feature. I don't need to cover my ass at this point; I don't care about that. You know the physician I am.

You need a statement.

Sometimes you're the good guy, sometimes you're the bad guy, sometimes you're just a guy in a shitstorm.

That's my statement.

I like you Tom, I do, I hope life's going better in your corner. You're in journalism, what could happen to journalism?

Sorry I will not confront the individual.

Because I am a doctor not a circus performer.

And that's all the time I can make right now. Poof.

Ray outside with his sign.

RAY: Well Tom!

I'm here to protest the telethon yes.

I feel for the sick children and their families, but Children's Hospital is not the place to give your money.

I hope Dr. Kagan will accept my request for a face-to-face conversation this afternoon. There may be others attending, so get ready for a crowd.

We trusted Dr. Kagan.

She was a warm person, for a doctor.

She wore a clown nose.

That sounds real weird, almost mean, but she set us at ease.

The boys were small when we came to Children's. Seven years old.

They saw her like a mom.

The 1970s were not the ideal decade for family responsibility.

We uh we lived through a lot of changes, if you were born around 1950, hoo boy. Evelyn and me—that's their mother—we're from Texas. You wouldn't know the town. We wanted to see California, the fruits and the nuts, that was us.

(*Little laugh*)

The first time Ray Ray banged his knee and his leg swelled up like a prickly pear, Evie *(EH vee)* knew to go right to the ER. When Mikey was diagnosed, Evie skipped to Hawaii. Her brother had it, so she thought she knew what was coming.

You move to San Diego for a beautiful life.

(*He holds up one finger in an "Excuse me a moment" gesture, turns his back*)
FUCK FUCK FUCK FUCK FUCK.

(*Turns back around*)

One of the rougher nights, Dr. Roz gave me a book, *When Bad Things Happen to Good People.*

First off it's written by this Jewish fellow, and secondly his son *died* so I'm thinking, "What's this got to do with me?" Because our kids were not dying.

I'll say that slow.

They were doing real well.

This was after the Factor 8 came on the market and I do mean market.

She promised me one hundred and forty years of my sons' combined lives.

Normal.

I hear that, I'm thinking, Evelyn is an asshole. To be so scared of blood.

I hear normal, I see my future:

(*A glorious fantasy*)

I'm dying of some shit I deserve. Lung cancer, or heart disease from too much steak, an illness of excess. I'm ancient, my boys are old, with bellies and grey beards; their kids bring *their* kids to sing me out with the King—I do an Elvis cover band that remains very popular, fuck this alternative shit, fuck the new wave, **the entire 1980s can suck my hairy hole**—my dynasty is crossing me over with *I Can't Help Falling in Love,* and in walks Evelyn, old pruny Ev and she's like, Ray I'm sorry.

And I go, That's okay baby. Meet your great grandson.

Sometimes bad things happen to good people.

And you fucking happened to me.

1977

A medical office. In memory.

ROZ: I thought you might want this book, Ray.

RAY: Huh. The kids are good people all right.

ROZ: I meant you.

RAY: Thank you, Doctor.

ROZ: You have a lot on your shoulders as a single parent.

RAY: Thank you.

ROZ: This book is about wrestling down the illusion that we get what we deserve.

RAY: I never held that illusion.

1991

Ray continues where he left off.

RAY: Bear with me, Tom. I'm getting there. Here's an example.

I learned to cook. I had to.

I cooked and Mikey and Ray Ray did the dishes.

That Ray Ray was a clown.

He didn't want to make enough trips table to sink, you know? Didn't want to make the trips drying rack to cupboard.

Not like our kitchen is large, five steps at most.

Ray Ray was king of the balancing act

I'd be, son, make two trips and he'd be

(*Balancing, Ray Ray macho*)

Pops, I got this.

He's maybe nine. And I'm going son, put the plates *down*. Make the *trips*.

Pops I got this.

And then Crash. Broken glass is a four alarm event in our home. Two hemophiliac third graders crouching on their chairs and I'm—

It's possible I'm raising my voice.

I won't let them down off the chairs till I've swept, mopped, wiped every inch with a wet paper towel, again and again. It takes hours. We have no room for shards.

By now Ray Ray's crying, Daddy it was an accident, and I say no, you didn't *care* enough to do it *right*.

That's not an accident, son, that's *negligence*!

My twin sons were born with a debilitating blood disease requiring ongoing medical care and sustained interdependence with doctors and blood products.

Hemophilia, a bad thing, happened.

It demanded the best available medical intervention.

Instead.

Instead, my children were injected with a blood borne plague.

Not once.

Not twice.

But up to three times a WEEK. For their entire CHILDHOOD.

That's not something that HAPPENED.

That's something she DID.

Do NOT give your money to Children's Hospital. They are liars and killers and please put that on the air.

YOU DID IT.

YOU DID IT.

DR ROZ KAGAN KILLED MY SON.

1978

Ray and Roz in Roz's office. She holds a piece of pottery made by a child.

ROZ: It's beautiful.

RAY: It's an ashtray. Not the ideal tribute to a doctor, but that's what he made.

ROZ: I'm honored.

RAY: They have the kids do ceramics for Mother's Day.

ROZ: Oh.

RAY: Mikey sent his to Hawaii, but Ray Ray thought of you.

ROZ: Thank you.

RAY: You have kids?

ROZ: Not yet.

RAY: Not *yet*? Sorry, don't mean to suggest that you—(are old)

ROZ: We're figuring it all out.

RAY: You and your husband?

ROZ: Me and my husband.

RAY: He a doctor too?

ROZ: Yes, actually.

RAY: He move from Ohio with you?

ROZ: Yes he did.

RAY: He as smart as you?

(*Roz hesitates*)

You paused.

ROZ: I did not.

RAY: You *paused!*

ROZ: (*The ashtray*) I will treasure this.

RAY: Now don't start smoking.

ROZ: I quit in med school.

RAY: Sensible.

ROZ: A lot of people start then. You'd be shocked.

RAY: I would not be shocked.

ROZ: Your pickup is here.

> She indicates a medical cooler.

RAY: I'll get along.

ROZ: No rush. You must not get too many breaks.

RAY: Work in the morning, boys afternoon, music by night.

ROZ: Music?

RAY: Cover band, nothing too creative. A few bucks.

ROZ: Still, you must be good.

(*Ray shrugs*)

What kind of music?

RAY: Golden Oldies.

ROZ: I would not have guessed that.

RAY: It was an era, it really was, I never get sick of it. Unlike this disco business.

ROZ: I'm with you there.

> Ray is about to leave.

RAY: You ever hear the term hemo-homo?

ROZ: Did someone tease your boys?

RAY: No, but Evie said kids used to pick on her brother.

ROZ: It was different, even ten twenty years ago.

RAY: Why did they say that? Hemo-*homo*?

ROZ: Before Factor, it used to be that hemophiliacs couldn't run, or even really walk. They remained dependent at home. Most were on crutches by ten, in wheelchairs by twenty, died before thirty.

RAY: That was Michael, rest in peace.

ROZ: So physically, their muscles—

RAY: Soft.

ROZ: Yes. And socially—

RAY: Separate.

ROZ: Sure.

RAY: Probably crying all the fucking time. Excuse me.

ROZ: There was a fair bit of that. Also the disease only affects males, so it was an image.

RAY: I want tough guys. Run hard. Play ball.

ROZ: You got one in Ray Ray. If you're concerned, we have a social worker on staff now, Marie. I hired her.

RAY: I don't mean to take up your time with feelings.

ROZ: No, ask me, tell me. I just want you to know the resources. I don't meet many fathers in your position. I admire your strength.

RAY: I come from a line of healthy people, Doctor Roz.

I ran track back in Texas. And in the service, whoo they work you. Body a temple, you don't poison it you push it.

My father taught me count on no one but yourself.

Yet here are my sons.

(*The medical cooler*)

Receiving in their need.

What a blessing, in its way. Everyone inside everyone else. I like that.

ROZ: I like it too.

RAY: Do you do the Red Cross drive?

ROZ: Sure, every three months.

RAY: *That* is civilization. My dad wants to talk about Jesus? A blood drive is Christ. Healthy people give to the sick, from their veins. My sons brim with the blood of the world.

ROZ: Actually, Factor doesn't come from the blood bank.

RAY: I thought Factor comes from cryo which comes from blood.

ROZ: Yes and no. Both are blood products, but—Think of a pitcher of orange juice.

RAY: Okay.

ROZ: Let's say you have your pitcher of juice but you just need the vitamin C. Making cryo is like starting with juice, separating out the water, and using the concentrate.

RAY: Okay.

ROZ: Which was a breakthrough thirty years ago, because instead of transfusing a hemophiliac with whole blood—

RAY: Gallons of juice—

ROZ: Right, doctors could give them cryo.

RAY: Less juice, same vitamin C. I follow you.

ROZ: Which was better, but severe hemophiliacs need a lot of cryo per transfusion.

RAY: I remember. Ten bags at a time. All day in the hospital.

ROZ: Now, imagine if you could take that pitcher of orange juice and extract just the vitamin C. That's what these commercial labs do today, when they make Factor.

RAY: So if cryo is the can of concentrate, Factor is a vitamin pill.

ROZ: Exactly. *And* whereas cryo relied on volunteer blood donation so was always in short supply, these new commercial labs have the technology to collect blood, remove the liquid that contains Factor, and reinfuse the donor with his own red blood cells. So he can donate more often, a couple times a week instead of every three months. They become like professionals.

RAY: Paid?

ROZ: Yes, I believe they are paid.

RAY: Who are these professionals?

ROZ: (*She really doesn't know and is unworried*) I don't know. We buy it from Baxter Pharmaceuticals.

RAY: Well bless them whoever they are.

ROZ: Yes, there's no going back to the dark ages.

RAY: Weeks in the hospital, uh uh. I'd rather pick up the Factor while Ray Ray plays ball.

ROZ: That's right.

RAY: (*The cooler*) Do I sign for this?

ROZ: Joanne will help you at the front desk.

RAY: Doctor Roz. You have worked a miracle in my home.

ROZ: I entered the field at the right time, when we have a good product, that's all.

RAY: That's not all. You actually care.

He leaves. Roz holds her ashtray.

1991

Same day. Roz in her office. We hear a bit of Ray's chant: "Dr Roz Kagan killed my son."

ROZ: Yeah Tom. You're having a good day huh? My worst day is your best day, that's why we're close.

He sounds personal, you noticed? Why would Ray Leon sound so personal?

Okay, lemme give you a for instance: when I began my career, hemophilia care was brutal. My first rotation in the ER, I'm a wide eyed doe of a thing—this was a couple centuries ago—ambulance brings in a child screaming, thrashing. My first hemophiliac. They strapped him to a board to keep him still for a transfusion.

I said this is a chronic disease, why is he being seen in the ER? And the attending doc says, "Fucking hemos, they're like fire drills, just get it done fast."

And I thought, no.

I will change this.

Children will not be afraid. They will understand their care.

Not because I'm female, Tom, but because I'm human.

I was way ahead of the curve; I brought new protocol to San Diego Children's. My mentor didn't believe little guys could handle a needle; I said, tell you what they can practice on me.

You want to talk about skin in the game? Every one of my patients stuck a needle in my arm. I rolled up my sleeve and *made it personal.*

Plus, we didn't let them go. Remember most hemophiliacs used to die in childhood, so only pediatricians learned their care. When our young adults tried to see regular internists, bad things happened.

So we let them stay with us at Children's. Informally. They were our long term cheerful success stories. We went to weddings and met babies. We grew up together. It was fun.

1980

A snatch of children's Christmas music of the era (i.e. Alvin and the Chipmunks). A big Santa suit hangs in Roz's office, complete with red hat and beard.

Roz pulls Ray into the office. The first time we see her out of her lab coat. She's in a state of mortal panic.

ROZ: Ray!

RAY: Merry Christmas.

ROZ: You have to be Santa!

RAY: I what?

ROZ: Dr. Lee is in surgery. He can't make the party. Be Santa.

RAY: You be Santa.

ROZ: I can't be Santa, I'm a woman.

RAY: Dr. Lee is Chinese.

ROZ: Ray I'm serious. The kids are yelling for Santa. Here's the suit.

RAY: I'll help you change.

ROZ: No no no no no. You change. Please?

RAY: The boys will recognize me.

ROZ: They'll recognize me.

RAY: They're eleven, they know there's no Santa.

ROZ: Great. So.

She holds up the suit.

RAY: Uh uh.

ROZ: But you *perform*.

RAY: So can you.

ROZ: No, no. I'm shy.

RAY: What did Dr. Lee say?

ROZ: He left a memo with Joanne.

RAY: What did it say?

ROZ: It said, I'm in surgery.

RAY: And?

ROZ: I'm in surgery. Be Santa.

RAY: This is your job.

ROZ: But you would be better.

RAY: Sure I would. But your *boss* told you to be Santa.

ROZ: He doesn't care who—

RAY: *Now* you're going to tell him, "I can't, I'm a woman?" After how hard
you work? How you achieved equality? Now you can't because you're a
woman?

ROZ: (*Hoping she's right*) It's just Santa.

RAY: Doctor Lee sees you as Santa. He didn't think twice. He said, Be Santa.
That's great! Don't get me to do it.

ROZ: But you do Elvis.

RAY: Different.

ROZ: Closer.

RAY: Ho ho ho.

ROZ: Come on.

RAY: Try it. Ho ho ho.

ROZ: I don't even celebrate Christmas.

RAY: You should come for Christmas.

ROZ: Really?

RAY: That would be fun, you and your husband right?

ROZ: He might have plans.

RAY: Okay just the four of us then, either way, or my mother might come in; I make a ham, does your faith—

ROZ: I eat ham.

RAY: Okay, oh boy, we are set. Dr. Roz is coming for Christmas!

ROZ: Terrific.

RAY: Right after you do Santa.

ROZ: I get stage fright.

RAY: Just think: I have what you want.

ROZ: I have what you want?

RAY: I have what you want.

ROZ: I have what you want.

RAY: I have what you want for CHRISTMAS.

ROZ: Ray—

RAY: Ho ho ho!

ROZ: Ho ho ho!

RAY: Lower. Ho ho ho!

ROZ: Ho ho ho!

RAY: Louder. Ho ho ho!

ROZ: Ho ho ho!

RAY: Good, let's try the beard.

ROZ: No one will believe me.

RAY: The little ones will believe you and the big ones already know.
(*He places the beard and hat on her, adjusting gently. She enjoys this*)
You are going to be the best Santa Claus the Children's Hospital Hematology Oncology Unit ever saw.

ROZ: Come on.

RAY: You know why? Because you're real.

ROZ: Ray.

RAY: You *do* have what we need. You *do* go child to child. You *do* pull each one close and ask questions. What do you want for Christmas?

ROZ: I don't even . . . (celebrate)

RAY: (*Santa voice*) What do you want for Christmas?

ROZ: (*Attempt at Santa*) What do you want for Christmas?

RAY: (*Santa*) What do you want for Christmas?

ROZ: (*Attempt at Santa*) What do you want for Christmas?

RAY: Ho ho ho!

ROZ: Ho ho ho!

RAY: Better. Ho ho ho!

ROZ: Ho ho ho!

RAY: **Ho ho ho what do you want for Christmas?**

ROZ: **Ho ho ho what do you want for Christmas?**

RAY: Get that suit on girl because you are SANTA.

ROZ: I'm Santa!

RAY: You want privacy?

ROZ: Just help me.

 (*He helps her put on the Santa jacket*)

 I'm Santa. I'm Santa.

RAY: You're Santa.

ROZ: I'm Santa?

RAY: Ho ho ho what do you want for Christmas?

ROZ: (*Best yet*) **Ho ho ho what do you want for Christmas?**

RAY: Go get em.

1982

 Club music.

 A phone rings very loudly in Roz's home. She answers, wide awake.

ROZ: This is Dr. Kagan.

 Ray is panicked.

RAY: It's Ray Ray!

ROZ: Start at the start.

RAY: I should *not* have gone *out*.

ROZ: Where are you, Ray?

RAY: I called Mikey. He said Ray Ray had a headache, fell asleep and won't wake up.

ROZ: I see.

RAY: I should NOT have gone OUT.

ROZ: Did Mikey try water—

RAY: Water, ice, a slap on the wrist—

ROZ: Can Mikey stay alone while the ambulance brings Ray / Ray to the emergency

RAY: I should NOT have gone OUT.

ROZ: Call 911. Make sure they go to Children's—

RAY: I should not have / done that.

ROZ: They'll want to route him to Edgemoor but there's no hemophilia care. Tell them Children's.

RAY: I can't tell an *ambulance* where to—

ROZ: I'll meet you there.

RAY: You will?

> *Roz yells as she prepares herself.*

ROZ: 911. You have an incoming medical call for Leon in Santee?

> Do not route the patient to Edgemoor. Take patient to Children's Hospital in San Diego. Patient is a pediatric hemophiliac and needs specialty care.

> It could be spontaneous intracranial bleeding.

> I am not a nurse I am his doctor.

> YES DO CONNECT ME WITH YOUR FUCKING—

> (*A supervisor*)

> Hello this is Doctor Rosalyn Kagan—please take pediatric patient Raymond Leon Jr. to Children's Hospital.

> I'll handle billing.

> I'll bring the supplies.

> Sir, I am recording this call.

> The child could die or suffer permanent brain damage, in which case my legal department will be up your ass so high we jump out your throat. **GET HIM TO CHILDREN'S.**

> *Same night. Children's ER waiting room, maybe an animal mural. Ray paces. He wears something that a gay man would wear clubbing at the time (i.e. a leather vest). The clothing outs him unmistakably without being too distracting.*

> *Roz barrels in carrying two medical coolers.*

RAY: They won't start surgery without the—

ROZ: I have the Factor.

RAY: That's good.

> *Roz blows past Ray into surgery. He holds an unlit cigarette in his palm. He paces alone.*

> *Roz emerges.*

RAY: Will Ray Ray be okay?

ROZ: They're looking for a head bleed.

RAY: I should NOT have gone out.

> *Ray paces. Roz looks at his clothes.*

ROZ: What are you—were you with your band?

> *A moment of Ray feeling exposed.*

RAY: Yeah.

> You got here quick.

ROZ: I was up.

RAY: Huh.

Do you help with the surgery, or?

ROZ: Nope. I called in a neurosurgeon.

RAY: You did?

ROZ: That's what he needs. Injections are about as far as my butterfingers go. But I can peek in on him for you.

RAY: That would be . . .

Roz leaves. Ray alone.

RAY: I have no right.

To pray to you.

I'm a sinner.

I'm a sinner.

But Ray Ray did no harm.

For him.

For him I pray.

In Jesus name.

Roz reenters.

ROZ: The surgeon found the bleed. They're infusing the Factor. They'll be ready to operate as soon as the clotting agent permeates his blood.

RAY: Will he be okay?

ROZ: The bleed looks moderate. It's well contained. They got him here in time. Ray Ray's oxygen levels stayed normal so he should recover fully.

RAY: Thank you. Oh god. Thank you for getting us to Children's. Thank you for calling the neurosurgeon. I don't know how you did that.

ROZ: Job description.

RAY: You should get some rest.

ROZ: I'll wait with you.

RAY: You would make a great mom.

ROZ: Jesus, Ray.

RAY: Now I scared you off.

ROZ: No.

RAY: You're still married, right?

ROZ: The advantage of "Doctor." You don't have to broadcast your business, and you don't piss anyone off using "Ms."

Ray's unlit cigarette is mangled in his fingers by now.

ROZ: Are you going to smoke that?

RAY: Do you want me to, *doctor?*

ROZ: I'm feeling sorry for your cigarette.

RAY: They changed the rules since last time. No smoking in the waiting room.

ROZ: Tough break.

RAY: Wouldn't you approve?

ROZ: People need their vices.

RAY: You used to wear a ring.

ROZ: He and I wanted the same thing.

RAY: What's that?

ROZ: A wife.

RAY: Oh.

ROZ: I don't mean—

RAY: Sure.

ROZ: An individual to defrost the chicken, sort the mail.

I've been told I leave my nurturing instincts at the office.

RAY: What happens to your mail?

ROZ: The mail will wait.

That's mail with an "I". The male with an "E" loses patience and returns to Ohio.

RAY: His loss.

ROZ: Thanks.

RAY: I should not have gone out.

ROZ: No blame game.

He takes her hand.

RAY: I should have stayed home.

I should not have been doing that.

ROZ: Whatever you did, it's okay.

RAY: I called you so late.

ROZ: I'm glad to help.

(*Personal*) I was glad to get your call.

They are suspended, holding hands, looking into each other's eyes.

RAY: What would I do without you?

Roz kisses Ray. The kiss develops, and looks mutual, but Roz drives it. Eventually Ray gently turns his head.

ROZ: Oh God.

RAY: You're so kind.

ROZ: Oh shit.

RAY: Smooth move, Raymond.

ROZ: No—

RAY: I let you walk right into that.

ROZ: Under no circumstance should I have—

RAY: We need you.

ROZ: Ray I love your kids. I'm the asshole to cross that line.

RAY: If I'm your Saturday night date what can I expect?

ROZ: Boundaries?

RAY: If you had boundaries you wouldn't answer the phone at midnight.

ROZ: I was up.

RAY: If you had boundaries I wouldn't know your home number. If you had boundaries my sons would have died. Probably a dozen times.

ROZ: I love those boys.

RAY: I love them too.

She takes him in, club clothes and all.

ROZ: Are you . . . ? You were married to Evie, but . . .

RAY: Come here.

He holds her. She's unnerved. She is in love with him. Every cell in her body wants him.

ROZ: I'll refer you to Doctor Morada.

RAY: No you will not.

ROZ: I don't know if I'm capable of making unbiased decisions for you and your boys.

RAY: Good. You're on our side. More than a doctor. Above and beyond, right?

ROZ: Always. But that's not / how it works.

RAY: Let me buy you some breakfast.

ROZ: He'll be out soon.

RAY: Just in the cafeteria.

ROZ: That's probably okay.

RAY: I appreciate you. So much.

ROZ: You know what, don't embarrass me.

RAY: Off base in Pleiku I wanted a tattoo: Love is not shame. But the guy didn't speak English and I thought he might mess up the writing. Which would defeat the purpose.

Ray is still holding Roz.

ROZ: Were you intending a military career?

RAY: Just the college money. Still untapped.

ROZ: Fantastic! Where will you—

RAY: Ah fuck I didn't want to tell you because I knew you'd be on me to go.

ROZ: You bet I will.

RAY: Why medicine?

ROZ: Good at science.

RAY: Why not nursing, or teaching?

ROZ: Really good at science.

RAY: Why not work in a lab? Why dying kids?

ROZ: Your kids are not dying.

RAY: Your cancer patients.

ROZ: Fifty percent survival rate. Up from zero a decade ago. That's a good feeling.

RAY: What about the other half?

ROZ: We've made medical advances, which are terrific; your boys benefit from the greatest medical product I've seen in my career, but I like to think there are human advances. In the way we communicate. Sometimes I don't have the cure. But even in the worst case, I can support the family's wishes, help a child pass peacefully.

RAY: Do the other docs see it that way?

ROZ: If you want to clear a room full of doctors, start talking about a good death.

RAY: You're miraculous.

ROZ: I'm feeling kind of stupid right now.

RAY: You, stupid?

ROZ: Stupid in my heart.

RAY: I said appreciate but I mean, I love you. We all do.

ROZ: That's okay.

RAY: We need you.

ROZ: Ray are you careful?

RAY: How I drive, what do you mean?

ROZ: It's a personal question, excuse me.

RAY: What do you mean?

ROZ: I'm not sure. Excuse me.

RAY: Okay.

ROZ: Just consider it a general medical—

RAY: A public service announcement.

ROZ: Wear / a—

RAY: Seatbelt.

ROZ: Sure.

RAY: Do you want that breakfast?

ROZ: I'm not hungry. I'd better go.

RAY: Be with me.

    Pause.

ROZ: I hope your kids will stay healthy, and we will see each other less.

RAY: I hope half of that.

ROZ: I'll call the hospital to check on Ray Ray. I'm glad for any help I could provide. Good night.

RAY: When can I see you?

ROZ: (*Small beat. A suggestion*) I'm in the office by seven each day, and clinic doesn't start until nine.

    Roz goes.

1991

    Same day.

RAY: It wasn't until much later that I learned everyone involved was making big bucks off the Factor 8, including Children's Hospital.

In the early 1980s this broker came to San Diego and was trying to permeate the hemophilia population locally so he could sell us the Factor. He was a hemophiliac too. He came to me and asked if I wanted to start utilizing his services. And I can't believe I said this but I did: "Well let me talk to Dr. Kagan because they have taken care of us so well I want to see what she says."

That is how badly I misunderstood the situation. That is how much I trusted her.

We're fucked. There is no nicer way to say it.

She is a killer and when I see her I will tell her to her face.

1982—The Next Morning

    Roz's office. Roz and Ray have just made love.

ROZ: Well.

RAY: Wow.

ROZ: I'm still—

RAY: Yeah.

    Are you happy?

ROZ: Yeah. I think I'm happy.

RAY: I want you to be happy.

ROZ: That was—

RAY: New.

ROZ: Which part was new, for you?

RAY: Well for one thing, the—(condom)

ROZ: Ray you need to use a condom, every time.

RAY: Please don't be the doctor, just for one minute?

ROZ: But we're in my office.

RAY: That's not my fault, I would have met you somewhere with more atmosphere.

> *Roz laughs.*

RAY: Marry me.

ROZ: Jesus.

RAY: This worked.

ROZ: It sure did. But / I'm your—

RAY: Once upon a time, you were not a doctor.

ROZ: True.

RAY: How old were you when you chose?

ROZ: Twelve.

RAY: Wow. But once upon a time, you were eleven.

ROZ: Stands to reason.

RAY: Just a girl of eleven who was very good at science. Little Roz . . . were you Kagan?

ROZ: Yeah.

RAY: Little Roz Kagan.

ROZ: Rosie.

RAY: Rosie! Rosie Kagan! Thank you for that.

ROZ: You're welcome.

RAY: Little Rosie Kagan—how does a girl of eleven even know she is good at science?

ROZ: My dad.

RAY: Ah hah! Doctor Dad?

ROZ: Sick dad.

RAY: Poor kid.

ROZ: It was a long time ago.

RAY: Hell of a science lesson.

ROZ: (*Shrugs*) My parents didn't speak perfect English, and the doctors explained everything in medical jargon, if they explained at all. So I looked up terms. I read his charts. My mother bought me a stethoscope. I listened to his heart.

RAY: Poor Rosie Kagan.

ROZ: Everybody lied. They said he'd be fine. He was not fine. He said, don't let me die alone in a hospital; guess what, he died alone in the hospital.

ROZ: I just want to kiss your little broken heart.

ROZ: You're doing pretty well.

RAY: I'm going to start calling you Rosie.

ROZ: You'd better not.

RAY: Rosie, Rosie, Rosie.

ROZ: What did you want to be when you were twelve?

RAY: A man of God.

ROZ: I see.

RAY: Some of us stray from the path. But not you.

ROZ: I'm straying now.

RAY: That's not straying, that's finding your way.

ROZ: We are feeling . . .

RAY: Love.

ROZ: Yes. Me too

RAY: So it's very simple.

ROZ: Under extreme circumstances, there can arise a form of . . . battle heat.

RAY: People meet in many ways, many combinations.

ROZ: You were in a war; you know battle heat.

RAY: I was a medic. I didn't kill anyone.

ROZ: (*Charmed*) You never told me you were a medic.

RAY: We're just getting started.

ROZ: That's lovely.

RAY: Yes, I'm lovely.

ROZ: You really are.

> Roz gives Ray a key.

RAY: Your home?

ROZ: Yeah.

RAY: Good, next time we'll be more comfortable.

ROZ: Do you know how many women were in the University of Cincinnati School of Medicine class of 1966?

RAY: One?

ROZ: Three. But I'm the only one who specialized. I'm the only one who opened a practice. If I wreck this, I wreck it for all women.

RAY: You're not going to wreck anything. You're going to have a beautiful life with a beautiful man, in your home.

ROZ: I want that.

RAY: Okay then.

ROZ: Are you gay?

RAY: (*The sex*) Did I seem gay, just now?

ROZ: You seem perfect.

RAY: I want to get married.

ROZ: I should pause.

RAY: You just gave me your key.

ROZ: That was bad.

RAY: You want it back?

ROZ: No.

RAY: What is wrong with you?

ROZ: A lot is probably wrong with me, obviously.

RAY: Obviously because of *me*?

ROZ: Not you. The category of you.

RAY: What category is that?

ROZ: Well, you're the father of my patients.

RAY: I know that part.

ROZ: That gives me a certain power—

RAY: No. Ray is in charge of Ray.

ROZ: And I don't understand . . . what type of man you are.

RAY: What's my category?

ROZ: Yeah.

RAY: What's your category?

ROZ: My category?

RAY: We are people. Human souls and bodies. That's all we need to know.
You heal my children; to me that's a plus. I want to heal you back a little.
Will you let me?

ROZ: Yes.

One Month Later, 1982

*Very early morning. Ray finds Roz in her office again. She is absorbed in
work.*

RAY: Good morning.

Earth to Roz?

Roz startles.

ROZ: Hi Ray.

RAY: You weren't at home.

ROZ: Right I'm here.

RAY: Did you sleep here?

ROZ: Resting.

Ray rubs Roz's shoulders.

ROZ: It's getting scary.

RAY: I'm harmless.

ROZ: I'm scared for the kids.

RAY: Let's tell the kids. No more sneaking around. It's time. *(Maybe he gets down on one knee)* Rosalyn Kagan—

ROZ: This bug.

RAY: What bug?

ROZ: I don't like the contagion pattern.

RAY: The gay bug?

ROZ: If it spreads the same way as Hepatitis B, which it might, then it is not only sexually transmitted but blood borne, and will reach the same populations as Hep B.

RAY: My boys both had Hep B.

ROZ: Yes. It's a risk of pooled blood products but Hep B is a prudent risk. It's treatable. As this bug is expected to be treatable. It is expected that most patients will carry it and clear it, very few will succumb. It is predicted to be a manageable disease, like Hep B.

RAY: Are you saying no panic.

ROZ: There is no general panic.

RAY: But.

ROZ: But I don't like it. There have been two hemophiliac deaths. Why did they die? Is that two out of a hundred cases or two out of two?

RAY: What will you do?

ROZ: I'm a hematologist oncologist not an epidemiologist.

RAY: Um what?

ROZ: I treat what presents. I'm not an authority on how it spreads.

RAY: What do the authorities say?

ROZ: Split. The Center for Disease Control flagged these two cases as a possible pandemic, but the National Hemophilia Foundation won't change protocol without more data.

RAY: And you're a hematologist so you keep protocol?

ROZ: Two deaths, eight reported cases; from a medical standpoint it's insignificant. But from an epidemiological perspective—which is not my field—that's how . . .

RAY: That's how what.

ROZ: I'm just reading two sets of journals side by side, there must be experts studying this, I didn't specialize in infectious disease, I'm practically a layman. I have a bad feeling. But who am I?

RAY: You? Are the smartest person I know. You know and I know you had to be twice as good as the other docs. They are home with their wives right now and here's Roz. You look like shit.

ROZ: Thanks.

RAY: You don't sleep. You don't cook. You probably never see the beach.

ROZ: San Diego has a beach?

RAY: You live on junk. You take too many pills. I think you're smoking again.

ROZ: So?

RAY: You give it your all, Roz Kagan, until there's nothing left.

ROZ: I'm sorry.

RAY: Don't apologize. Get your act together and stand up for my kids.

ROZ: Well. One doctor in Philadelphia—one—is insisting his patients go back to cryoprecipitate.

RAY: Cryo? The transfusions?

ROZ: He won't give Factor anymore. He's sticking with his local blood bank, taking hemophilia care back twenty years. They're calling him a dinosaur.

RAY: Sure.

ROZ: Do I want that? Would I take away everything your kids can do, their health, their whole lives, because of a hunch?

RAY: It's not a hunch, it's *your* hunch. And one guy in Philly has the same hunch.

ROZ: He's a senior doc; he runs that practice. I'm low on the totem pole.

RAY: So?

ROZ: I'd have to convince the whole department, starting with Dr. Lee.

RAY: Okay, I'm Dr. Lee. You be you. What do you say?

ROZ: I might say, "Phillip. There are eight hemophiliacs in the United States presenting symptoms of Gay Related Immune Deficiency. Two have died. While that is not even a tiny fraction of the hemophiliacs in this country, I am worried—" I can't say worried.

RAY: Why not?

ROZ: It's a feeling word.

RAY: Doctors are weird.

ROZ: Yeah.

"The Center for Disease Control hypothesizes that these cases were contracted from commercial blood products. I suggest we break with the National Hemophilia Foundation and cease treatment with Factor 8, now."

RAY: And he says?

ROZ: "What do we give our patients instead?"

RAY: And you say—

ROZ: Cryo.

RAY: *Cryo?*

ROZ: And he says:

"Do you suggest that we withhold a miraculous product that sustains these children's normal lifestyles, to reintroduce a painful and ineffective treatment that will leave some of them crippled?"

RAY: Hmm. And you say:

ROZ: "Yes. Yes I do." And he says, Why? And I say, because I have a feeling—not feeling—I say, because there's a chance, a tiny chance, that this bug could be worse.

RAY: Worse.

ROZ: So he says, "Worse than the debilitating symptoms of juvenile hemophilia unchecked by Factor? Do you remember the history of this disease?"

I say of course I remember, but I feel, I think, I—

He says, "Families will leave. They will go to Los Angeles to get Factor. Two hundred miles round trip is easier than the cryo."

He says, "I brought you here to start a state of the art medical practice. If our patients leave, what's your practice?

"The National Hemophilia Foundation follows protocol but Roz Kagan follows her *feminine intuition.*"

(*Beat. A decision*) I can't do it. I don't have the numbers. I don't have a tolerable alternate plan of care. I don't have anything to offer.

RAY: You will figure this out.

ROZ: Ray. Use condoms.

RAY: We do.

ROZ: Out there.

RAY: You think I have a lot of free time.

ROZ: Ray. Let's stop.

RAY: Okay.

> *Roz heartbroken.*

ROZ: Okay.

RAY: (*Not unkind*) Am I supposed to say something else?

ROZ: No. No you're perfect. I screw everything up.

RAY: What are you talking about?

ROZ: I don't know how to be close, or when, when to be close. I don't know when to be difficult, when to make a scene, when to keep my mouth shut, how to see what's right in front of me.

I wanted to be a different kind of doctor.

RAY: You are.

ROZ: (*Their relationship*) This was not what I had in mind.

RAY: We're stopping.

ROZ: It's easy for you.

RAY: Easier, maybe.

ROZ: Of course it is.

Thank you for even . . . I've been told I'm a tough . . . I'm probably just not—

RAY: Roz. There is nothing wrong with you.

Roz takes in this possibility, maybe for the first time.

ROZ: Ditto.

RAY: You have a nice house. You should go there sometime.

ROZ: Yeah I'll try that soon.

RAY: Are you okay?

ROZ: Oh god, I'm great! You should not be worried about me! You of all people.

RAY: You will fight for those boys. I know you.

ROZ: I'd better start my day.

RAY: And I came in here thinking we might take the next step. Tell the kids. Become a family. Share it all. But we won't.

ROZ: (*This costs her*) Probably for the best, given the givens. Right?

RAY: Maybe. Should I pick up the Factor while I'm here?

ROZ: Might as well. The new batch is in the fridge. Joanne isn't in yet. I'll sign for you.

RAY: Thanks.

ROZ: You bet, Ray.

Ray exits. Roz jerks herself into action for the day.

1991

RAY: Every word that came out of her mouth was very measured because she supposedly didn't know what was going on either. Now I see this isn't true.

Certain people knew in 1983 that there was a problem with the Factor. The Cutter memo proves that. Cutter is one of the companies that manufactures blood products, and they had a legal memo in hand in 1983 that said, "There's a large potential problem here; we should put in a warning label and an instruction sheet to the doctors, stating that the Factor could be contaminated." But Cutter fought the *warning label* for two years.

"We didn't know." That's how they all do it. That's how the pharmaceutical people do it, that's how the blood bank does it, the medical enterprise in total, down to Roz Kagan. That's the whole defense. Well I don't accept it.

It was her job to know.

Furthermore she did know.

Blood for money and money for blood. They swapped.

1984

A hospital meeting room. Roz addresses patients.

ROZ: Ricky would you mind joining Marie outside, this talk is just for parents and the patients over twelve.

(*A little pause. Roz is good at this*)

Gentlemen. I've known some of you guys since you were babies; it's awkward. But here we go: If you are sexually active or even sexually hopeful, you need one of these.

(*The condom*)

Even if you're married—congratulations James. Go ahead, laugh. But let's control what we can control here. And sexual behavior, despite rumors to the contrary, can be controlled.

Now. Regarding the Factor 8.

We don't need to panic. But if you are taking Factor regularly to prevent bleeding, don't do that anymore.

A new heat-treated Factor developed in Germany is now available in the US. Heat seems to kill the AIDS virus. It's considered experimental, as there is still no reliable test. But here at Children's we will switch to the heat-treated Factor now; we will not wait for guidelines from the National Hemophilia Foundation.

I urge you to discard whatever supplies you have at home. We don't know which lots are bad. I realize there is a cost. We are working with our pharmaceutical suppliers on a buyback, a formal recall. That's been slow.

Meanwhile it is an option to go back to cryoprecipitate. That would mean that in case of a bleed you would come to the hospital for a transfusion, rather than treating at home.

We held a regional meeting, LA Childrens, LA Orthopedic, San Diego Children's. We reached a consensus. Adopt the heat-treated factor, but wait for a bleed. Use less.

Marie is available if anyone wants to talk.

This is somber and upsetting news. But let's not panic.

> *She gathers her things. A sense that the room is clearing out. Ray approaches her.*

RAY: That was on message.

ROZ: It's good to see you.

RAY: Consensus, huh?

ROZ: As a smaller clinic it makes sense for us to work in step with the other programs.

RAY: You can't test for this?

ROZ: Center for Disease Control is working on a test.

RAY: It's been two years.

ROZ: There's no money for research. There is nothing. The President has not said the word AIDS.

RAY: No one gives a shit about the gays.

ROZ: I go over and over this with my colleagues in LA. I'm up all night.

RAY: If you were their mom what would you do?

ROZ: I would treat for the bleed. With heat treated Factor 8. The trials look very good.

RAY: What about cryo?

ROZ: We can make that available to you.

RAY: But you said a long time ago there isn't enough to go around.

ROZ: Sure if everyone went back on the cryo we'd have a supply problem. But that's unlikely because it's inconvenient.

RAY: If my kids want cryo there is cryo for us?

ROZ: Yes.

RAY: And it's safer?

ROZ: Well, the odds are better. Fewer donors per bag.

RAY: It's from our local Red Cross.

ROZ: Should be.

RAY: I still donate every three months. Least I can do.

ROZ: Ray, if you're sleeping with men you should stop donating blood.

RAY: Wow you just want to be in every part of my business.

ROZ: It's common sense. I'm not sure why the gay leaders haven't been more emphatic on this point.

RAY: I don't know the GAY LEADERS, Roz.

I hang out here. In the hospital. In these waiting rooms listening to the other parents whose sons have been STRUCK LIKE MINE, who want to put the faggots in concentration camps. Blame the queers for the dirty blood. I hear this EVERY TIME I WAIT WITH MY KIDS. That our boys are the innocent victims. The poor Ryan White kid kicked out of school. Innocent. I hear ENOUGH ABOUT FAGGOTS POISONING THE BLOOD.

ROZ: Okay.

RAY: I will tell you something else, Doctor Roz.

The nice buttfucker piano teacher donors are probably safer. Than the "professionals" who sold their blood off the street?

That's the poison.

I'm reading up.

Blood the source of life was bought and sold. Bought from junkies and hookers and prisoners. Sold to Cutter, Baxter, Bayer, etcetera. Repackaged and resold to me, to my children.

The poison is cash.

Don't blame the faggots for participating in the gift of blood donation.

Don't blame the faggots for participating in civilization as is our their RIGHT.

ROZ: I see your point Ray but if you belong to a risk group—

RAY: Plus I barely have sex!

And when I do I heed your doctorly advice about the rubbers.

ROZ: Good.

RAY: Oh it's great.

ROZ: The gay community is doing almost all the work on this, all the advocacy.

RAY: I see those freaks. Acting up.

ROZ: Our kids have the potential to shift public sympathy. If hemophiliacs and their families can join the larger movement, we might be able to speed up the research.

RAY: I'm not going to handcuff myself to a blood bank in San Francisco.

ROZ: That's where the main effort—

RAY: (*End of conversation*) I don't have the time.

My boys are fifteen. They're just starting out.

ROZ: I missed Ray Ray at the meeting.

RAY: He has a game.

ROZ: Great, but he needs to understand sexual transmission.

RAY: You ever try to control a boy who's fifteen?

ROZ: All the time.

RAY: The kid's on the bench these days, still yells his head off. Mikey's in band.

ROZ: Wonderful.

RAY: Trumpet.

ROZ: Fantastic.

RAY: I've been listening to him practice five years and I'm just now able to stand it. A lot of potential, my kids. All potential.

ROZ: We can switch them to cryo. Or the heat treated Factor looks good.

RAY: Insurance charges us double for the heat treated.

ROZ: Is that right?

RAY: One of the Hemophilia chapter guys says he can sell it to us cheaper.

ROZ: I would prefer you buy from the hospital.

RAY: Gotta make that buck.

ROZ: It's an issue of medical control. Though the Factor sales do give us a tiny bit of clout.

RAY: Uh huh.

ROZ: Children's wants to close the hemophilia clinic. Send you up to LA.

RAY: Motherfuckers.

ROZ: We run at a loss.

RAY: You're telling me.

ROZ: It's all moving to a new model. The HMOs. The for-profit hospitals. Partnerships with the big pharma companies.

RAY: Fucking Reagan.

ROZ: Fucking Reagan. Everything's supposed to run in the black.

RAY: Sick kids don't run in the black.

ROZ: We're on the same side.

RAY: My boys got taller than me.

ROZ: I know. I don't even do their physicals anymore because they're young men.

RAY: They are so close. So close to grown.

ROZ: I've known all of these guys since they were small.

RAY: Promise me you'll get them there.

ROZ: All I can tell you is the truth.

RAY: (*Turns his back*) Fuck fuck fuck fuck fuck.

ROZ: Come here. Can I?

RAY: Fuck fuck fuck fuck fuck.

(*Roz physically comforts Ray in a doctor/patient way*)

We should put them on the cryo.

ROZ: Fine.

RAY: But then they're hemo-homos again. The bruising, the bleeding, the hospital.

ROZ: I know.

RAY: Maybe just for a time, till you have a test.

ROZ: We can try it.

RAY: They've been on the Factor eight years. How many vials?

ROZ: Thousands.

RAY: How many donors per vial?

ROZ: Sixty thousand.

        Silence. Roz is still close to Ray.

RAY: They all have it already, don't they?

ROZ: There is no reliable test.

RAY: What's your gut?

(*Roz can't answer*)

What's your advice?

ROZ: Stay with the heat treated Factor 8.

RAY: That's what we'll do.

ROZ: Continue to buy from Children's? At least I know our supplier.

RAY: Okay.

ROZ: It's an issue of medical control.

RAY: You have everything under control?

ROZ: I'm trying.

RAY: I trust you.

1991

RAY: In 1985 she secretly tested the boys for HIV. She never told them and she never told the families. It was all done underhanded. The only reason I found out was because in 1987 another boy with hemophilia saw results of that 1985 test in his own records, with everybody's name, and Mikey's name was negative. Of course by 1987, over 90% of the hemophiliacs in this country were positive.

ROZ: You want to know about *nineteen eighty fucking five*? Fine. In 1985, just prior to the development of a reliable test for the AIDS virus, I got a call from a colleague in research, "I have an investigational test kit for HTLV-3. I would like some specimen to test." I said okay. We sent blood samples and he sent results back in an informal, collegial way, and we put it in each patient's chart. For better or worse that's how we did it. Mikey came back negative on that test.

On that test also was a girl, not a hemophiliac, a transplant patient. She was clearly dying of AIDS. And her test was negative. So we retested that sample. Again, negative.

Huh.

I knew that child had AIDS. She was wasting away.

So here I was with a test that was unproven, and which I knew had missed this patient.

What would you do?

Even if it was a good test, let's say it was reliable. What would one do in 1985 for a hemophiliac with a negative HIV test? Keep him on the best product available. And the best product available was heat-treated Factor 8. By then we knew the heat treatment worked.

So that's what we did for Mikey.

And that's what we did for the positive ones too.

We weren't testing the patients. We were testing the test.

1987

Roz's office. It's the nicer office from 1991. Ray enters, out of breath.

RAY: Sorry we're late. Ray Ray needed a hand. Mikey's got him.

ROZ: Are you okay?

RAY: I ran from the parking lot. Ray Ray's had the flu, it isn't too bad today, but he's moving a little slow. Then I forgot about the new office . . .

I don't think I was ever late, all these years.

ROZ: I think you're right. Catch your breath.

RAY: The boys can drive, but I want to be part of the consultation. Since you got Mikey's results back.

ROZ: Yes, we tested at the patient's request.

RAY: Well?

ROZ: Your son is eighteen, so I need to speak to the patient himself.

RAY: Of course we have to play by the rules.

ROZ: The new anonymity laws are serious, Ray. I can lose my license for even noting a patient was tested.

RAY: I understand the HIV test was a formality, more or less, at this point?

ROZ: (*Delicate*) It was.

> *Ray is crushed.*

RAY: I knew that.

It's just that Mikey is so strong, he's filled out so much you wouldn't believe, it even the last six months. Eighteen years old.

ROZ: We should discuss that.

RAY: You take a look at that big lunk and then we'll discuss it!

ROZ: Michael and Raymond are adults.

RAY: Thanks to you. You're a good doctor.

ROZ: This is a children's hospital.

RAY: Why are you telling me things I already know?

ROZ: They need to be seen with other adults.

RAY: The hemophiliacs don't age out. We went over this years ago. They stay under your care.

ROZ: That was the informal system. But we are a children's hospital. We don't have an AIDS ward—

RAY: Ward?

ROZ: I mean we don't have the expertise. We are not the best facility.

RAY: But you know us.

ROZ: The decision now is whether to continue this warm relationship or find your sons the most advanced medical care.

RAY: You're dumping them /

ROZ: I am moving them /

RAY: —because of the HIV.

ROZ: —because they are adults.

RAY: Where will we go?

ROZ: To University Hospital.

RAY: University? That's not a hospital it's a city.

ROZ: It's the best local hospital for AIDS research.

RAY: What about hemophilia care?

ROZ: I am in touch with the staff over there. I'm sending all the information.

RAY: So it's done.

ROZ: It will be a transition. It may take about a year to cross the adult / patients over.

RAY: Can you promise a year?

ROZ: The timeline also depends on what your sons need.

RAY: They need you. You're supposed to support the family, treat them like people. Be a different kind of doctor.

ROZ: I have to take emotions out of the picture. At this point Ray Ray's care is complicated. Mikey's care could get there too.

RAY: So you dump us. It's over.

ROZ: There is a lot being done right now.

RAY: "There is a lot being done right now." You sound like a pamphlet.

ROZ: I am not an AIDS doctor.

RAY: No one's an AIDS doctor, right? This thing is only a few years old. You're all learning as you go, that's what you said.

ROZ: I can't focus on this properly. I can't keep up with the research. Over at University they're seeing case after case. Building the science.

RAY: You're good at science.

ROZ: Most of my patients have childhood cancer, Ray. What about them?

RAY: What about Mikey and Ray Ray?

ROZ: Michael and Raymond are adults.

RAY: They have zits. They have terrible judgment. Ray Ray's still setting his farts on fire.

ROZ: You're kidding me.

RAY: I wish I was.

ROZ: Well. If childish behavior qualified you for Children's Hospital, we'd need a lot more beds.

RAY: Good one, Roz.

ROZ: Raymond is an adult AIDS patient. Michael is an HIV positive adult.

RAY: He wasn't positive two years ago.

ROZ: Ray we went over this.

RAY: That test was negative.

ROZ: Now with a reliable test they're finding batches of contaminated Factor dating back to the seventies.

RAY: What about the children with AIDS? You hanging on to them?

ROZ: They have nowhere else to go. Your sons have an alternative.

RAY: It's a maze over at University. It's a zoo. You're throwing them in with all kinds of . . . AIDS people.

ROZ: What's your support system?

RAY: I'll talk to Marie.

ROZ: We had to let Marie go.

RAY: *Now?* You cut our social worker *now?*

ROZ: It's horrible. I hate it. I'm asking Ray, what is your backup?

RAY: I thought it was you.

ROZ: I mean on a personal level.

RAY: You have been available on many levels.

ROZ: Yes.

RAY: When did you move to this office?

ROZ: Dr. Lee retired last year.

RAY: So you're running the show.

ROZ: I wouldn't go that far. There wasn't even budget for a new junior hire, so—

RAY: But you got the big desk.

ROZ: I got the big desk.

RAY: (*Sexual*) I liked your old desk.

ROZ: We stopped.

RAY: You did not want to stop.

ROZ: Want was not the dominant reason for stopping, no.

RAY: You wanted to keep going.

ROZ: Of course I did.

> *Ray touches Roz's thigh.*

RAY: We could. We could keep going.

ROZ: Ray don't do this.

RAY: Why not?

> *Ray touches Roz more. She responds.*

ROZ: I can't give you what you need. I can't give your sons what they need.

RAY: Let's try. Let's keep trying.

ROZ: Mikey and Ray Ray will be here.

RAY: I told them to wait in the lobby.

> *She pulls away.*

ROZ: You *what*?

RAY: I heard a rumor.

ROZ: So you purposely came to see me alone?

RAY: **Don't make us go where no one knows my kids.**

> *Silence. Roz composes herself.*

ROZ: This was an agonizing, soul searching, very difficult decision made on medical principles alone.

RAY: Their own mother left them. Why wouldn't you?

ROZ: I understand this feels like abandonment. I will talk it through with Mikey and Ray Ray.

RAY: No. During the transition my family prefers to see Dr. Morada.

ROZ: We have an appointment.

RAY: I will reschedule.

ROZ: I need to say goodbye.

RAY: Nope.

> *Roz is as generous as possible.*

ROZ: If you must leave angry, I accept that you leave angry. I cannot afford any principles other than medical, in making decisions now. It's too dire. University is a research hospital, it's where your sons belong.

RAY: Fuck research. My kids are going to be lab rats.

ROZ: If I'd been in research I might have called this five years ago.

RAY: You did call it.

ROZ: I might have been able to do something. I might have had the confidence, or the clout—

RAY: Poor Doctor Roz on the big desk without the clout.

ROZ: If I had grown children I would send them to University Hospital.

RAY: But you don't. You have no one.

> *Ray walks out.*

1991

RAY: I've gotten very cynical since my boys / were victimized so badly with this whole thing.

Kagan denies this but the way I see it developing, I can envision the administration and Kagan getting together with the other docs / maybe '82, '83.

And I could see them doing exactly what the Red Cross did— that's another memo look it up— / and viewing this whole thing in pure economics.

ROZ: I will speak with Ray Leon if he will make an appointment, with counsel. But he cannot stand on hospital grounds and / scream.

Nor may he disrupt an event that is a more important part of our budget every / year.

This hospital receives less funding every year, as our costs increase. The telethon keeps families together and saves lives.

RAY: They held onto my kids while they could still make a buck, then dumped them to / University when they got too expensive. If University was the best place why didn't they go sooner?

Maybe there was a trial my son could have gotten, maybe AZT, / if that was the best place why weren't they there in 1985?

They decided to roll the dice, / save a buck, and hope they lucked out.

But they lost.

We lost.
My sons paid with / their lives.

We pay, not the hospital and not the doctor.

Practically every hemophiliac in this country born before 1985 is either HIV positive or dead.

Ten thousand people.

That's a genocide.

ROZ: I'm being faulted for transferring them to University and I'm being faulted for not transferring them sooner. It's difficult to keep up with the criticism but I'm going to go down swinging.

They should have been given the best AIDS treatment available at that time? Well what was the AIDS treatment?

AZT was being worked on, but only with very sick gay men who were basically dying, not hemophiliacs and not / children.
AZT is a highly toxic drug. You don't give this for a cold, / okay?

Eventually it was tested on gay men who were HIV positive but asymptomatic. / *Then* the study came down to hemophiliacs.

But in 1987 no one was giving AZT to asymptomatic people. It would have / been crazy.

I too am devastated by the outcome but we must respect established channels.

Children in this building are gravely ill.

1991

Same day. Roz enters her bedroom and flicks on the lights, revealing Ray in her bed.

ROZ: Jesus.

RAY: You snuck out the back.

ROZ: I need you to leave my home.

RAY: Aren't you curious how I got in?

ROZ: I need you to leave.

RAY: I used my key. The one you gave me.

ROZ: That was years ago.

RAY: You didn't change the locks.

ROZ: No, this is my home.

RAY: New master bath.

ROZ: Yes.

RAY: What'd that run you? The tile alone—

ROZ: Get out of here, Ray.

RAY: You wouldn't *meet* with me today. You wouldn't *face* me.

ROZ: It's out of my hands.

RAY: Ray Ray is dead.

ROZ: I learned that. I'm very sorry.

RAY: He got married.

ROZ: I heard.

RAY: High school sweetheart. Who'd think kids in the nineteen nineties would be so old-fashioned. It was a real pretty wedding. In Presidio Park, looking at the ocean.

ROZ: He loved that park.

RAY: She died first.

ROZ: Jesus.

RAY: Four months pregnant.

> *Pause.*

ROZ: Can we, continue this conversation over a meal?

RAY: You cooking?

ROZ: Let me take you out.

RAY: How many plates of pad thai will it take, Doc Roz?

ROZ: I'm not implying the food—

RAY: You want me gone.

ROZ: I care about you Ray. But we can't do this.

RAY: Heard that before.

ROZ: We need boundaries.

RAY: You gave me your *key*.

ROZ: That was a mistake.

RAY: Exhibit A.

ROZ: You're going to do what you need to do, Ray.

RAY: What do you think that is?

ROZ: I'm planning to resign, so—

RAY: Early retirement?

ROZ: An academic appointment.

RAY: Good for you.

ROZ: It's a job.

RAY: You were a tourist.

ROZ: Ray I can't even imagine what you're going through.

RAY: No you really can't.

ROZ: On a personal level . . .

RAY: Finish your sentence.

ROZ: I lost a lot too.

RAY: Oh is that how we're going to play it?

ROZ: Boys I knew twenty years.

RAY: My son is dead. His wife is dead. My grandchild will not be born.
Mikey watched the whole thing, knowing he has the same virus. Saw his
brother go blind, go crazy, shit himself in a ward with a couple of AIDS
skeletons while the skin fell off his face. So Mikey's feeling cheerful.

ROZ: I want to talk about the facts and the feelings.

RAY: Remember the Tylenol scare?

ROZ: Of course—

RAY: Someone died after taking a Tylenol and it was a national alert—
boom—Tylenol off the shelves overnight.
Remember the Pinto started catching fire?

ROZ: Sure.

RAY: They pulled the cars and *then* they found the flaw.
But you kept selling us your Factor.
That's a crime.

ROZ: Let's take a walk.

RAY: Sorry.

(*Ray is handcuffed to Roz's bed, both hands*)
You got me trapped. Right where you like me.

ROZ: Okay that—this is not how we talk.

RAY: You wouldn't meet.

ROZ: Ray it turned into a mess. I started getting advice—

RAY: Called in the lawyers. Kagan, Rothstein, and Jewstein.

ROZ: I am so sorry for your loss.

RAY: I bet you are.

ROZ: I wanted to be there for Ray Ray. I didn't know he had been hospitalized.

RAY: Were you waiting on an invitation?

ROZ: I was not waiting on an invitation.

RAY: You wanted to speak at the funeral?

ROZ: No.

RAY: About bad things happening?

ROZ: I met you at the hospital, I *redirected the ambulance* for crying out loud, I found you in the middle of the night.

RAY: Several times.

ROZ: I met you in the hospital with a dozen vials of Factor. Two coolers.

Was one of those vials the contaminate?

Maybe.

But I would do it again.

I would have to.

Ray Ray had a brain hemorrhage.

He was dying that night.

What could I give him except what I had?

RAY: You knew.

ROZ: Ray that's not true.

RAY: You knew the risk. You said so. In 1982 you said it mirrored Hep B, you said AIDS could act like Hep B.

ROZ: We didn't even have a name. I did not say AIDS.

RAY: You made me use a condom in 1982 and you didn't tell the boys until 1984.

ROZ: What can I do for you, Ray?

RAY: Pay up.

ROZ: There's a class action lawsuit / you can—

RAY: You. Pay.

ROZ: No wrongdoing.

RAY: Pay my tuition.

ROZ: You're in school?

RAY: Planning on it.

ROZ: Ray that's fantastic. What subject?

RAY: Biology.

ROZ: Wonderful.

RAY: I have the time.

> *Pause.*

ROZ: But to make use of that. Good for you.

RAY: You have condescended to my sons and me from the day we met. Arrogant fucking doctors.

ROZ: I'll pay your tuition.

RAY: Can you afford it?

ROZ: Where will you study?

RAY: Mesa.

ROZ: Yes.

RAY: Then that's not what I want.

ROZ: I figured.

RAY: The first hemophiliac AIDS case was 1981. Why did you keep giving them Factor until 1985?

ROZ: It's a valid question.

RAY: I know it's a valid fucking question.

ROZ: You have to respect time and place and process.

RAY: I don't have to respect fuck all anymore.

ROZ: (*The handcuffs*) Tell me there's a key to that thing.

RAY: I'm acting up.

> You inspired me Roz.

> I'm sitting in.

> I'm locked down.

ROZ: You hurt a lot.

RAY: I HURT A LOT.

ROZ: Let's get you help.

RAY: Do not manage me. I will not be managed.

ROZ: Where's the key?

RAY: Up my butt.

> (*Beat*)

> Get your latex gloves, Roz.

ROZ: I am a doctor and I will do that.

RAY: I'll kick in your head.

ROZ: I did not give your sons AIDS.

RAY: No you taught them to give it to themselves.

ROZ: There are medical mistakes, there are changes in knowledge, there is—

RAY: The babies born now are safe.

ROZ: We think so.

RAY: My kids were in that lucky slice, that lucky few years.

ROZ: You want to kick my head in.

RAY: I want to kill you.

ROZ: Yeah.

RAY: All of you. Fucking Cutter, Baxter, Bayer. Motherfuckers.

ROZ: Motherfuckers.

RAY: You. You're the motherfucker.

Collected a paycheck every day of this plague.

Sold poison for profit.

ROZ: That was never my personal profit.

RAY: Hemophilia care stayed open. You got the big desk. Now you're off to the University.

ROZ: I've been to a lot of funerals, Ray.

RAY: **I've been to two.**

Roz leaves.

RAY: Where are you going?

WHERE ARE YOU GOING?

Raymond you did not think this through.

Roz returns with a medical cooler.

RAY: What's this?

ROZ: Baxter finally gave out the contaminated lot numbers. Issued a recall. In *1989.*

RAY: Jesus.

ROZ: I kept these because I learned they were selling the bad batches overseas.

RAY: What the fuck?

ROZ: Yup. Japan, China, Korea.

They're selling it now.

RAY: Motherfuckers.

ROZ: Motherfuckers does not begin to describe it, Ray. Pure evil.

RAY: But I'm sure there is some nice lady over there just doing her best.

ROZ: We don't know.

You came to my home and not the drug company.

You came to my home and not the White House.

RAY: Because you personally are a killer.

You are a killer and I can say that to your face.

Killer. Killer. Killer.

Roz wipes off her arm with an alcohol swab.

RAY: What are you doing?

ROZ: I'm cleaning my skin with antiseptic.

I'm opening the disposable needle.

I'm drawing the contaminated Factor.

You want to kill me?

Get out of your handcuffs and do it.

RAY: The key is in my pocket.

ROZ: I hoped so.

RAY: It would be physically impossible to put it up my butt. Wearing handcuffs.

ROZ: May I touch you?

RAY: Yeah.

Roz retrieves the key from Ray's pants pocket. She unlocks his handcuffs.

Roz uncaps the syringe and hands it to Ray.

ROZ: Go ahead. You can't hurt me.

Ray holds the syringe.

RAY: How could you test them and not tell me? Just tell me it was a bad test. Tell me something.

ROZ: I was wrong.

RAY: Yeah, you were.

ROZ: I have felt utterly helpless with you. I do not like that feeling.

RAY: You promised to tell the truth.

ROZ: What good is the truth if there's nothing you can do?

RAY: How could you send us away?

ROZ: I believed it was his best chance.

RAY: A nurse at University didn't know how to find the vein on a hemophiliac; she stabbed and gouged, and pushed, and pulled. His arm swelled this big with black blood. I complained; the doctor said, "This can happen with hemophiliacs," I said, "Not anymore. This is a new age." Ray Ray died suffering from that arm.

ROZ: There's no excuse.

RAY: Wasn't there a doctor who went back to cryo, early?

ROZ: Yeah. In Philadelphia.

RAY: What happened?

ROZ: His patients have a twenty percent rate of infection. Compared to
ninety five percent.

RAY: But not you.

ROZ: No.

RAY: You reached consensus.

ROZ: Yes.

RAY: Did you ever talk to Lee?

ROZ: I waited too long.

RAY: You played it safe.

ROZ: Yeah I did.

I thought experts knew better than me.

That's a safe way to think.

As if grownups are in charge.

I did that.

Go ahead.

(*Roz extends her arm*)

I'm numb.

I'm done.

I buried too many.

I have a professorship yeah but fuck it.

I'd rather give you the satisfaction.

I'd rather give you what you want.

You're right I'm bad with boundaries

I'd rather die of exposure

Die of whatever

Die of thrush, pneumocystis, diarrhea

I'd rather die letting you in.

I'd rather die giving you

Whatever part of me

You want.

Ray considers.

RAY: Better put the cap back. It's a hazard.

And get that shit out of your house.

ROZ: Okay.

RAY: Dammit. I don't know who to kill.

Quiet.

ROZ: How have you been?

RAY: I've been like shit.

ROZ: Me too.

RAY: I told Mikey I see men.

ROZ: That was brave.

RAY: He worried I would get AIDS.

Hilarious.

Why is shit distributed how it is?

ROZ: I have no theory.

RAY: I was waiting for the twins to grow up. I thought, hold out. Don't put them through anything more. Just hold out and then they'll be grown, I'll be forty, I'll have a few years to join the party.

ROZ: It's a bad time to join the party.

RAY: What are you gonna teach?

ROZ: Medical history.

RAY: Like, this?

ROZ: No. Maybe. Maybe eventually, this.

RAY: (*New thought*) One day this will be history.

ROZ: And we will be the survivors.

RAY: Not because we are good.

ROZ: Nope.

RAY: That shitty book, Shit Happens to Good People.

ROZ: I was young when I gave you that book.

RAY: There are no natural disasters.

There's evil. There's ignorance. There's profit.

ROZ: They're working on a cure.

RAY: Sure they are. Drug companies made money on the bad blood, now they make money on the disease, one day they'll peddle the fucking cure. Cash cash cash.

Shit happens but humans decide who takes the hit. What fires get put out right away, what burns for years before anyone lifts a fucking finger. There is nothing random about it. Nothing natural.

ROZ: But in how we respond? In who we become to each other?

RAY: Are you still talking about that fucking book?

ROZ: Maybe.

RAY: Because I didn't fucking read it.

ROZ: I don't blame you.

RAY: You don't blame me. How generous.

ROZ: The syringe is there. The offer stands.

RAY: I'm not going to kill you. Or even myself. Though it's tempting.

ROZ: What will we do, Ray?

RAY: I could die of this.

ROZ: Have you been tested?

RAY: Negative. Again last month.

ROZ: Me too.

RAY: Oh.

ROZ: Health worker. High risk.

RAY: Mikey has no symptoms.

ROZ: That's significant.

RAY: We're waiting for the other shoe to drop but.

ROZ: Every year he holds out he could be closer. Research money is in.

RAY: A little late.

ROZ: A lot late.

RAY: You promised us seventy years and we got about twelve.
   But those twelve were something.
   My kids got started as men.
   Ray Ray found love.
   Mikey is Mikey.
   I study biology.
   I have one son.

ROZ: You are a spectacular father. Do you know that?

RAY: I miss him.

ROZ: He was your tough guy.

RAY: Tough at the end.

ROZ: We might have a lot of life left.

RAY: I feel a thousand years old.

ROZ: But you're not.

RAY: I should get out of San Diego.

ROZ: Great.

RAY: The best hospitals are in San Francisco anyway.

ROZ: Huge capacity. Fine doctors.

RAY: So maybe I get there.
   And Mikey survives.
   And maybe I find a lover.
   And maybe you find a lover.

ROZ: And maybe someone will care this happened.
   And maybe the ones who don't care now will care then.

And maybe the ones who care now will not care then.

And a cure will come, but not for all.

RAY: And the baths will shut.

And the bars will shut.

And the culture will shift, and we will behave.

And gay couples will buy condos

And we will want fucking condos

And I don't want a condo.

I waited to be free.

I can't recall why.

To protect my kids

from shame?

from harm?

from me?

And maybe I will be free and maybe I won't.

And there will be no reason any of them died.

ROZ: And these deaths were preventable, but death is not preventable.

RAY: And one day I will be old and you will be older—you're older than me right?

ROZ: I'm pretty sure.

RAY: I will be old and you will be older and maybe—can I say this?

ROZ: I will be dying.

RAY: Possibly here.

In the bed.

ROZ: Possibly I was a professor for many years.

RAY: And let's say Mikey makes it.

And let's say times are different.

And I will talk to you on a television phone.

ROZ: And I will catch your eye on the television phone and beckon you.

Ray, come here.

We shared so much.

RAY: And I will show up with my guitar

And the lines my boys cut near my mouth.

Lines I will not fix although we gays can be a little vain.

I will kiss my lover in our condo and I will board a plane to see you.

To sing you out.

Because you deserve it.

ROZ: Because this is a love song.

And if it's not I don't want to hear it.

RAY: And I would not trade one hour with my sons for a year in Hawaii.

Evie was an asshole.

She missed everything.

ROZ: I'll be blind.

RAY: You'll be blind?

ROZ: I will be completely dependent.

I will be led around by others.

I will profess history in my blindness.

RAY: Okay you'll be blind.

And you will be—

ROZ: I will be dying. As we do. In our time.

Ray holds Roz.

He sings the beginning of Elvis's "I Can't Help Falling in Love With You." It's slow and sentimental.

Ray sings for Roz, then for the boys, then for the world.

END OF PLAY

ELIZABETH HEFFRON's plays include *Bo-Nita*, which closed an extended run at Urbanite Theatre in Florida last April. The play was a 2014 Edgerton New Play Award recipient, received its world premiere at the Seattle Repertory Theatre, and was also produced at Portland Center Stage. Her most recent work, *Portugal*, was selected for Northern Stage's New Works Now program in January 2017 in Vermont and received a 2016 Holland New Voices MainStage reading at the Great Plains Theatre Conference. Her play, *Mitzi's Abortion: A Saint's Guide to Late-Term Politics and Medicine in America*, was first produced at ACT Theatre in 2006, and has since been performed across the country, and published by Original Works Publishing, and the Rain City anthology MANIFESTO v.3, edited by Naomi Iizuka. She is a staff writer of short radio plays for Sandbox Radio Live, and teaches at Cornish College of the Arts and Freehold Theatre/Lab, where she also works with incarcerated women on collaborative performance pieces. She is an alumna of the Seattle Rep Writers Group, a member of the Sandbox Artists Collective, and the Dramatists Guild.

Elizabeth Heffron

Bo-Nita

A Play Performed by One Woman

CHARACTERS:

BO-NITA 13, scrappy, matter-of-fact, but still a child. The role is meant for an adult actor who can play the emotional quality of a 13-year-old, not the exact age.

The actor playing Bo-Nita will also need to be able to convey:

MONA mid-30's, Bo-Nita's mother, white.

GRANDMA TINY late 50's, Bo-Nita's grandmother; Mona's mother, white.

GERARD mid-30's to 40's, a nice enough guy, but has trouble with boundaries, 1/8 Cajun, mostly white.

LEON
(a.k.a. WHOZZITS-#47) 40's, Tile Salesman. Skinny, fastidious, married, knows his tile, African-American.

COLONEL T 60's, Grandma Tiny's brother; Mona's uncle, white.

JACQUE 50's, Gerard's half-Uncle, urban Cajun.

NOTE: The song used for Mona's anthem is a suggestion. Rights to use this song in performance can be secured by contacting BMG Rights Management.

Bo-Nita, a straightforward girl of 13, stands on the sidewalk, in front of her school. She is waiting for someone. It is a bright afternoon, and we can hear the sounds of traffic, and the school environment. Bo-Nita looks down the street, sees no one, then takes her backpack off her back, and sets it on the ground beside her. Even though it may be hot, she is wearing long sleeves.

Bo-Nita looks down the street again for a long time. She seems to be willfully conjuring the person she's waiting for with her mind, but to no avail. To relieve some unknown tension, she suddenly does a tiny, intricate clapping-rhythm-stomp. She sees that we are watching her. She stops. She takes us in. She really looks at us. Then, she speaks.

BO-NITA: There's this guy. . . . He's like my . . . well, this guy, you know? And he says in America, you gotta find your own personal beat. Like your own rhythm. 'Cuz without your own personal beat in America, you just get totally snowed by everybody else's beats. 'Cuz they're maybe a lot *louder* than yours, or whatever. I mean without your own beat in America? You're basically toast. According to him. So . . . yeah . . .

She does a little more of her stomp/beat.

BO-NITA: And he says if you got your rhythm-thing going, then no matter where you find yourself . . . no matter how scared or freaked out you are . . . if you can just get back to your personal beat, then everything'll be okay. It's like some natural miracle just sitting around in your life . . . like an aloe plant or something . . . and you're completely stupid if you don't take advantage of it. Yeah. That's his philosophy on that. (*beat*) He also steals snow tires off parked cars? And sells them to people on E-Bay. He says E-Bay's miraculous too . . .

She does one more bit of stomp, then checks for the person she's waiting for. No sign of them. Her shoulders sink a little. Bo-Nita looks at us again, and decides to trust us.

BO-NITA: Personally . . . ? I've only ever witnessed an *actual* miracle once. It was back in St. Louis . . .

During the following, the sound of the street and the school subside, and the lights slowly begin to change. They get softer, less harsh, as Bo-Nita draws us into her story.

BO-NITA: See my semi-ex-stepdaddy, Gerard? Well, he was on top of me. About to punch me in the face. When he all of a sudden gets this light around his head. Like a 'Touched-by-an-Angel' kinda thing. And he stops, with his arm up, like this—

She demonstrates this mid-swing, frozen pose.

BO-NITA: And starts clawing away at his chest, then dives off me—like "Man Overboard!"—and lands on the floor with a thud, yelling—

GERARD: Bo-Nita!

BO-NITA: That's how he sounds, like—

GERARD: Bo-Nita! Call a doctor! I think I'm havin—Ah! Ah!

BO-NITA: He's squirming all over the place. *Writhing*. Not many times you get to use a word like 'writhe', but this was one of those opportunities. Gerard's like this snake, trying to sidewind his way across my bedroom floor. I guess he was inching towards the bathroom. 'Cuz he still had some medicine in there, from before when Mona kicked him out.

GERARD: Bo, please baby! I got . . . I got some nitro in the . . .

BO-NITA: He keeps working this whole 'life' deal . . . fighting for all the angles, hoping I'd just *forget* the pounding he was about to give me for having a smartass mouth—'cuz I joked about him not being able to get it up to poke me. Like I was gonna go get his nitro!?

Bo-Nita turns to Gerard and yells.

BO-NITA: No way, sucker, *writhe!*

GERARD: Bo-Nita . . . ! Bo, I swear to God, man.

BO-NITA: Writhe!

GERARD: I'm gonna—Ah! Oh shit—

BO-NITA: (*she's watching him*) Gerard's movements start to mutate. From . . . some flabby-ass rattler, to that of a fish. Like maybe a Walleye, big fat one, that's jumping for air at the bottom of your boat, before you go and wonk it on its head. And he's like—

GERARD: (*demonstrates the fish described above*) Bo! Bo! Bo!

BO-NITA: Me, I'm glued to my deluxe twin bunk bed. The one Mona got me after she came back from California? Yeah. I'm in the upper bunk, safe from dying Walleyes. Gerard gives me big, moon eyes and stops moving so much. Now he seems, like, less concerned about this sudden change of plans. Almost peaceful, like he had this on the itinerary when he started the day. He stares up at me . . . taking these shallow breaths . . . gulping down whatever air he can, and he says—

GERARD: Ugh . . . ugh . . . You're okay kid.

BO-NITA: Shut up, Gerard!

Bo-Nita claps her hands on her ears, humming loudly to avoid hearing Gerard.

GERARD: You're . . . ugh . . . g-gonna be . . . ugh—okay. Don't go around with . . . ugh . . . this. (*his eyes close, and his head droops*)

BO-NITA: (*to audience*) And he sorta sputters out, and I think: "Great. Okay, well *that's* over." But then he suddenly pops back up with—

GERARD: I . . . I forgive you! (*Gerard loses consciousness completely*)

BO-NITA: Like he's the Pope or somebody. Like he's got *any business* forgiving *me*. And that's when I could feel it start . . . how my blood goes hot and angry, like a red wave . . . like this *tsunami*, I've tried to explain to Ms. Shabazz and all those stupid counselors about a billion times.

It picks you up, and there's nothing you can do but ride it. So Gerard goes and "*forgives*" me and I'm gone.

Bo-Nita turns to Gerard on the ground and shouts.

BO-NITA: F-you, Gerard! (*back to audience*) I shoot off that bed like a bullet and land on his big mound of a body, and I beat him. Balled-up fists, I hit him where it counts at first, his stupid little pecker.

Bo-Nita beats him.

BO-NITA: (*there is real rage in this*) Bam, bam, bam!

(*to audience*) Then I change course, aim for his nose, his eyes, those fat lips that are 1/8 Cajun. I'm like this green-bean-canning-machine I saw on a field trip in the 5th grade. I'm there on top of Gerard, and I'm a *robot*; smooth, clean, *effective*.

Bo-Nita beats him again.

BO-NITA: (*more rage*) Bam-bam-bam-bam-bam!

Bo-Nita stops herself, takes a breather, assessing the damage.

BO-NITA: Gerard always bragged about his lips. They were soft and fleshy, with a kinda double-curve, like a two-humped camel that ran along the upper line. He'd be like—

GERARD: Hey Bo . . . I'm taking a survey. It's part of my annual self-examination. What's the sexiest part about me? Don't be shy, girl, you gotta right to your opinions. But I know you're gonna say my lips. I *know* you're gonna say my lips. Check 'em out from the side . . . here . . .

Gerard turns and shows us his lip profile.

BO-NITA: He was always doing these surveys and classes and stuff, to improve his mind or whatever, 'cuz he didn't plan on staying a dope-smoking, wood refinisher forever. Him and Mona were the same that way . . . always looking for that extra step-up. Like with his lip-improvement exercises. He was always going—

GERARD: (*this is a lip exercise, he starts by puckering up*)

Scrunch-'em-up.

(*now he stretches his mouth wide in a huge smile*)

Spread-'em-out

Scrunch-'em-up

Spread-'em-out . . .

Bo-Nita stares back down at Gerard.

BO-NITA: Now you wouldn't even know he was born with a pair, they were just gone. And where lips usually went was a pulpy pink mess, like what happens to earthworms in a blender. And I can see some bit of tooth mixed into the muck. And my own fists are beginning to look a lot like his muck, but still, I can't help myself. I keep going—

Bam-bam-bam-bam-bam!

We hear a doorbell that sounds like a chirping bird.

BO-NITA: Even after I hear our tweetering-bird doorbell do the same goddamn phrase of 'Oh, what a Beautiful Morning' and Mona's heels, clattering on the front hall tile. And Mona calls out—

MONA: *(calling)* Bo . . . ? You-hoo! Bo-Nita-baby . . . ! *(she giggles, then says to someone else)* She's probably reading some damn opus in her room. *(she stumbles)* Whoops . . . ! *(she giggles again)*

BO-NITA: She's giggling, way too girly, and I hear this sound come back, like some kinda male static. Like—

LEON: Hey now, baby . . . let's try and stay vertical.

BO-NITA: Crap. Must be some guy she's dragged in.

MONA: 'Try and stay vertical'! That's soooo funny, Leroy!

LEON: Uhhh . . . it's Leon.

MONA: Leon! There you go again! You. Are. A funny-bunny!

Another burst of giggles from Mona.

BO-NITA: And I'm like, great. Mona's gone and got herself some new 'Whozzits'. First time she brings them home? She always gets super-shitfaced. Even like now, when it's the middle of the day. I don't know why she does that, and it kinda *really* burns my butt, and we even discussed the whole issue over a meatloaf dinner a couple months ago . . .

A kitchen timer goes off . . .

MONA: *(at the dinner table)* Bo-Nita, are you gonna eat that loaf, or just mess with it?

Bo-Nita keeps messing with her meatloaf.

MONA: Hmmm . . . ? *(beat)* You know I hate it when you get pissy. Specially after I go to all the trouble of cookin' you a whole goddamn dinner.

BO-NITA: I'm not pissy.

MONA: Yeah, you are. Look at you. Pass me the bowl.

BO-NITA: *(to audience)* I pick up the pipe? But I don't pass it to her. Instead, I . . .

Bo-Nita deliberately lights the pipe, and takes a hit.

MONA: What are you doing?

BO-NITA: *(holding the smoke in)* What's it look like?

MONA: It's a school night, young lady.

BO-NITA: *(exhaling)* Duh.

MONA: (*an old irritation*) I can't believe your grandma let you start.

BO-NITA: (*an accusation*) You weren't there. Remember? You were in California.

MONA: (*snapping at this*) *I know that!* I know I was.

BO-NITA: So. Whatever. And it helps me sleep.

MONA: (*trying to be a good mother on this*) Well, two hits is your limit, young lady.

BO-NITA: I believe we've already established that.

MONA: Don't be a snot.

BO-NITA: I'm not a snot.

MONA: Snot-snot-snot.

BO-NITA: Stop.

MONA: Look at that little persimmon-mouth. Something big's on your mind, so just spit it out.

BO-NITA: Mom . . .

MONA: Yeah?

BO-NITA: (*beat*) Why do you always gotta get so super-shitfaced when you bring new guys home?

MONA: What are you talking about? I don't get super-shitfaced.

BO-NITA: Yeah, you do.

MONA: No.

BO-NITA: Every time. (*counting them off*) Bobby, Dwayne, Lavon, Gerard, *Mike*—

MONA: You *know* not to mention that man's name! His name's been ix-nayed from our vocabulary.

BO-NITA: (*sticking to her question*) Super-shitfaced. Every time. (*to audience*) Mona sort of pauses, and pushes her plate back, and takes her own hit from the pipe that Dead-Grandma-Tiny made in 'Senior Pottery' a couple Christmases ago, and she says—

MONA: (*exhaling*) You lookin' to go deep tonight, Bo? Is that it?

BO-NITA: I'm just . . . wondering . . .

MONA: (*there's some bite in this, a warning*) Would you rather I switch vices?

BO-NITA: No.

MONA: Go back to the white stuff—

BO-NITA: No! That's not what I'm saying! God! Never mind.

MONA: (*complete change of demeanor, suddenly loving, cajoling*) I'm just teasing you, baby! That's all! C'mere-c'mere-c'mere!

BO-NITA: Cut it out.

MONA: Come sit on your mama's lap.

Mona reaches over to pull Bo-Nita onto her lap.

BO-NITA: And Mona sort of drags me onto her lap. And I sort of let her.

MONA: (*she tickles her, makes baby voices*) Yeah . . . That's my baby . . .

BO-NITA: (*liking it*) Stop that, it tickles!

MONA: My wittle-wittle baby!

BO-NITA: (*still laughing*) I said stop.

MONA: (*beat*) You *know* that was the best day of my life, right?

BO-NITA: I know.

MONA: When they brought you out. After all that twisting and screaming, and there you were . . . just . . . the perfect little pink thing. Little bow in your cap—

BO-NITA: Bo-

MONA: And your grandma called you 'pretty as a penny, and neat as a pin'.

BO-NITA: -Nita.

MONA: Like a fresh start just gazing up at me . . . no judgment . . . nothing but love. All the crap of the world's waitin' right outside that hospital room, but none of it mattered when I was lookin' at you . . .

BO-NITA: Soooo . . . how'd I get my hyphen? (*to audience*) I already know exactly how I got my hyphen. Mona's told me like 8 million times . . . but somehow . . . hearing her say it again? Never gets old.

MONA: You got your hyphen because . . . one, they're British and totally sexy. And two, hyphens are all about hanging on and keeping things together. And that's an art, Bo. That's something I want you to learn better'n me. And the last reason? Hyphens don't let go. I don't want you ever, *ever* to let go. You hear me?

BO-NITA: Yeah.

MONA: No, I mean it.

BO-NITA: I know. I hear you.

MONA: Goddamn, I love you on my lap, baby. You just feel fucking good!

BO-NITA: (*soaking this up, but to audience*) And whenever she gets touchy-feely like this? I can tell what's coming next. Mona's anthem. Next thing out of her mouth is—

MONA: Sing with me, Bo . . .

(*she sings the beginning to a song, like: "Dreaming" by Blondie*)
WHEN I MET YOU IN THE RESTAURANT
YOU COULD TELL I WAS NO DEBUTANTE
YOU ASKED ME WHAT'S MY PLEASURE
A MOVIE OR A MEASURE?
I'LL HAVE A CUP OF TEA AND TELL YOU OF MY—
Hit it, baby.

Bo-Nita shakes her head, no.

MONA: C'mon!

BO-NITA: You do it.

MONA: Alright, if I have to . . .

DREAMING

DREAMING IS FREE

DREAMING

DREAMING IS FREE

Yeah . . .

They both sit in the silence for a second. Then Bo-Nita gets off her lap and back to the question at hand.

BO-NITA: So . . .

MONA: What?

BO-NITA: *Why* do you always get so super-shitfaced?

MONA: You really want me to answer that?

BO-NITA: Yeah.

MONA: (*eyeing Bo-Nita wearily*) This isn't gonna wind up in one of your Gifted Program essays, is it? Where I get a phone call and DCS suddenly breathin' down my neck again . . . ?

BO-NITA: No. God! I *told* you, I was just doing my '*life observations*' like the teacher *asked*, I didn't know it would ring some kind of bell! And besides . . . they cut that whole program.

MONA: Good.

BO-NITA: I'm just . . . it just . . . I don't know . . .

MONA: What?

BO-NITA: It just really *bugs* me.

MONA: 'Bugs' you, huh . . . Well lemme think . . . Why do I always get shitfaced . . .

BO-NITA: (*to audience*) I watch Mona chew on a piece of her meatloaf, slowly pondering this dark, metaphysical question, like it's the first time she's ever really thought about it. She starts nodding, her head forward—the way people do when they've been waitressing for 16 hours straight and then have to sit in a warm emergency room 'cuz of their kid's asthma? They nod like that, bolt upright in their chair. Her brow's all furrowed too. Like it's the most important insight she could ever have about herself and it's just not coming. Finally, she sighs, like . . .

Does a Mona sigh.

MONA: I don't know. I don't know, Bo-Nita. Maybe . . . it just depresses me.

BO-NITA: What depresses you? Me?

MONA: No, not *you*. Jesus, you're always so goddamn *sensitive*.

BO-NITA: Then . . . what then?

MONA: I don't know . . . *It*.

BO-NITA: *It*?

MONA: Yeah, just . . . *IT*. The whole, sad cycle . . . the knowing that I'm not doin' anything *new*. I'm just doin' the same lame goddamn thing I've always done, over-and-over, and I got no . . . *exit plan*. You know? I got no . . . *ulterior motive*. Some day, Bo . . . (*she stops*) Never mind.

BO-NITA: No. Tell me . . .

MONA: Some day, I gotta feeling I'll be 65 and I'll still be bringing these guys over.

BO-NITA: Pretty old guys by then, huh?

MONA: Yep . . . Yeah.

Mona makes a sweeping gesture.

MONA: And this is *not* how I wanted us to end up.

BO-NITA: I don't know. It's not so bad.

MONA: (*not hearing her*) And that makes me wanna get drunk or high or some goddamn thing, before I start back in again. I guess . . . I guess that is *exactly* why I like to get super-shitfaced . . .

BO-NITA: (*to audience*) And Mona finally swallows that piece of loaf she's been moving around in her right cheek. She swallows it like that puts the seal of approval on the answer . . . And suddenly I'm in that sad-blue-place that Ms. Shabazz had me draw, and it feels like the floor's gone and I'm being sucked down a drain, and there's no point to even breathing. Watching her swallow that meat felt like some kind of death sentence, where the death never stops, where you're never *finally* dead. You just keep dying and dying real slowly, fizzling out, like a leaky birthday balloon.

We hear something that reminds Bo-Nita of Mona's giggle in the hallway.

Bo-Nita shakes herself out of this memory.

BO-NITA: (*to audience, with more urgency*) Now Mona's heels have stopped clicking on our front hall tile. And she and Whozzits-#47 are moving into our living room—which is covered in a forest-green, stain-resistant carpet that we only paid 94-cents-a-yard for—'cuz Mona got to know the carpet salesman in the biblical sense? Unfortunately, things petered out before she could get the roll installed, so we wound up putting the whole thing down ourselves. That's why it curls up in a couple of the corners. We tried working with those carpet staples? But they're a joke without that professional gun. Eventually, Mona had to go out and buy us an industrial-size tub of Gorilla Glue, so anytime some section wants to spring back up, we're ready.

MONA: (*calling*) Bo . . . ?

BO-NITA: (*calling to Mona*) Uhhh . . . In here, Mom! (*back to audience*) The Whozzits says something cautious, but Mona puts him at ease.

MONA: (*giggling, to Whozzits*) She's 13! Not like she's 8! She's not gonna be scared of you, baby . . .

BO-NITA: I've stopped pummeling Gerard, and I'm breathing real hard. I hear the shuffle of their shoes on the carpet coming this way, but I can't seem to move. I look down. My hands are fisted-up, like bloody stumps on the ends of my forearms, and I can't get my fingers to open. So I just cross 'em over my chest, like this? Kinda nonchalant . . .

> Bo-Nita crosses her arms across her chest.

BO-NITA: . . . hoping to hide the worst parts, just as Mona and #47 pop through the door. And Mona's all—

MONA: Boneeetah! I'd like you to meet . . . (*beat*) Uhh . . .

BO-NITA: I watch her mouth go south as she takes in the Nancy-Grace-Special that's laid out before her . . . me and my messed-up stumps, straddling her fat, semi-ex-husband Gerard, who no longer has what you'd call a functional face.

MONA: Oh my God . . .

BO-NITA: This guy? #47? Turns out to be a sorta skinny-Eddie-Murphy-poindexter-type. I nail him for a salesman right away. A married one. He wasn't expecting this picture when he turned the corner, and already you can tell he's doing the math and wondering if his wife could accidentally end up reading about this in the St. Louis Post-Dispatch, and what was it all gonna cost him in child support and emotional duress. That's what I'm thinking he must be thinking . . . Either that, or he's got some *serious* facial tics that have all decided to go off at once, like some kind of facial tic fiesta. Like—

> Bo-Nita demonstrates Leon'S serious facial tics.

BO-NITA: They don't seem to wanna say much. So I try and volunteer something off-the-cuff, like . . . (*to Mona, extra casual*) Hey Mama. Gerard stopped by. He had a heart attack.

LEON: A heart attack?! That don't look like no heart attack to me. You just beat the *shit* outa that guy!

BO-NITA: I can see Mona's doing some quick figuring now too.

MONA: Leroy, please don't jump to conclusions.

BO-NITA: She's still in her 'high-polite' voice, but heading towards 'TV-lawyer'.

MONA: Yes, it appears Bo-Nita's done some disfigurement on Gerard's face—

LEON: Done some disfigurement?!

MONA: But there's no way she would have been able to wail on him like that, without him having a full-on heart attack. Gerard's over 300 pounds, and strong too. He was a full-back at Frontenac in the 80's. The man's got telephone poles for thighs . . .

BO-NITA: Mona trails off, reminiscing a little I guess, Gerard's thighs could do that to her. Until all of a sudden . . . the whole picture of what we were looking at wooshed right back into view—including her personal probation situation—which probably didn't include dead, fat guys in her kid's bedroom.

MONA: Oh my god . . . Oh my *God*, baby. We . . . we can't have this! We gotta get him *outa* here! Maybe . . . maybe we can . . . put him in his car or something.

LEON: Put him in his car . . . ?! What's the *matter* with you people? Look at him! We need to call an *ambulance*!

BO-NITA: So I say, just to shut him up . . . (*to Leon*) Oh yeah, Mister, and are *you* gonna sign for him? Your fancy-ass *wife* would *love* that!

LEON: You need to wash out that mouth, girl—

Bo-Nita makes a face and sticks her tongue out at Leon.

LEON: Stop that! What the hell's the matter with you? I'm not going to jail for this.

MONA: Nobody's goin' to jail, Leroy.

LEON: **Leon.**

MONA: You're *completely* overreacting. Bo-Nita-honey, make sure Gerard has really checked out.

BO-NITA: So I bounce up and down on the mound a couple of times, and lean forward to where his mouth normally is, and listen for some sound of breathing. (*to Mona*) "Nope, nothing."

LEON: Goodnight, nurse! That man is dead? Are you telling me that man is *dead?!*

BO-NITA: Me and Mona, we just look at him like he must be retarded or something.

LEON: I'm outa here. I'm sorry, honey, but this is *not* my thing!

BO-NITA: (*suddenly angry, to Leon*) No, your thing is porking my Mom real good behind the China King.

LEON: You best watch your manners, young lady—

Mona does a loud, piercing whistle.

MONA: Alright you two, now can it! We gotta . . . *situation* in front of us here that requires *community effort. We've all gotta pull together!* Bo-Nita, go into my closet and get out one of your grandma's old belly dancing costumes, and some fishnet stockings!

LEON: Fishnet stockings?!

BO-NITA: (*to audience*) #47 is back at his old game, but I don't care. I just feel a deep sense of relief with Mona finally shouting out orders. It means she's hatching one of her plans. Maybe even a good plan, hopefully . . . Hopefully . . .

> *Sound from the school environment intrudes slightly into Bo-Nita's story. She looks down the street. Still nothing. She kicks her backpack around a little, then reconnects with us a little deeper . . .*

BO-NITA: When . . . Mona was out in . . . (*she uses air quotes*) "California"? They had . . . they had this Pet-Project-thing. Where they'd, like, instruct all the women how to be dog trainers? Like vocationally. And Mona *loved* it. When I finally got to come visit, I'd never seen her so happy. She learned exactly how to give orders so that dogs would really listen and do whatever she said, which is like a pretty commercial skill. Unfortunately, the state funding dried up before she could finish the full course, so she never got her certificate. And that's, like, so not fair, 'cuz once you've been somewhere . . . like "California"? There's all kinds of jobs that you just can't get anymore. Like most of the good-paying ones, in health care and finance and stuff. And sometimes this just flattens Mona, and she stops trying and just becomes like this big human bucket-of-slop, and you could tell her she'd just won a million bucks and she wouldn't even turn her head. When she's 'low' like that, she's like this run-over slug, dying in the street, cussing at pedestrians, her antennas barely even moving. But, then, there are the other times, you know? When she's what she calls 'up'—and the world's just bursting with fresh possibilities—

MONA: I'm *up*, Bo-Nita! Up, up, up!

BO-NITA: She's like this bottle-rocket, all spark and surprise. Her thoughts are light-years ahead of her mouth. And her brain cells just spew out ideas like a mental machine-gun. Dead-Grandma-Tiny used to question whether it was all her own natural energy, but I didn't care how she got that way . . . when it was good like that? I just liked it.

MONA: (*in an 'up' phase, speaking fast*) Jesus Christ, look at the sky! You're not looking, baby.

BO-NITA: I'm looking.

MONA: Looks like cotton candy, don't it Bo-Nita? Like you could just stick your tongue out there and work it. (*completely different subject, hatching a plan*) Okay, back to business . . . Here's how we handle all that 'peddlers license' BS. We buy a llama.

BO-NITA: What?

MONA: Yeah, cute South American giraffe, big eyes, sheep fur.

BO-NITA: A llama?

MONA: We'll put our display for the 'Rain Forest Rejuvenating Creams' on the llama's back! I'm still pissed they sent us all our supplies C.O.D., but we're gonna make the best of it. Fuck them and their whole supply chain. We're a perfectly good credit risk. I don't care what their computer says. And never take that kind of rejection personally, baby, that's one thing you gotta remember if you're going to make a killing in sales. You can't take anything personally. We'll have to construct a saddle of some kind . . .

BO-NITA: Why do we—

MONA: A saddle, a saddle! For the llama! Possibly silk, lots of tassels and whatever else, South American things! *That's* how we'll get into (*she puts her pinkies up and uses them to make air quotes, and says this word as if she's stuck-up*) "Ladue." We'll make a spectacle of ourselves. I swear to God, we'll make a mint, Bo-Nita, if we can just get this shit to those super-rich ladies in "Ladue!"

BO-NITA: Well . . . how much do llamas cost?

MONA: That's the wrong question, baby. The question is *not* 'what do llamas cost?' The question is: 'How much can we *make* with one?'

BO-NITA: But where's it gonna live?

MONA: Nope, I'm not goin' there. That's a detail! I'm not gettin' bogged down in the details. It'll live where it lives. West County! They got tons of llamas out there, on all those fake farms. Oh! Better yet. We'll *lease* a llama! You know how the DVD said to visualize your first commission check? Well, I want you to visualize a flat screen TV! Are you seeing it Bo? Are you seeing us eating popcorn and watching 'Avatar' on some honkin' 3-D, flat screen TV?

BO-NITA: Some of her ideas actually pan out—like how I got my bunk bed—but some really suck, and set us way back . . . like the one where we snuck over to Concordia and trapped crawdads in their big pond all night, then tried to sell them to the fancy restaurants in the Central West End. Gerard was in on that one. We were gonna have a whole line of poached seafood products, and sell 'em all over St. Louis. And Gerard was, like, racking his brain for a good name, but Mona just kept knocking him down.

GERARD: How 'bout . . . 'Crawdads du Carondolet'.

MONA: Too French.

GERARD: 'Crawdads, Inc.' . . . ?

MONA: How 'bout we put 'em all to sleep. (*she makes a big overblown snoring sound*)

GERARD: Oh, I know! 'Cajun Crawdads' . . . !

MONA: Gerard, you know we can't say 'Cajun'.

GERARD: Why not?

MONA: That'd be dishonest. You're not Cajun enough to put it in the name.

GERARD: Not Cajun enough?! I sure as shit am! I'm in the book, honey, look me up! 17.5 percent is *more* than enough!

MONA: (*totally dismissing this*) Pffft—

GERARD: Hell, it's less dishonest than that city health certificate you rigged up!

MONA: We *needed* a health certificate, Gerard. What was I supposed to do? *Apply* for one?

BO-NITA: Even when the idea was way-off, even when I could feel it was gonna be a giant bust before she got the whole thing out of her mouth, it was still . . . *exciting*. That's how I like Mona best, when she's positive. When she's charged and moving.

We hear some tinkle of Grandma Tiny's belly dancing costume.

BO-NITA: Now Whozzits pipes up with—

LEON: Uhh, look Ladies, I hate to state the obvious, but belly dancers don't wear fishnets—

MONA: (*to Leon*) What . . . ?

LEON: Actually, yeah, I've seen my share of belly dancers, and none of 'em wore fishnets.

BO-NITA: Oh good, he's stepping onto thin ice . . . I'm thinking, while I'm rummaging through Dead-Grandma-Tiny's side of the closet.

MONA: Well, obviously Leon, you weren't witnessing authentic, St. Louis Middle Eastern Dance.

LEON: Everybody knows they dance *barefoot*.

MONA: Not in Missouri.

LEON: They sure as hell don't wear fishnets.

MONA: Have you ever heard of Princess Shazzah Lola?

LEON: (*beat*) No.

MONA: No. Obviously not. I was *raised* by Princess Shazzah Lola, that's my mother's *stage name*. You know 'The Parthenon' on Lindell?

LEON: Uhhh—

MONA: You know 'Zorba's' in The Loop? My mother was *featured* at those places, and a bunch of others, on Gravois, Gaslight Square in the 70's. This was someone, Leon, my mother was someone who *dedicated her life* to this art form—along with her herb business—and she *always* wore fishnets! So, I would suggest you stop blabbin' on about topics where you've basically got your head up your ass.

BO-NITA: I come out of the closet with two of the costumes . . . (*holding up them up, to Mona*) Okay . . . '1001 Nights', or 'Cleopatra's Revenge' . . . ?

MONA: Revenge.

BO-NITA: I hand Mona the costume, with all the coins on the bra part clinking like crazy, and still reeking of that patchouli oil Grandma Tiny seemed to bathe in after she lost all her hair. The Cleopatra outfit was a good choice. It was Tiny's last professional bedlah, when she'd bloated up past 200 pounds, after they'd started the chemo? I bring out the controversial fishnets, plus a pair of platform shoes, which Missouri belly dancers also wear, and me and Whozzits are charged with getting Gerard naked, while Mona cleans up his face. Mona's got experience in this department. She's a whiz at patching you up, so nobody asks nosy questions at school. She pulls out a couple of ice packs from the freezer, plants them on the floor, then rolls Gerard onto his stomach, so his face lands smack on the packs, and they start to work their magic.

MONA: I gotta go find the Preparation H.

BO-NITA: Mona heads for the bathroom, leaving me and Whozzits to puzzle out the clothes deal ourselves.

LEON: Just . . . how are we 'sposed to do this?

BO-NITA: Undress him?

LEON: Yeah.

BO-NITA: Not that hard. Start at the top and work down.

LEON: Okay . . .

BO-NITA: We peel Gerard's clothes off him like a 300-pound banana, moving him this way and that 'til he's down to pink skin.

LEON: Oh my . . . well . . . ain't that somethin' . . .

BO-NITA: Yeah . . . (to audience) And we're both staring down at the butt-naked Gerard . . . (she shakes her head) I don't know . . . What is it about mostly white guys, when you get their clothes off . . . ? They always look like some kinda uncooked dinner roll. Something's just not quite done about them, and it makes you feel sorta like you do when you see a puppy at the pound? Because the thing is, most of them never get finished. Least, not as far as I can tell. Mona and her girlfriends, they keep changing it up. Evolving. Gettin' nose rings or whatever. But these dough boys, it's like . . . however their mamas plopped 'em out, that's how they're gonna stay their entire lives.

LEON: What happened to his foot?

BO-NITA: His friend ran over it with an edger.

LEON: Hell . . .

BO-NITA: We put Gerard in the fishnets, Whozzits and me, working together. We each take a leg and bunch up our bit of the stringy stockings by his toes, then slide them over his swollen ankles and up his boulder-like calves. It's amazing the thing about fishnet stockings. They can make any leg look better. Even Gerard's are coming out pretty fine, until we hit those thighs of his, and suddenly its like swimming up the Meramec in May.

LEON: (*struggling to get the fishnets up Gerard's thigh*) Well shit . . . (*calling back to Mona*) Hey Mona—you gotta shoe horn or something we can use to squeegee these things up? It's like Falujah over here!

BO-NITA: Mona goes to the kitchen and tosses us a couple of spatulas, and we wedge the fishnets up Gerard's thighs, and stretch the panty part over his big hairy behind. On some silent signal, #47 and I roll him over on his back, for the final adjustments, and run right into a big, old surprise.

LEON: Damn . . . that's a nasty-looking hard-on.

BO-NITA: You can hear this sorta hushed respect in his voice. And for just a second, I feel really sorry for Gerard. 'Cause of his weight or his diabetes or all that weed he smoked, he'd had all kinds of trouble gettin' his number up when he wanted to. Now, here he is, flat out dead, and Mr. Piggy? Decides to salute the entire planet. It feels like this giant, philosophical statement on how the world is. How sometimes your entire life turns out to be a sort of mean joke. Like the whole situation with Mike-the-Ixnayed. Or those 28 months when Mona was away, and me and Grandma Tiny had to go live with her brother, Colonel T., in a stinky-ass trailer, outside Grubville, Middle-of-Nowhere, USA.

A cow moos.

BO-NITA: Tiny was pissed we had to leave the city, 'cuz it screwed up her distribution networks, and she hated living so far away from her artistic opportunities.

GRANDMA TINY: Just so's we're straight, baby girl, you set up your things on that side of the room, and I'm here, by the heater, 'cuz your grandma needs the heat. And no touchin none of my bedlahs, or anythin' that jingle-jangles, or hell, if it even *smells* like belly-dancin', you stay clear, 'cuz I got it all in performance-order, just in case there's an emergency call. And I'll know if your grubby, little hands have been messin 'em up. You got that?

Bo-Nita nods.

GRANDMA TINY: And another thing, you ever mention Mike's name again, I'll slap you straight through to tomorrow. You hear me?

COLONEL T: (*keeps a toothpick permanently in his mouth*) Now Tiny, that's not Christian.

GRANDMA TINY: T! That man cooked up more ammonia than Union Carbide! If there was any of him left, I'd be spittin' on his bones.

COLONEL T: Suit yerself. Prolly saved yer girl's life . . . when his split-level blew.

GRANDMA TINY: How can you say that?!

COLONEL T: Got her where she's at. Prolly'll save her life, if you ask me.

GRANDMA TINY: Well, I ain't askin' you.

COLONEL T: If she's smart about it. If she takes advantage of her time.

GRANDMA TINY: T—

COLONEL T: I seen it happen.

GRANDMA TINY: (*changing the subject*) Bo-Nita, you get over here!

BO-NITA: Grandma Tiny hands me a dirty-looking box. (*to Tiny*) What's this?

GRANDMA TINY: I got you some sifters and dicers. You're gonna be sortin' out seeds.

BO-NITA: All the seeds?

COLONEL T: Now, Tiny, she's gonna need time to go to school, and whatnot.

GRANDMA TINY: (*waves him off, then new thought*) They don't have sniffer dogs at these farm schools, do they, T?

COLONEL T: Dogs?

GRANDMA TINY: We better make sure you get a good shower every morning, Bo-Nita, before you head for town. Just in case they got some fancy equipment at that school. Don't wanna be smellin' like product, settin' off a bunch of alarms.

COLONEL T: Hell, there's no fancy equipment, Tiny. They barely got books.

BO-NITA: Colonel T had his driver's license revoked some time back in the 90's 'cause of some government plot regarding his consumption of alcoholic beverages. So he'd taken to driving his suped-up Cub Cadet Lawn Mower whenever he needed to go into town for 'fuel and fresh perspectives.'

COLONEL T: (*big whistle*) Hey there, Girl, stop messin' with them snakes and get your butt over here! I'm takin' ya for a *mow*!

GRANDMA TINY: (*calling after them*) Colonel? Colonel! Where you goin' with Bo-Nita?!

COLONEL T: (*calling back*) Fuel and fresh perspectives!

GRANDMA TINY: (*continuing to call*) Don't you have deliveries to make? And what about that prayer meeting?

COLONEL T: All in good time, my pretty. All in good time.

GRANDMA TINY: Well, don't go back to that library, you hear me?! I ain't payin' for any more of them fines! And use your goddamn hand signals on that highway!

COLONEL T: (*waving her off*) Keep your tits on, Tiny, this ain't a mission to Mars!

    A cow moos again.

BO-NITA: The Colonel had this old cow. Her name was Fetch? And for some reason, Grandma Tiny decided I had to milk her every morning and every night, and that animal had these thin, hanging nipples, that felt like tired rubber bands that might just snap right off if you pulled too hard. And the milk she offered up was thin too. Thin and kind of blue-looking, and it stunk of all the onions she'd eat all day long. But Grandma Tiny? She made me *drink* that milk, everyday. *Everyday* for the 28 months my mom was gone, like *I* was the one that ran the paper-scam for Mike, like *I* was the one that needed to be punished . . .

Sometimes, at night, I still have this sudden flash of me milking that cow, knowing I was gonna have to drink what came dribblin' out, and I get that same, old pukey feeling . . . like a humid nausea that comes back and back . . . and you just have to *force* yourself to think about something *'positive'*, like they said in that counseling class . . . like *Dairy Queen* . . . or *Dr. Phil*, or *something* . . .

We hear a little TINKLE from the belly dancing costume.

BO-NITA: Old Whozzits is staring at Gerard's woodie, like it's some sorta spectacular puzzle.

LEON: (*scratching his head*) I don't know about this . . . I'm thinking you better stuff it down your side.

BO-NITA: Me?

LEON: Not right for a man to do it.

BO-NITA: I'm not touchin' it.

LEON: Well, it can't stay like that.

BO-NITA: Why not?

LEON: Poking straight up like a stick shift? Hell no! Where are your manners? The man's *dead*, for chrissake.

BO-NITA: So I go and get a paper towel, and try and do something with Gerard's jimmy, which wasn't of a mind to be pushed around. Finally, me and Whozzits wrestle the panty part of the fishnets into place and just let Mr. Piggy land where he may, tucked up against Gerard's big belly.

LEON: (*relieved*) There. Snug as a bug in a rug.

BO-NITA: Mona's making final adjustments on the Cleopatra top. As she stuffs up the big boobies with some of her scented underwear, it finally occurs to #47 to ask . . .

LEON: Uhhhh . . . just *where* exactly we headed with all this, Mona . . . ?

MONA: Need-to-know-basis, Leroy. Now help me lift him up. Bo-Nita, I need you to fasten the harem belt around back. You got it?

BO-NITA: (*to Mona*) Yes, ma'am. (*to audience*) The two of them heft on 'three' and I wrap the bottom half of the costume around Gerard's hips, with the coins, and pink sequins and fake-turquoise-beads all dancing around his middle. Mona orders me to get her make-up bag, while she applies the

Preparation H under Gerard's puffed-up eyes. #47 starts to flutter around the room, like a stunned finch.

MONA: (*to Leon*) Leon, just help me get him in the car, and follow us down to the Landing. That's all I'm askin'.

LEON: Oh, that's *all!* Look, I'm a tile salesman, ladies! And there's a large order of easy-maintenance, fusion tiles I'm *supposed* to receive any minute!

BONITA: And Whozzits goes for the door, but Mona's not gonna have it.

MONA: (*she bellows*) **Hey!**

> *We hear a door slam, hard.*

BO-NITA: She kicks my door shut, and gives Leon that dog-command-glare of hers, that sort of cuts you in half and sucks the breath out of you, all at the same time.

LEON: (*wind out of his sails*) What . . . ?

BO-NITA: We stand around for a few seconds, til we're all sure Leon's not gonna make a run for it, then Mona goes back to refurbishing Gerard's face. She carefully scoops up his lip material and smooshes it back around his gum line, cementing most of it in place with our handy tub of Gorilla Glue. She even tries to rebuild his two-humped-camel, and improvises an extra little hump on his bottom lip.

MONA: There. Just for effect. You like it . . . ?

BO-NITA: All three of us blow on Gerard a bunch of times, to let the glue set. And Mona covers up the whole shebang with her "Passion Ruby" lipstick. She blues his eyelids, adds some big, fakey lashes, and dabs him all over with Tiny's remaining supply of patchouli oil. Then, we stand back and admire her handiwork . . .

> *All three of them scrutinize Gerard.*

BO-NITA: It's something to see . . . Gerard in 'Cleopatra's Revenge' with the fishnets, and the platforms, and his face made up like Tammy Fae Baker's 1/8-Cajun-twin-sister.

LEON: One more time . . . (*more cautious*) What *exactly* is the *point* to all this . . . ?

BO-NITA: Mona answers slooooow, like maybe the guy's retarded *and* deaf . . .

MONA: (*slowly*) We'rre gonna take him down to the Lannding, near the jazzz clubs . . . leave him in his carr, and make it look like he was looking for a hookk-up, and a bunch of Southside Polllllacks spied him for queerr and beat him up, and because of this obvious *trauummma*, he went into carrdiac arrrest. Voila. Self-explanatory.

LEON: (*beat*) That's . . .

MONA: What?

LEON: That's not gonna work.

MONA: There you go with the *negativity* again. That kind of thinking gets you nowhere. See Leroy, it's gonna work because people will get *waylaid* by the get-up. It's a psychological *fact*, distraction is 9/10's of the art of survival. Now, help me stand him up. Bo-Nita-honey, go wash your hands.

BO-NITA: I do as she says. The water hurts. I soap up, and wash the dried blood away, wanting to scream. It's like a million tiny little knives cutting into my fingers. I come back out and they've dragged Gerard to the front door. Mona's taken the old, pink plastic roof from my Barbie Dream House, and draped it over his head, I guess so no one will recognize him. We all proceed out the door, like a guilty Fat Tuesday parade, to Gerard's Cherry Red Chrysler Sebring, and we stuff him into the passenger seat. Mona's about to hop in the driver's side, but stops and turns to Leon, and hands him the keys.

MONA: (*handing him the keys*) You drive his car, I'll drive yours.

LEON: What? *Me* drive him?! I got nothin' to do with this!

MONA: Leroy, you think I'm a complete idiot?

BO-NITA: It's not Leroy. It's never been Leroy.

MONA: Shut up Bo-Nita. (*to Leon*) Leroy, look . . . I need you to drive us home once we drop him off, and I can't guarantee that you'll do that, unless Gerard rides with you.

LEON: Sweetheart, I'll dog your ass all the way to the Landing, I *swear* baby, cross-my-heart!

MONA: Really . . .

LEON: (*triple crosses himself*) Oh yeah. Hundred percent. No doubt.

MONA: (*squinting, judging his face*) I don't believe you.

LEON: Well . . . shit, Mona! That don't say much about our level of trust.

MONA: Level of *trust*?

BO-NITA: Trust is like a foreign country to Mona, and after they have a two-minute staring contest, Whozzits finally takes the keys and grumbles in that way where you know he's pissed and resentful, but not enough to actually stand up for himself. And you kinda sense he's probably a little pussywhipped back home, which Mona says is one of her biggest turn-offs, but I don't necessarily think it's such a bad thing . . . 'cuz I've seen first-hand what the other-way-around looks like? And that's got some serious drawbacks too.

MONA: (*to Leon*) You're gonna buckle him up, right?

LEON: Yeah, I'll buckle him up. Sure, I'll buckle him up. Anything else? You want me to wipe his big-ass behind?

MONA: Hardy-har-har—

BO-NITA: Mona slams the door shut. We walk back to Leon's lime-green Geo Metro and follow Leon and Gerard down Lindbergh to 40. We drive in this awful kind of silence. My hands are really starting to throb and puff up. I look over to Mona and try to say something funny, something that'll put everything we're going through into perspective and bring us closer together, but I see how she's gripping the little Geo wheel and the way she's running her lower jaw back and forth across what's left of her molars, and I just can't think of the funny thing I want to say . . .

(*beat*) If Gerard wasn't dead and tarted-up in the other car, he'd have a theory on all of this. He's got, like, tons of theories, that just sprout out of him when you're somewhere like Pontoon Beach, floating around on inner tubes, just enjoying the day . . .

We hear the sound of a beer can opening.

GERARD: (*taking a swig of beer, relishing it*) Ahhhh . . . You know, Bo-Nita . . . why your mama's gotta work so much?

BO-NITA: (*dragging her hand in the water*) For the money?

GERARD: Yeah, for that. But—ultimately—it's the system. The system's keeping her down. It's all fucked up.

BO-NITA: It is?

GERARD: I mean, look around . . . You see these good ol' boys all boozed-up and red-faced? They don't know it, but they've all bought into that 'unspoken agenda'.

BO-NITA: Yeah . . . ?

GERARD: They've done what's called "internalizing their shame." All that corporate bullshit about self-reliance and pulling-yourself-up-by-your-bootstraps. They've made these boys think that if they haven't made it by now, here in America—with all that white skin hanging off their bodies—then they got no fucking excuse. They speak the language. They got two hundred years of privilege under their belts. They think—hell, I'll tell you *exactly* what they got them thinking. They're thinking: "Shit, if I ain't ridin around in an Escalade *by now*, if I'm still stockin shelves or pumpin septic, then it's my own goddamn fault. There must be something wrong with *me*." You see what I'm saying, Bo?

BO-NITA: How do you know that?

GERARD: I can see it all real clearly 'cuz I'm 1/8th Cajun. (*beat*) You want a sip of my Bud . . . ?

BO-NITA: No.

GERARD: See . . . the system wants people feeling guilty. So you don't start questioning where all the fucking money is going. And your rage stays aimed at all the *other* animals in the circus, the lions and tigers and whatnot, but you don't even *think* to question the *fucking ringleaders*. You catchin' my drift?

BO-NITA: Ummm.

GERARD: The system's screwing your mom, Bo. It's screwing all of us, right up the ass.

BO-NITA: Well okay, but, *what* 'system'?

GERARD: (*beat*) You really want me to spell it out?

BO-NITA: I guess.

Gerard looks around carefully to make sure no one can hear him.

GERARD: I'll tell you, but you gotta keep this hush-hush. 'Cuz what I'm about to say could get us kicked off the lake.

BO-NITA: Okay . . .

GERARD: (*he whispers this*) Capitalism.

BO-NITA: (*she whispers too*) Capitalism?

GERARD: Yeah, the big money boys. The goddamn Capitalists.

BO-NITA: The goddamn Capitalists?

GERARD: Shh! Jesus-fuckin—! You wanna get us killed?

BO-NITA: Sorry. (*lower voice*) So Capitalists are bad?

GERARD: This is probably a discussion for another time, but I been reading some serious shit, Bo-Nita. Some *serious* shit, on the internet. And one of these days? All these good ol boys are gonna *wake up*, and get over their shame, and look around at the freeways and the school systems, all crumbling down around them, and say 'what the fuck, man'? They're gonna start to *see*, Bo-Nita. They'll be eyeball-to-eyeball with the reality of the situation, and when that happens . . . when that happens, well, *watch out.*

Sounds of a tinny Geo Metro on the freeway.

BO-NITA: So . . . I'm sittin shotgun in the rinky-dink Metro, and Mona yells—

MONA: (*behind the wheel of the Geo, over the noise*) He's driving about 14 miles an hour!—

BO-NITA: (*in the seat next to her*) He probably doesn't wanna get stopped.

MONA: It's the *interstate*, Bo-Nita, you drive this slow, you're *gonna* to get stopped. We look like a 2-car funeral procession!

BO-NITA: Well we kinda *are* a 2-car funeral procession.

MONA: Don't start with me, Bo, I'm not in the mood.

BO-NITA: Mona's cranky, and I can tell she and Leon are totally kaput as a love-item. Which feels like sort of a waste, considering how much they've already been through together. I start to envision the rest of the day, with us dumping Gerard at the Landing and then drivin' back to Ballwin in Leon's ratty, little Metro, and then him makin' a bunch of lame-ass excuses for why he can't sell us the tile we need for the bathroom at employee rates, when—*whoa!*—all of a sudden, I see my Barbie Dream House roof come flyin' out Gerard's car window and bounce off down the highway!

Bo-Nita watches the dream house fly by.

MONA: What the hell . . . ?!

BO-NITA: Up ahead, there's *definite* movement coming from Gerard's side of the Sebring! And you can even see he's starting to wake up. He's doing something like . . .

We hear softer muffled freeway sounds, inside Gerard's Chrysler Sebring.

GERARD: (*blinking, looking around him, groggy*) Errrrrr . . . err . . . errrrrrrr. (*shakes his head like a bulldog*) Awaaa-awawaa . . . (*working hard to focus, talking through stiff, Gorilla-Glued lips, winds up mostly vowels*) (Wh)aa . . . da . . . (f)uck . . . ?

BO-NITA: And Leon's sorta like—

LEON: Oh Jesus-God-Jesus! Oh man!

GERARD: (*blinking hard, then staring at Leon, confused*) (Wh)o are (y)ou . . . ?

LEON: Uhhh, Gerard, right?

GERARD: Yeah . . . (*looking around, finally recognizing his vehicle*) Hey, (th)is is (m)yyy car . . . !

LEON: Gerard, I can explain—

GERARD: (*revving up*) (Wh)o are (y)ou?! (Wh)o da hell are (y)ou!

LEON: I'm, I'm Leon, man. I work down at the Tile Implosion.

GERARD: (*looking down, noticing the fishnets, lifting one of his legs*) (Wh)aaa?

LEON: Look man, I'm an innocent bystander, here.

Gerard's attention turns to bedlah, he cups his hands around his big boobies.

GERARD: (Wh)aa da (f)uck are (th)ese . . . ?!

LEON: They thought you were dead, and, and I tried to tell 'em, ahh— oh shit—

Gerard pulls the rearview mirror his way and looks into it.

GERARD: (*seeing his painted-up face in the mirror*) Son of a (b)itch . . . !

LEON: I'd just gone over there—you know—for a little lunchtime-lay with Mona. And there you were in the kid's room.

GERARD: (*leaning closer to the mirror, tenderly touching his lips*) (M)y (l)i(p)s . . . ?! (Wh)ad da (f)uck did (y)ou do to (m)y (l)i(p)s?!!

LEON: Not *me*, man!

GERARD: (Y)ou (f)ucked 'e(m) u(p)!

LEON: I had nothin' to do with it!

GERARD: (F)uckin' (p)ervert!!!

LEON: What?!

GERARD: (P)ervert!!!

LEON: Ow! Whoa! Stop it! STOP!

BO-NITA: You can tell Gerard's attacking Leon, but he's buckled in pretty tight. And Leon's weaving this way and that, trying to evade the blows and stay on pavement, all at the same time! It looks like one of those backyard cockfights Gerard used to sneak me into, when Mona was pullin' a triple at the restaurant. We'd drink Cokes, watch these birds tear each other to bits, and hear people talk about life-and-death, and how they ought to just shoot people, rather than raise their taxes.

MONA: Oh crap, Leroy, no, no, no . . .

BO-NITA: What?

MONA: He's exiting! He's taking the friggin' cloverleaf . . .

BO-NITA: We're chasing them over the interstate, and back down around the other side, when all of a sudden the Sebring jumps a guardrail, and starts four-wheeling-it up the freeway shoulder.

MONA: Where the hell do they think they're goin'?!

BO-NITA: (*to audience*) It don't look like they got much of a plan. Gerard's car's darting back and forth, like this . . .

Bo-Nita demonstrates the Chrysler's chaotic path with her hand.

BO-NITA: Like a jackrabbit. And we're bouncing along after their freshly-mowed trail. We cross an access road and continue upcountry, towards some trees and a huge, white, saucer-type building.

MONA: What is that?

BO-NITA: Kinda looks like the Planetarium.

MONA: It *is* the Planetarium. It's the goddamn Planetarium! Jesus Christ, this is Forest Park! They're gonna hit picnickers soon.

BO-NITA: (*to audience*) Right as Mona says this? The Sebring sideswipes an empty picnic table, then swerves left, and bashes into an oak tree, smashin' up Gerard's Cherry Red hood real good, and bringin' the car to a stop.

GERARD: (*to Leon*) I'(m) gonna ki(ll) (y)ou . . . !

BO-NITA: We hear Gerard say in his new language. Leon has unbuckled himself, and is haulin' some *serious* butt towards the Planetarium, yelling—

LEON: (*yelling, waving his arms*) Help! Maniac! Call 911! Call 911!!!

BO-NITA: Gerard's right on his tail, goin' as fast as a Missouri belly dancer can in fishnets and platform shoes. Mona runs after them both with her arms outstretched.

MONA: Gerarrrrd . . . ?! Gerard, honey, stop . . . ! Gerard-baby, there's been a *big* misunderstanding!

BO-NITA: I get out of Whozzit's Metro, and walk up to the Sebring, sit down in the driver's seat, and shut the door. (*she does a little, abbreviated bit of her rhythm/beat to calm herself down, she looks around*) The world gets all quiet, and inside it smells like leather and Gerard's cigars. I finger the Cherry Red upholstery and look out the windshield. Another thing Gerard was teachin' me about—before we got the restraining order—was those old, Swedish movies, with the guy walkin' around in the black robes, carrying a sickle, and moaning, and saying all this dark, depressing stuff in Swedish. He'd be like—

GERARD: 'Igmar Bergman' . . . say it.

BO-NITA: What?

GERARD: Say 'Igmar Bergman'.

BO-NITA: 'Igmar Bergman' . . .

GERARD: Yeah, that's right, 'member that, Bo. Igmar Bergman, and 'The Seventh Seal'. That's now part of your cultural heritage. Like droppin' nukes, and jell-o shots, or any of the other stuff we've talked about. You got it?

BO-NITA: Uh-huh . . . (*to audience*) I get a hit of that movie, 'The Seventh Seal' as I watch Mona, Leon, and Gerard through the windshield. They look like old-fashioned puppets as they disappear over the crest of the hill, dancin' the way all those Swedish villagers did right before the end . . . And it's suddenly even quieter and kinda creepy in the Sebring, and I start to shiver, and right then, Gerard's glove compartment goes off and starts singin' the French National Anthem . . .

We hear the French National Anthem as a ring-tone.

BO-NITA: I open it up and sure enough, there's his Cherry Red Motorola singing and flashing a mile a minute. I check the number, shoot, it's his half-Uncle, shoot, what do I do . . . ? (*BO-NITA cautiously answers the cell phone*) Hello . . . ?

JACQUE: (*in an urban-Cajun mixed accent, few teeth, mostly gum*) Allo? Gerard?

BO-NITA: Uhhh, no . . .

JACQUE: Who dis, ah?

BO-NITA: Uhh, I think, maybe—

JACQUE: Bo-Nita? Dat you, girl?

BO-NITA: Wrong number?

JACQUE: Dis Bo-Nita, oui?!

BO-NITA: (*reluctantly*) Yeah.

JACQUE: Yah, Boo, es Jacque! Put dat Gerard on, a-sap!

BO-NITA: Well . . . he's . . . kinda tied up right now.

JACQUE: Tied-up? Mais, wha you said?

BO-NITA: Yeah, he's sorta in the middle of something.

JACQUE: Ah, crap myself! He know wha time we got?!

BO-NITA: Well, I think—

JACQUE: He back doin' Mona?

BO-NITA: Not exactly.

JACQUE: Mais, *wha* den? Oo-ay da hell you at?

BO-NITA: (*softly*) The Planetarium.

JACQUE: Wha you said? Speak up!

BO-NITA: (*loud*) The Planetarium.

JACQUE: Planetarium?! Wha da fuck he doin' dere?! He 'sposed be in *Florissant*, re-finishin' a *floor!*

BO-NITA: He says he's real sorry, but—

JACQUE: Sorry?! Sorry, my fad ass! I got dat mad-moselle chewin' me a new one! I got dem Bosnian boys low-ballin' me all over Creve Coeur! He don't show, dat lady gon' get herself a Bosnian boy—put dat Gerard on!

BO-NITA: I'm telling ya, he's unavailable!

JACQUE: (*much darker*) You jerkin' my chain, ma cherie?

BO-NITA: (*quickly*) Okay! Yeah! Goodbye!

> She snaps the cell phone shut, throws it down on the seat next to her, and breathes out.
>
> We hear the sounds of birds.

BO-NITA: Some birds start fighting over something outside. I hear their little, greedy squaks. I'm lookin' down towards the steering wheel and I notice that the car keys are still in the ignition . . . I check out the set-up . . . doesn't look that much different than the Colonel's Cub Cadet . . . so . . .

> Bo-Nita tentatively turns the key in the ignition. It starts right up.
>
> There's the sound of the car turning over.

BO-NITA: I start her up, and that Sebring purrs just like it never even *felt* the picnic table *or* the tree! It purrs like it's saying, see, this is American Know-How, you can bash me up from here to Kingdom Come, but I'm gonna keep on goin', just to mess with you. Just like those batteries, just like Gerard. I'm thinkin' all this stuff, as I reverse out of the oak tree, put it in 'drive' and start climbing the hill, honking every once in awhile to alert any dumb-ass picnickers who might be in my way. By the time I reach the Planetarium, Mona, Leon, and Gerard are at some kind of an impasse. Sorta like high noon at the OK Corral or something. They've surrounded a couple of wide Mexican ladies and their kids on a plaid blanket that are dishing up huge wads of that German potato salad with the vinegar and bacon bits and stuff? And I'm thinking, you know, who taught these people to make German potato salad? Then, I hear Gerard say—

GERARD: (*to Mona, accusing*) So . . . you (w)ere (j)ust gonna du(mp) (m)e at the Landing, huh?!

MONA: Nooo, Gerard, baby, *nuthin'* like that!

LEON: (*to Gerard*) Yeah, she was! Oh yeah, she was!

MONA: Gerard, you know those Jazz Clubs down there . . . They attract all those intellectual-doctor-types!

LEON: She was makin' it look like you were gay-bashed, man!

MONA: Shut up, Leroy!

LEON: (*to Mona*) No! You were about to leave him for dead!

MONA: (*to Gerard*) I was *tryin'* to attract *medical* attention!

LEON: (*to Gerard*) She's a black widow! That's what she is!

MONA: There's doctors, Gerard—*doctors* that listen to all that 'Kenny G.' crap. They woulda had you resuscitated in no time!

LEON: No, the plan was—

MONA: Leroy, I swear to God, I'm callin' your wife!

LEON: Fuckin' A, it's *Leon*, bitch. *LEON!*

GERARD: (*to Mona, truly hurt*) Lea(v)e (m)e (f)or dead . . . ?

MONA: What?

LEON: (*to Mona*) He's asking were you gonna leave him for dead?! (*to Gerard*) The answer's *yes*, man!

MONA: Gerard, honey, now just *think* about it . . . How could we take you to a legitimate hospital, without you gettin' arrested? You're not 'sposed to get within 500 feet of Bo-Nita, you *know* that. So you go and surprise her like that—

GERARD: (Wh)at . . . ?

MONA: Now we won't press charges, will we Bo-Nita, but that's a blatant violation of the—

GERARD: Sur(pr)ize her? She (f)uckin' *in(v)ited* (m)e!

MONA: (*beat*) What?

LEON: He said she fucking invited him!

BO-NITA: (*to everyone*) No, I didn't. (*to Mona*) I didn't . . .

GERARD: (*to Bo-Nita*) (Y)ou (s)ure as hell did!

LEON: He said you sure as hell did!

BO-NITA: I didn't!

GERARD: (*to Bo-Nita, indicating Mona*) Tell her!

BO-NITA: I didn't, Mom . . . I swear to God.

GERARD: (B)ullshit!

LEON: He says bullshit!

GERARD: Tell her the (f)uckin' (tr)uth, (B)o.

LEON: He says—

MONA: (*blows up*) Leon! We can all understand what he's saying, so just shut the fuck up!

    PAUSE.

BO-NITA: (*to audience*) I look down and see the wide ladies and their kids all huddled together, sorta frozen, watching us, and letting the flies crawl all over their wads of potato salad. And the way they're sitting there, quiet and sweaty, and giving us those scaredy-cat-innocent-eyes, like *we're* the foreigners, or hoods, or something to be afraid of, that really starts my old typhoon churnin' . . . I can feel it heating up, deep down. Like how it feels when Colonel T borrows a rusty LTD and takes you and Grandma Tiny down to Maryville for deer-hunting in the off-season, and you've got an entire, illegal dead deer stuffed in your trunk, and you have to stop for gas on the way home. So you pull into the station, and you see this family in a brand new, Midnight Blue Mercedes SUV, and they start giving you those same horrified eyes and they're pointing at your rusty trunk, so you roll down the window and look back, and there's all this bright red illegal deer blood just drip-drip-drippin' down to the pavement, and you turn back to see the judgment just *oozing* from their goody-two-shoes faces and it makes you want to get out of the car and bash their stupid heads together. *That's* how I'm feeling right now, with this Mexican-potato-salad-family. So I try and do the 'stepback' and think of some calming phrase, like what Ms. Shabazz would say, and I think: "Big breath . . . count backwards . . . don't bash their faces in . . ." Which works in a way, so instead, I turn to them and go—(*to the picnickers, sudden, vicious, the last one very loud and prolonged*) BOO! BOO! BOOOOOOOOOOO!!!

    Bo-Nita's storm blows all the way through. She's winded.

BO-NITA: The birds have stopped chirping, and I notice that everybody's looking right at me . . . (*to Mona, Gerard, and Leon*) What? All I said was 'Boo' . . .

    The sound of the school environment forces its way back into Bo-Nita's consciousness. She goes to her backpack, pulls out an inhaler, takes a quick puff, then stuffs it back in the pack. She maybe takes a swig from her water bottle. She looks back down the street, but still sees nothing. She then turns back to us.

BO-NITA: So . . . now . . . old Whozzits now sees a crack in the situation.

LEON: Alright, I'm outa here, people. I got tile comin' in.

GERARD: (*to Leon*) Hey. (M)ister "Lunchti(m)e-Lay" . . . (Wh)ere you think *you're* going?

LEON: (*to Gerard*) She's all yours, man.

MONA: Leon . . . ?

LEON: (*to Mona*) That's right, baby, it's Leon. And I'm done. Don't come waggin' your ass at the Tile Implosion ever again.

GERARD: (*to Leon*) Hey (m)an, (w)atch that tone.

MONA: But what about our discount?

LEON: No way, sister. I'm tellin' the boys. We got your scam down. You're 86'd *forever!*

MONA: Then I'm callin' your wife!

LEON: Call my wife! Call my fucking pastor, for all I care!

GERARD: (*to Leon*) Hey asshole.

LEON: What?

GERARD: A *(p)ologize!*

LEON: What? Can't understand you, man.

GERARD: I said *a(p)ologize!*

BO-NITA: Gerard takes off after Leon again, who's waving his arms, calling for 911 *and* a taxi all at the same time.

MONA: (*calling*) Gerard, don't kill him, baby!—

BO-NITA: They disappear around the side of the Planetarium, and their exit somehow changes the whole shape of the day. Now, it's just me and Mona and the picnickers. Mona's got her silent-evil-eye on me, which I hate.

MONA: (*quiet, low*) Get in the car, Bo-Nita.

BO-NITA: You want me to drive? I can drive . . .

MONA: No.

BO-NITA: Mona and I get in the Sebring and slam our doors. Her hand goes up to start the car, but then she stops . . .

MONA: Did you invite Gerard over to the apartment, Bo-Nita?

BO-NITA: (*to audience*) My stomach starts to cave in, and I suddenly feel real dizzy. (*to Mona*) No. Jesus. I swear to God, he just showed up. (*to audience*) And I'm about to continue down that line, but I see Mona's hand go out and grab Gerard's Cherry Red Motorola that's sittin' between us in the front seat, and instead I say: (*to Mona*) Mom, don't . . .

MONA: Why not? You got nuthin' to hide, right Bo.

BO-NITA: (*weakly*) I didn't . . . (*to audience*) She's working that phone like a pro, beep-beep-beeping back through his whole, stupid call history.

MONA: You didn't do nuthin', butter wouldn't melt in your mouth, so *a'course* there won't be a received call in here from our number, right Bo-Nita?

No response.

MONA: Right?

BO-NITA: (*beat*) Mom . . .

MONA: Oh, but lookey here . . . 10:46am . . . Today. This morning. Oh my God.

BO-NITA: I just . . .

MONA: You called him?

BO-NITA: I just—

MONA: You called him. After all we've been through—

BO-NITA: I just kinda missed him . . . that's all.

MONA: You *missed* him?! Bo-Nita, he was tryin to *mess* with you!

BO-NITA: I know, but—

MONA: You know, *but?*

BO-NITA: Never mind!

MONA: Uh-uh baby, no 'never mind'. What the fuck were you *thinking?*

BO-NITA: Don't get mad.

MONA: I'm not mad!

BO-NITA: Yeah, you are.

MONA: Don't tell me what I am. Now, I'm gonna ask you again . . . why did you call Gerard?

BO-NITA: I just . . . I missed all the *other stuff* we did . . . you know?

MONA: The 'other' stuff.

BO-NITA: Like tying flies, and sending away for those online starter kits.

MONA: What?

BO-NITA: And the card games he'd teach me.

MONA: *I* teach you games.

BO-NITA: Yeah, but you're always working so much—

MONA: I'm always workin'—

BO-NITA: I don't mean—

MONA: I'm always workin'—that's right!—fuck you—I'm *scramblin' 24/7* just so I can keep fucking *custody* of you, Bo-Nita! Just so I show that goddamn *judge* I've become a responsible mother! So *once again*—this is all my fucking fault?! Is that it?

BO-NITA: No! That's not what I meant!

MONA: There's *no way* to set things right.

BO-NITA: *I'm not saying that!*

MONA: I might as well just fucking give up. Hand you over. Throw in the towel! Is that it? Is that what you want from me, Bo-Nita?

BO-NITA: (*trying to stop her tirade*) He *likes* me, that's all! And he thinks I'm good at stuff! And it feels *good* when someone says that you're good at stuff! And he *said* he wasn't gonna try that anymore! *He promised me!* He said he was *sorry.*

MONA: *Sorry . . . ?!*

BO-NITA: And it's like those Swedish movies, you know? How everybody's sort of tossed around by all their fates and stuff, and he *said* he wasn't gonna give into his *fate* anymore! He said—

Mona can't take this anymore, she shakes Bo-Nita hard.

MONA: *Bo-Nita, are you just a fucking idiot?!*

BO-NITA: *No!*

MONA: *A complete, fucking idiot!*

BO-NITA: *I'M NOT THE IDIOT! I'M NOT THE ONE THAT GOT WITH MIKE!*

MONA: *(beat)* Don't you go there—

BO-NITA: Why not?! Why can't I go there?!

MONA: I'm warnin' you—

BO-NITA: Least Gerard never moved us to some split-level in Jeff County!

MONA: Stop it!

BO-NITA: Least Gerard didn't have nothing to do with this!

MONA: *Don't you dare!*

BO-NITA: *(to audience)* Me and Mona struggle, 'cuz I'm trying to get my sleeve up, but she wants it down, and she's like—

MONA: *(wrestling with Bo-Nita)* Stop, baby. Please!

BO-NITA: *(working against Mona's resistence)* What's wrong? Can't you look at it? *Look at it!*

BO-NITA: And I wrestle free and get my sleeve up, and give Mona a nice, close whiff of the 3rd-degree burn that runs from my shoulder, all the way down to my wrist . . .

MONA: Please.

BO-NITA: *(to Mona)* I gotta look at it the rest of my fuckin life, so you should have to look at it too!

MONA: I have *apologized* over and over for what Mike—

BO-NITA: Fuck you! I don't care! You're a bad fuckin mother!

MONA: Bo—

BO-NITA: You are! You are! I fucking *hate* you!

Bo-Nita swings at her mother, but Mona doesn't fight back.

BO-NITA: *(to audience)* And I swing at her a few times, but Mona's like this soft lump, and doesn't even protect herself, and after awhile I stop bashing her, and pull my sleeve down . . . And I, like . . . *really* wish I hadn't gone there, you know? I'd even made this pact with myself, *never* to go there. And I really wish I hadn't,'cuz sittin' there, in the Sebring, I watch my mom wrinkle up right before my eyes . . .

She gets the same dead, ancient look Grandma Tiny did five years ago, the day we had to say goodbye to Mona behind the electric fence. We watched her disappear, like a little mouse with her head down, into a mean-looking cinder block building. Mona turned and waved to us, and gave us this kinda 'thumbs-up' before the guard pulled her inside by the elbow . . . That was . . . that was the first and only time that Grandma Tiny held my hand. It felt too warm and real boney, not soft like you'd think a grandma's hand would be. She held my hand all the way back to the car, and then she let go and started bawling and she didn't stop the whole six-hour trip home. She drove and cried and drove and cried and even when we stopped at the 'Steak 'n Shake', and ordered two steakburgers and two peanut-butter shakes, she cried through the entire meal . . .

Seeing that same kind of achey-breaky face on Mona right now hurts, and it's like there's no escape from all this pain or something, and . . . I know I'm not supposed to, but it makes me think on what Gerard told me, during one of his cultural history lessons—

GERARD: So Bo-Nita . . . here's the deal . . . Missouri . . . is right smack dab in the middle of *everything* and *nothing*. You get where I'm headed?

BO-NITA: Ummm.

GERARD: It's like your cereal bowl there. What was in that?

BO-NITA: The kind of cereal?

GERARD: Yeah.

BO-NITA: Captain Crunch.

GERARD: Exactly. Now let's examine the bowl . . .

BO-NITA: What do you mean?

GERARD: Take a look in the bowl. What do you see?

BO-NITA: Uhh, I see the leftover milk . . .

GERARD: Describe it.

BO-NITA: The milk?

GERARD: Yeah.

BO-NITA: (*peering into the bowl*) Well, it looks sort of stale . . . and it's got these little brown specks in it, and it's kind of stained yellowish, from the Captain Crunch that was there.

GERARD: Good. Now let's say . . . let's say a *fly* lands in the milk. He's not gonna like it, right? 'Cause it's old and warm and it's getting his wings wet.

BO-NITA: Yeah, probably.

GERARD: So what does he do?

BO-NITA: Umm . . .

GERARD: He starts to swim to the *sides*, correct? He's gonna try and crawl out.

BO-NITA: Right.

GERARD: (*moving a little closer to her*) But just like those of us with roots in Missouri, he's gonna find that there *is no way out*. Those walls, man, are slick and inconsiderate, and every time he makes a dash for it, BAM, he slides back down into the milk. So . . . what does that fly have to do *now*?

BO-NITA: (*beat*) I don't know . . . what?

GERARD: Think, Bo.

BO-NITA: (*nervous*) I *am* . . .

GERARD: (*this is very personal*) He's gotta learn to *like warm milk*. You see where I'm headin here . . . ?

BO-NITA: (*to audience*) And Gerard gets real close and puts his big hand on my knee . . . (*to Gerard*) Like warm milk . . .

GERARD: Yeah, see that fly needs to find something in its situation that it can live with, 'cause it's stuck either way . . .

BO-NITA: (*beat*) I don't . . . like warm milk . . .

    Bo-Nita purposefully wipes his hand off her knee.

GERARD: (*leaning back*) Well . . . that could be a problem . . .

    We become aware of muffled park sounds and picnickers.

MONA: (*to Bo-Nita, low and snarky*) So did he get what he came for, Bo-Nita?

BO-NITA: (*to Mona*) I told you, he promised he wouldn't try anything.

MONA: But then he didn't keep his promise, according to you, so I wanna know, did you give him what he came for?

BO-NITA: No, his thing wasn't working. I laughed, and he was about to punch me, when he had the heart attack.

MONA: Alleged heart attack.

BO-NITA: *Real* heart attack!

MONA: And then you beat the shit out of him.

BO-NITA: Don't say it like that.

MONA: I actually *married* that man, Bo-Nita. He was the light of my life. Every time . . . *every time* something *good* finally shows up for me, there you are.

BO-NITA: You're going low, so just stop.

MONA: With your needy-little-greedy face.

BO-NITA: Just shut up!

MONA: Don't tell me to shut up!

BO-NITA: Then *shut up* then! *Shut up!*

There is sudden, loud banging on the car.

BO-NITA: Just then, Gerard starts pounding on the Sebring's crunched-in hood.

GERARD: (G)irls!!! (G)irrrls! Ahhh!—

BO-NITA: He's clutching his chest, like—

GERARD: (*having a heart attack*) Ah! Ow-Ow-Ow! Ah!

MONA: Gerard . . . ?!

GERARD: (Th)is is the—Ow-Ow!—the (b)ig one!

BO-NITA: Me and Mona scramble out of the car, grab him, and stuff him into the back seat. (*to Mona*) We've gotta get him to the hospital!

MONA: I know that!

BO-NITA: And before we're even thinking about it, Mona guns the Sebring over the grass 'til we finally hit Clayton Avenue and start barreling down a real street again.

Mona drives and shouts orders into the rearview mirror.

MONA: Keep his head up! Press down on his heart or something! I think, or blow into his—hang on we're making this light! (*she guns it*)

BO-NITA: And maybe . . . Gerard having another heart attack? That's like the second miracle in one day. 'Cuz—unlike most moments in life—this time we get a do-over. We get the chance to do it again. And this time we take him to the hospital, and practically park that Sebring right in the ER.

MONA: Out of our way! Dead man walking!

GERARD: Ah! Ah! Slo(w) do(w)n!

BO-NITA: And we act like there's nothing weird about a beat-up, belly dancer in drag having a heart attack, and we stay with Gerard 'til the technicians lay him on the stretcher, and we all wave and blow each other kisses, like we're real family.

GERARD: (*blowing kisses, through chest pains*) Ahhhh! Oh Christ! See you! (B)e good . . . Ahh!

MONA: (*blowing smooches back*) Bye baby . . .

BO-NITA: Bye Gerard!

GERARD: Lo(v)e you! Your (m)y girls . . . !

BO-NITA: (*waving, genuine*) Bye Gerard. We love you too!

MONA: (*waving, under her breath*) Don't overplay it, Bo-Nita.

GERARD: Hey! Ahh! (B)o . . . !

BO-NITA: Yeah?

GERARD: Don't (f)orget . . .

Gerard starts to do a prone version of Bo-Nita's rhythm stomp.

BO-NITA: Yeah. Okay . . . ! (*to audience*) We watch Gerard get wheeled down
the hallway. He keeps waving back at us the whole time, 'til his stretcher
turns the corner and he's finally gone . . .

They stop waving. There's a beat, and then Mona turns slightly to Bo-Nita.

MONA: You . . . okay . . . Bo-Nita?

BO-NITA: Yeah. (*short beat*) You okay . . . ?

MONA: Yeah. (*beat*) Jesus-H-Christ . . . whatta day . . .

Mona sighs and stands there a moment longer.

MONA: C'mon Bo-Nita, let's get outa here.

Mona puts her hand out, and Bo-Nita takes it. Together, they turn to go.

BO-NITA: (*back to audience*) We walk back to the Sebring, hand-in-hand . . .
And even though his whole entire family thought he should, Gerard
declined to press charges against us. But me and Mona . . . we left
St. Louis anyway, about a month later. 'Cause his Uncle Jacque has a
memory like an Ozark crow, and I had explained Gerard's whole theory
about the fly and the cereal bowl to Mona, and she wasn't into warm
milk either. So one day, we walked into the Tile Implosion and pressed
old Whozzits for some quiet money, which wasn't hard at all, and we
just decided to drive west, wherever the fates would take us. And when
we ran out of gas and couldn't pay for any more, that's where we'd drop
anchor. And that's what we did. That's how we wound up here . . . just
outside Phoenix . . .

Bo-Nita looks around her, like she's waking up. The lights begin to go back up.

BO-NITA: Mona met this guy named Alonso? At a NA meeting. And he's,
like, letting us stay in his rec room, until we can get our own place. He
raises ferrets professionally, like all different kinds. I didn't even know
there were *that many* kinds of ferrets. And he told me he's like this
vegetarian, but I'm not so sure I buy it 'cuz he's like constantly watching
Monster Truck stuff on TV. Mona says she loves it out here. She's wearing
sunglasses, and all these weird, floppy hats. She had on a pink one this
morning, when she dropped me off for school . . .

MONA: (*her hands on the wheel of the car*) Smell that desert air, baby! Are you
smelling it?

BO-NITA: (*sitting next to her in the passenger seat*) Yeah . . .

MONA: So clean. Not a whiff of humidity. None of that river odor either.

BO-NITA: Yeah.

MONA: You gotta start eating tortillas now, Bo.

BO-NITA: I know.

MONA: (*beat*) What's wrong?

BO-NITA: We're sittin in the car, in front of my new school. (*to Mona*) You're tapping your leg again, like you used to . . .

MONA: No I'm not . . . !

Bo-Nita shrugs.

MONA: (*going for upbeat, making a joke of it*) Jesus Christ, Bo-Nita, you gotta stop worryin over every little thing!

BO-NITA: Maybe I should've stayed home today.

MONA: (*really chipper*) Now that's just crazy. I told you I've got 3 job interviews lined-up for today, and I can feel something spectacular's gonna happen for us, Bo-Nita. Okay? *Okay* . . . ?

BO-NITA: (*reluctantly*) Okay.

MONA: 'Cuz it's *our* turn, baby. 'Cuz we're hanging on, right? We're hanging in there.

BO-NITA: Yeah.

MONA: That's my hyphenated girl.

BO-NITA: I get out of the car, and turn back to say—(*to Mona, with an insistence*) You're picking me up at 4:30, right? (*leaning towards the car window*) Right, mom? (*to audience*) But Mona's thrown the car in gear, and is blowing me a mountain of kisses in front of all these stupid Arizona kids, which is like super embarrassing. So I just wave, as she drives off, nice and loud, with the muffler smoking . . .

We begin to hear the opening school noises, and the lights reach full reality brightness once more. Bo-Nita looks down the street. The person she's waiting for still hasn't come. She picks up her backpack and puts it on her back.

BO-NITA: So, yeah . . . So there's not much I can tell you about Phoenix yet . . . except the streets are all, like, 8 lanes wide, and they call waitresses 'servers'. And the Junior High School I go to? Looks like some kind of fake Indian pueblo. And . . . I don't know . . . the whole place just feels about ten years old and sort of what they call 'adobe-temporary'. Like it's trying really hard to make itself up as it goes along . . . Which . . . according to Mona . . . might just fit us to a 'T'. You know . . . ?

Bo-Nita looks back down the street one last time. She turns toward the building behind her, and contemplates going inside, but hesitates, and faces back toward us again. She checks her watch. Thinks. Then slowly starts to do the rhythm-stomp she did at the top of the play. She goes a few rounds, before we can hear that she is singing something. It turns out to be Mona's anthem, "Dreaming". And the lyrics tuck neatly into the rhythm of her stomp.

BO-NITA: WHEN I MET YOU IN THE RESTAURANT
YOU COULD TELL I WAS NO DEBUTANTE

YOU ASKED ME WHAT'S MY PLEASURE
A MOVIE OR A MEASURE . . .

Blondie's version of the song takes over, as Bo-Nita continues to beat out her rhythm, and the lights go all the way down.

END OF PLAY.

DON X. NGUYEN's Full-length plays include *Hello, From the Children of Planet Earth* (2018 world premiere The Playwrights Realm), *The Man From Saigon* (A.C.T New Strands Festival, NYSAF 2012 Founders Award, Naked Angels workshop), *The Supreme Leader* (developed at Roundabout, Labyrinth Theatre, and Ma-Yi), *Red Flamboyant* (Firebone Theatre, GAP Prize Winner – Aurora Theatre, Ojai Playwrights Conference), *Sound* (Azeotrope/ACT, BAPF, Playwrights Realm Fellowship, Civilians R&D, finalist – Princess Grace Award), *The Commencement of William Tan* (Yale Cabaret, NYSAF). Nominations include: the Laurents/Hatcher award and the L. Arnold Weissberger Award. Don is a current member of the Ma-Yi Writers Lab, the Public Theater's inaugural Emerging Writers Group, The Civilians inaugural R&D Group, the 52nd Street Project, and a co-founder of Mission to (dit)Mars, a Queens based theatre arts collective. For more information, please visit: thenuge.com.

Don X. Nguyen

Sound

CHARACTERS:

GEORGE	(male, 35) A deaf fisherman. Proud of his Deaf culture. Intense and bull-headed.
BARBARA	(female, 35) Hearing but signs. George's ex-wife and Allison's mother. Does what she wants and will stop at nothing to provide for her daughter.
ALEXANDER GRAHAM BELL	(male, late 30s) Inventor and teacher of the Deaf. Hearing.
MABEL HUBBARD	(female, 25–30) Wife of Alexander Graham Bell.
ALLISON	(female, 13) George and Barbara's deaf daughter. Precocious with a little attitude.
MR. PEASE	(male, mid 30s) Bell's interpreter and guide on Martha's Vineyard. The Actor playing this role must be hearing and fluent in ASL.
TECHNICIAN/ AUDIOLOGIST/ NURSES/SPEECH THERAPIST	Can be played by one actor or several.

SETTING:

Chilmark, Martha's Vineyard, 1885 and the Present.

PRODUCTION NOTES:

Signed dialogue appears in brackets [ ]

It is crucial to have an ASL Director in charge of creating the ASL Gloss for the actors, and please allow extra rehearsal time to do so. While it's possible to create the ASL Gloss before the beginning of rehearsals, each signing actor will have their own preferences for how they want to sign a phrase, so it's best to include them in the glossing process wherever possible.

The number one goal for any production should be 100% accessibility for both Deaf and Hearing audiences. This entails a mix of voicing for anything that is signed on stage, and shadowsigning/super-titling anything that is spoken.

PART I

Scene I

> *Moonlight. Water. A boat.*
>
> *Projected across the night sky:*
>
> *"Chilmark, Martha's Vineyard. Today."*
>
> *A Man stands on the bow of the boat, staring into the still water.*
>
> *The thumping of loud bass-driven music is heard/felt. In a basement is Allison, a deaf thirteen year old girl. She bounces up and down to this music. While she does this, she vehemently signs "George."*
>
> *Spilling in is a woman's voice calling out George's name. And perhaps his name is projected across the sky.*

WOMAN (BARBARA): (*growing in intensity*) **George! George! George!**

> *Lights shift to:*
>
> *Barbara (hearing) and George (deaf) in a kitchen of an old Vineyard farmhouse. George stares into the water-filled sink, filled with dirty dishes. The thumping music can be heard/felt below them.*
>
> *Note: When Barbara is in a room with only Deaf people, she will sign and not speak. Another actor can voice for her during these scenes.*

BARBARA: (*waving at him*) [George!]

> *George snaps out of it and gathers dishes.*

BARBARA: (*waving*) [George, look at me!]

> *George scrapes food off the dishes.*

BARBARA: [I know you see my hands.]

> *George dunks the dishes into the sink.*

BARBARA: [Either you're mad at me or you really like doing the dishes.]

> *No response. Barbara stomps her foot.*
>
> *He stops.*

BARBARA: [I know you have something to say.]

GEORGE: . . .

BARBARA: (*to herself*) [Fine.]

   (*to George*) [I'm done talking to you.]

   George pulls his hands out of the sink and rapidly signs back.

GEORGE: [Fine? This will never be fine!]

BARBARA: [Your hands are spitting on me.]

   George pats his hands on his pants.

BARBARA: [I'm sorry you had to find out this way.]

GEORGE: [Or maybe you're sorry I found out at all?]

BARBARA: [Don't do that. You know how hard it is to contact you when you're out there.]

GEORGE: [You knew I'd be away for months and this was the perfect time to do it.]

BARBARA: [That is absolutely not true. I'm only doing what's best.]

GEORGE: [For you or Allison? We share legal custody. Remember?]

BARBARA: [But she lives with me.]

GEORGE: [Only because I can't be here everyday. You know that.]

BARBARA: [She's thirteen, almost fourteen. The longer we wait, the harder it will be for her to adjust.]

   (*turns away*) God, we should've done this the moment she lost her hearing.

GEORGE: [Stop using your voice!]

BARBARA: (*collecting herself*) [We should've done this the moment she lost her hearing.]

GEORGE: [When she was two?]

BARBARA: [Yes! We should have gone ahead with the implant.]

GEORGE: [You want doctors to drill a hole in her head and stick that . . . that thing—]

BARBARA: [It's not a "thing!" It's called an implant—]

GEORGE: [You want her to be a machine?]

BARBARA: [No! I want the doctors to help her become . . .]

GEORGE: [Become what? N-O-R-M-A-L?]

BARBARA: [No.]

GEORGE: [You were going to say normal.]

BARBARA: [I was not going to say "normal!"]

   Beat.

GEORGE: [Was this Mark's idea?]

BARBARA: [No!]

GEORGE: [You want to know what I see?]

BARBARA: [Do I really have a choice?]

GEORGE: [I see your new husband, who is hearing, and has hearing children of his own—]

BARBARA: [Mark and I have been married for ten years! He's not new.]

GEORGE: [Sorry. Your NEWEST husband—]

BARBARA: (*throwing up her hands*) God!

GEORGE: [He wants to change my daughter into something unnatural.]

BARBARA: [She was born hearing.]

GEORGE: [Then she became deaf. Naturally.]

BARBARA: [You're like that annoying person at parties that you can't win any arguments with.]

> *Barbara turns away.*

GEORGE: (*clapping for her attention*) [How would you pay for this operation? Those implants are fifty thousand or something.]

BARBARA: [Eighty.]

GEORGE: [Eighty thousand? Your husband doesn't make that much more than me.]

BARBARA: [The insurance pays for it.]

GEORGE: [What about after? What about speech therapy? Doctor's visits? Insurance doesn't cover that!]

BARBARA: [For someone who's against the CI, you seem to know a lot about it.]

GEORGE: [That's why I win all my arguments at parties.]

> *Lights up on Allison in the basement, still bouncing. She stops and turns off the music. She senses the vibrations of the fight above her. She looks up.*
>
> *George stomps to get Barbara's attention. She turns to him.*

GEORGE: [So how would you pay for the rest?]

BARBARA: (*meekly*) [. . . there are grants.]

GEORGE: [Grants?]

BARBARA: [Yes, grants.]

GEORGE: [What grants?]

BARBARA: . . .

GEORGE: [What grants?]

BARBARA: [AG Bell Association.]

GEORGE: [WHAT?]

BARBARA: (*stronger*) [AG Bell.]

GEORGE: [AG BELL?]

BARBARA: [Yes. There's an AG Bell Speech Center in New Bedford.]

GEORGE: [AG Fucking Bell? Patron saint of the Deaf.]

BARBARA: [You're impossible!]

GEORGE: [No, you're impossible! You and your husband both want to take my daughter away from me. I won't let that happen! Never!]

George throws a dish against a wall.

Silence.

Allison cautiously enters with her backpack.

BARBARA: [It's okay honey. Say goodbye to your father and then go wait in the car.]

ALLISON: . . .

BARBARA: [Allison. Say goodbye.]

ALLISON: [Bye GEORGE.]

Allison exits.

GEORGE: [Why is she calling me George?]

BARBARA: [She's thirteen. Everything happens overnight with thirteen year olds.]

GEORGE: [Does she call you Barbara?]

BARBARA: [I would never let her call me Barbara.]

GEORGE: . . .

BARBARA: [She hasn't seen you in a while.]

GEORGE: [You know I've been working.]

BARBARA: [I know. I'm just saying, maybe that's why she calls you George now. To prove a point.]

GEORGE: [Well I have a few points I'd like to prove.]

BARBARA: [I have to go.]

GEORGE: [If you go through with this, she won't be a hearing person and she won't be a deaf person—]

BARBARA: [Stop.]

GEORGE: [-She'll be stuck in the middle of two different worlds.]

BARBARA: [Stuck in two worlds? Yeah, I know how that feels.]

GEORGE: [Yes you understand. I thought you could handle it but I was wrong.]

Silence.

BARBARA: [. . . On our wedding day, before we marched down the aisle, grandma Bebe whispered to me "Barbie, it's hard enough living in one world when you're married. You'd be living in two with him. You sure you want to do this?"]

GEORGE: [What did you say?]

BARBARA: [I said I do.]

GEORGE: . . .

BARBARA: [And I did. For as long as I could.]

GEORGE: [Your family was difficult.]

BARBARA: [Yours too.]

> They almost share a laugh.

BARBARA: [You used to say to me there's all kinds. All kinds.]

GEORGE: [All kinds of what?]

BARBARA: [There's congenital. Hard of hearing, Deaf who speak clearly, Deaf who don't.] (*beat*) [You're not just deaf or hearing. There's everything in between. I understand there's a grey area.]

GEORGE: [I know you do.]

BARBARA: [Then why do you always treat this as a black and white issue with me? Give me a little credit. I married a deaf man.]

GEORGE: [And then you married a hearing man.]

BARBARA: [We tried for a very long time. But it wasn't all bad. Look at her.]

GEORGE: [She's a firecracker.]

BARBARA: [Yes. But she's also full of wonder. And it's not going to stop.]

> Beat.

GEORGE: [I told you not to move off island.]

BARBARA: [This is not about who lives where—]

GEORGE: [I begged you not to.]

BARBARA: [We're right across the Sound. It's not that difficult to get to us. You're a fisherman. You have a boat for God's sakes.]

GEORGE: [Our daughter became deaf and then you remarried and moved her into a hearing home. You've never given her a chance to get comfortable with her deafness.]

BARBARA: [We can have the same conversation over and over again, or we can have a new one. I'd like to—]

> A car honks.

BARBARA: [Mark's honking.]

GEORGE: [What?]

BARBARA: [I said Mark's honking.]

GEORGE: [I didn't hear anything.]

BARBARA: [That used to be funny. I have to go.]

GEORGE: [Hey. She's my daughter too.]

> Another honk.

Barbara exits.

George remains in the kitchen as lights come up on Alexander Graham Bell, standing on the deck of a ferry on the Vineyard Sound. Bell looks up at the sky, feels the rain with his hands, then opens an umbrella.

George crosses to an open window, where rain is beating against the window sill. He lets the rain bounce off his hand, then shuts the window.

Flashes of lightning. There is no thunder.

Scene 2

Shift to an implant center in New Bedford, MA. Barbara and Allison are seated with a Technician. Barbara interprets for them.

TECHNICIAN: You'll wear a microphone on the outside which picks up sound and lets it inside where it is turned into an electric signal.

ALLISON: (*to Barbara*) [This is the tenth time she's told us this.]

BARBARA: [Then it must be important.]

TECHNICIAN: The microphone on the outside sends a signal to a device on the inside—

TECHNICIAN: —which bypasses the damaged structures of the inner ear.	ALLISON: [bypassing the damaged structures of the inner ear.]

BARBARA: (*to Allison*) [Stop]

(*to Technician*) I'm sorry, but I was told there would be an interpreter, so I wouldn't have to.

TECHNICIAN: Oh. I wasn't aware of that. I don't have anything in my notes. Um . . . (*beat*) We can reschedule this if you'd like.

BARBARA: It's okay.

TECHNICIAN: Are you sure?

BARBARA: Yeah.

The Technician pulls out a clipboard.

TECHNICIAN: (*to Barbara*) Just a few checkpoints. She's been through a series of audiological tests to establish her level of hearing loss, correct?

BARBARA: Yes.

ALLISON: [July is striped bass, bluefish and sea trout, I think.]

TECHNICIAN: And Allison has been counseled regarding the potential benefits and limitations of the Cochlear Implant?

BARBARA: Yes.

ALLISON: [Not sea trout. That's June. Fluke. Fluke is in July.]

TECHNICIAN: Great. We just have to run one more test to make sure she can successfully undergo general anaesthesia for her surgery and then that will conclude this preop evaluation.

(*to Allison*) Allison, do you have any final questions?

BARBARA: Do you have any questions?

ALLISON: [He didn't come.]

BARBARA: [Mark's flight was delayed, otherwise—]

ALLISON: [George.]

BARBARA: [Oh. I didn't press him about it. I didn't think you wanted him to be here. I'm sorry.]

ALLISON: [It's okay. He's probably on his boat. I guess I can't compete with the fish.]

BARBARA: [Let's finish this up and we'll stop at Friendly's for ice cream. Okay?]

ALLISON: [Sal's.]

BARBARA: [That's out of the way.]

ALLISON: . . .

BARBARA: [Fine. Sal's.]

Allison nods.

BARBARA: (*to the Technician*) We don't have any questions.

Scene 3

On the Vineyard Sound. Bell stands on the top deck of a ferry, staring at his pocketwatch. He begins to write a letter.

After a few moments, MABEL, his wife, appears. She writes back. They naturally drop this convention as the scene progresses.

NOTE: Any spoken scenes should also be shadow-signed or at the very least super-titled for Deaf audiences.

MABEL: During my daily readings today I discovered each head of a sunflower is made up of hundreds of tiny flowers called florets.

BELL: Your voracious appetite for knowledge is as dazzling as a sunflower.

MABEL: The high-bushes needs some work . . .

BELL: The gardener can tend to it . . .

MABEL: You're much more thorough at examining the high-bushes then the gardener . . .

BELL: Then leave them. I'll get to it soon enough . . .

MABEL: I'm beginning to think that word does not exist amongst you inventors.

BELL: Which? Soon or enough?

MABEL: Both, actually.

BELL: . . .

MABEL: Come home.

BELL: You know I can't. Not yet.

MABEL: Yes, I'm sure the island misses you as much as I do.

BELL: We've discussed this a thousand and one times over.

MABEL: Then what's a thousand and two?

BELL: . . .

MABEL: Why return to this island, Alec? Why not in Salem, where you'd be near?

BELL: Mabel, you know all the deaf islanders are here.

MABEL: The Deaf are also in Salem.

BELL: There is something about this island.

MABEL: You've spent years tracing their heritage, digging holes on the beach, taking soil samples. Years, Alec. When will it be enough?

BELL: When you can hear again.

MABEL: You've taught me to read lips. You've taught me to speak. Is that not enough?

A ferry horn blows.

BELL: The first time I stepped foot on the island I was standing at the Mansion House listening to the harbor. Do you know what I heard? Storm waves billowing upon the shore.

MABEL: That is not unique to an island, Alec.

BELL: It was an unmistakable surging of storm waves, yet the water on my side of the island was quiet and still. How do you explain that?

MABEL: How do you?

BELL: According to Mr. Pease's grandfather, it's due to the ocean waves after the storm of the preceding day, dashing on the other side of the Island, to the south. Nearly nine and a half miles away.

MABEL: Wonderful. Now you know. Come home.

BELL: But how does the sound of those waves come from the other side of the island? How does it travel nine and a half miles through the atmosphere and be audible? It's not loud enough to do that.

MABEL: I don't know.

BELL: There has to be a conductor of some kind to carry it over that far distance.

MABEL: The clouds perhaps.

BELL: The clouds are not solid enough to carry sound like that.

MABEL: Then I give up.

BELL: The sound of those storm waves pass through the island, from one side to the other. Mabel, the island is the conductor!

MABEL: Topiaries for the front yard would be nice, don't you think?

BELL: The island works exactly like the liquid transmitter inside the telephone. That is why the work must be done here.

MABEL: If only you could travel the speed of sound, like the telephone, then I think the distance between us would be bearable.

Bell crosses to Mabel and without touching her, examines her neck.

BELL: All the telephone does is give people the ability to speak more than they probably should. I don't consider that an accomplishment. But to invent . . . something that would allow you and . . . and perhaps all the Deaf to finally hear? Now that would be an accomplishment. That would be enough, Mabel. For me, that would be enough.

MABEL: I'll give you the word "enough." If I can keep the word "soon."

BELL: How soon is soon?

MABEL: Elsie's birthday is six weeks away. Promise me you'll be there.

Mr. Pease enters. He's a young, lanky man.

MR. PEASE: Mr. Bell. Good to see you again.

BELL: Likewise Mr. Pease. Only five trunks this time.

MR. PEASE: I'll have my boys fetch them for you.

MABEL: Promise me.

BELL: (*to Mabel*) Mabel, there is so much work to be done here.

MABEL: You can tell me all about it when you come home.

Bell exits with Mr. Pease.

Scene 4

Lights up on George cleaning fishing gear.

Barbara enters.

GEORGE: [She's downstairs.]

George turns away, attempts to untangle fishing line. He can't. He pulls out a pocket knife. She taps him on the shoulder.

BARBARA: [I know she's downstairs.] (*beat*) [Stop. Let me.]

He does.

BARBARA: (*to herself*) [You're so quick to cut things that you can simply untie with your hands.]

She untangles the lines.

BARBARA: [See?]

GEORGE: [Your claws must be sharper than mine.]

George tries to exit but she taps his shoulder.

BARBARA: [Hey. Don't blame me for surrounding Allison with hearing people. I'm hearing. That's who I am.]

GEORGE: [No, what you are is a mother to a deaf child.]

BARBARA: [You're right. And as a mother to a deaf child, I look at the world my daughter is growing up in and I am terrified of its speed.]

GEORGE: . . .

BARBARA: [You can say I don't know what it's like to be deaf—fine. That's fair. But you don't know what it's like to hear.]

GEORGE: . . .

BARBARA: . . .

GEORGE: [What about her Deaf friends?]

BARBARA: [What about her Deaf friends?]

GEORGE: [She won't be deaf anymore. Is she prepared to lose them?]

BARBARA: [She's not going to lose her Deaf friends because of the CI.]

GEORGE: [You don't know that.]

BARBARA: [And you don't know either.]

GEORGE: [She was MEANT to be Deaf!]

BARBARA: [How can you say she was meant to be Deaf?!]

Allison enters and watches them.

GEORGE: [There's no guarantee an implant will work a hundred percent.]

BARBARA: [I know there's no guarantee. But we have to take this chance for Allison!]

GEORGE: [I'm not backing down.]

BARBARA: [What are you going to do?]

GEORGE: [We might have some legal issues here that we haven't even begun to talk about.]

BARBARA: [Why pay lawyers to destroy each other in a court room? We do that now for free!]

Allison stomps her feet.

ALLISON: [Stop fighting! This isn't mom's fault.]

GEORGE: [ALLISON—]

ALLISON: [It wasn't her idea. It was mine.]

GEORGE: [You don't have to protect your mom.]

ALLISON: [She's protecting me.]

GEORGE: [From what?]

ALLISON: [You!]

GEORGE: . . .

ALLISON: [This was my decision. Not hers.]

GEORGE: (*to Barbara*) [Is this true?]

BARBARA: (*to Allison*) [Stop.]

ALLISON: [No. I'm tired of him yelling at you.]

GEORGE: (to Allison) [This was your idea?]

ALLISON: [Yes. So if you want to take someone to court, I guess it will have to be me.]

> *Beat.*

GEORGE: [Why do you want to hear?]

ALLISON: [Because I just want to.]

GEORGE: [That's not good enough.]

ALLISON: [Nothing is ever good enough for you!]

GEORGE: [Do you understand the amount of work you're going to have to do if you get this? This is not like getting braces where you just wear it and after a few years, everything is fine.]

ALLISON: [I know the difference between braces and an implant.]

GEORGE: [I'm trying to tell you it's constant work.]

ALLISON: [I know it is!]

GEORGE: [Why put yourself into the hearing world? It's so complicated and difficult. In the deaf world, you have no difficulties communicating.]

ALLISON: [That's not true.]

GEORGE: [What's not true? Name one deaf person you can't communicate with.]

ALLISON: [You.]

BARBARA: [Allison. Tell him what you told me.]

ALLISON: [He won't understand.]

GEORGE: [I'm your father.]

ALLISON: . . .

GEORGE: [Please. PLEASE.]

> *George sits.*
>
> *Allison hands him a notebook.*

ALLISON: [My notes from school. Go ahead, look.]

> *George skims through the notebook.*

GEORGE: [Remember when you helped me catch all these different fish and then you drew them in your notebook?]

ALLISON: [I prefer math to fish.]

GEORGE: [Why?]

ALLISON: [Math is less slippery than fish.]

GEORGE: (*to Barbara*) [She has my sense of humor.]

ALLISON: [I've been taking AP classes in mathematics.]

GEORGE: [AP?]

ALLISON: [Advanced Placement classes.]

BARBARA: (*to George*) [Gifted.]

GEORGE: [That's great.]

ALLISON: [It's great when I can understand it.]

GEORGE: [What do you mean?]

ALLISON: [The classes are at a different school. A hearing school. All the kids record the lectures. I can't do that. So I have to have an interpreter to understand what the teacher is saying and a notetaker to write it all down because I can't look away from the interpreter otherwise I get lost. Somedays, the notetaker must leave early, so I only get half the notes.]

GEORGE: [Can't you ask the teacher to give you her notes? I'm sure your teacher would make an exception for you.]

ALLISON: [I'm already an exception when I walk in the classroom with my terp and notetaker and they all look at me. I hate that. So I'm not going to ask for the notes.]

GEORGE: [You want to become a hearing person just so you can take notes without help?]

ALLISON: (*to Barbara*) [I told you he wouldn't understand.]

BARBARA: (*to George*) [You know it's not that simple.]

GEORGE: [School is not forever. The CI is.]

ALLISON: . . .

GEORGE: [It's just a few classes!]

ALLISON: [It's not just a few classes! It is my life!]

GEORGE: [You're thirteen years old. Your life is being thirteen, like your friends.]

ALLISON: [I want to go to a good college. That college will probably be hearing. I want to walk into a classroom by myself and take notes by myself and learn the things I need to learn to make sure I don't end up stuck here for the rest of my life! Like my friends.]

GEORGE: [You never acted like you were "stuck" when we were together on the boat. Remember that? You loved fishing with me. What happened?]

ALLISON: [I outgrew you.]

Scene 5

The Gay Head Cliffs, Martha's Vineyard

Mr. Pease sits on a stump eating a tomato.

With a spade and canvas bag, Bell stands in a hole, digging.

BELL: I must warn you, there's going to be much trial and error, so we'll need to build several hundred prototypes. But not just out of any clay. The subsoil in this area is made up of very curious variegated clays, which means they exhibit different colors. The clay crops out like fingers and are boldly colored.

MR. PEASE: Mmmm. (*offering*) Tomato?

BELL: No thank you. (*referring to the islanders*) Would you mind translating what I just said to them?

MR. PEASE: [He's digging for clay.]

Bell gives Pease a curious look and returns to digging.

MR. PEASE: Your speech method you use in Salem, you've had much success with it?

BELL: I have. Mabel is a prime example. She lip reads wonderfully and speaks quite well.

MR. PEASE: [His wife is deaf.] (*to Bell*) And you don't sign at all?

BELL: I don't need to.

MR. PEASE: Signing is quite useful for us. And not just for speaking to the deaf here on the island. Us hearing folk use it all the time.

Bell continues digging.

MR. PEASE: When I'm in church, I can converse with my friends across the room without disturbing the whole congregation . . . or the Lord.

BELL: They can't rely on their hands all the time to speak.

MR. PEASE: But they do.

BELL: What if they get tired? Ask them that.

MR. PEASE: [What do you do if your hands get tired?] (*relaying to Bell*) Then we stop talking.

BELL: What about at dinner, when they have to set the table and they have both hands full and need to ask for assistance?

MR. PEASE: [What about at dinner . . .]

BELL: No, stop.

MR. PEASE: [Ignore.]

BELL: We're focusing on practicalities when we should be discussing the more important matter.

MR. PEASE: Which is?

BELL: That the people of this island are isolated from the larger society, which if you want the deaf to integrate, they'll need to be taught to speak.

MR. PEASE: Is the larger society planning on moving here to the island?

BELL: No, but eventually these deaf islanders need to go to proper schools, off island.

MR. PEASE: We have schools here.

BELL: Mr. Pease, the deaf are already at a disadvantage. Would you rob them the opportunity to receive the finest education possible?

MR. PEASE: No, I guess not.

BELL: Integration into the larger society is inevitable. I simply want the deaf to be prepared for that inevitability.

MR. PEASE: There are many deaf here who have stayed on the island, built farms, started families.

BELL: Yes, families. That's another thing. They simply cannot continue to do so.

MR. PEASE: Start families?

BELL: With each other.

MR. PEASE: Who would they start it with?

BELL: Deaf-mutes should not marry other deaf-mutes. That's how deafness is propagated.

MR. PEASE: Propa . . .

BELL: Passed on from one generation to the next.

MR. PEASE: I see.

BELL: Good.

MR. PEASE: Forgive me, are you . . . proposing a way to get rid of the Deaf?

BELL: Their deafness, Mr. Pease. Their deafness. (*beat*) Now if you don't mind, I would really like to dig this hole.

MR. PEASE: Do you need assistance?

BELL: I'm quite capable of digging my own hole.

    Beat.

MR. PEASE: Can I be candid with you Mr. Bell?

    Bell throws the shovel down and straightens himself.

MR. PEASE: I don't see why it's so important for the deaf to speak.

BELL: We deny them speed if we do not teach them to speak.

MR. PEASE: But signing is just as fast. Back at the general store, there was no delay.

BELL: Yes, but it was the middle of the day where the light was abundant. What happens at night when it's difficult to see each other's hands?

MR. PEASE: There are other things to do in the dark than speak.

Pease laughs. Bell is not amused.

BELL: The fact is, Mr. Pease, we should not be living in two different worlds. We should be thriving in one. Now would you please dismiss them.

MR. PEASE: (*to the islanders*) [That's enough for today.]

(*to Bell*) I don't mean to challenge you. My curiosity sometimes gets the best of me.

Beat.

BELL: My wife, Mabel. The reason she cannot hear is due to the bout of scarlet fever she had as a child. It slowly took her hearing. That scarlet fever, even though it is gone, is now causing her to slowly lose her sight. If she cannot hear nor see, well, you understand . . . she'll be completely isolated from the world. This is why I am here. To find a way to restore her hearing. So that once blindness takes her, at least she won't completely be in the dark.

MR. PEASE: I'm sorry, Mr. Bell.

BELL: Let's enjoy the silence for a while, shall we?

Bell resumes digging as Pease sits quietly, eating another tomato.

Scene 6

Allison is chatting with her friends on the internet. She is sitting in the dark, lit only by the glow of her laptop. Allison's screen name is AlleyCat2002.

ALLISON: yeah watched sum of the vids

THEDEAFSTAR99: they drill into yer head n make lots of incisions

IMKATNISSBITCHES: shes seen the vids

THEDEAFSTAR99: n they keep cuttn away all the flesh 2 put the implant in

IMKATNISSBITCHES: she made her decisn. stop tryn 2 scare her

ALLISON: no itz fine.

THEDEAFSTAR99: i jus wanna make sure u know what ur gettng into

ALLISON: between you n George!

THEDEAFSTAR99: whos george?

ALLISON: my dad dummy

THEDEAFSTAR99: O dam my dad would nvr let me call him by his first name

ALLISON: George hates it :)

IMKATNISSBITCHES: arnt u being a little disrespect 2 yer dad?

ALLISON: me? what about him? he's always on his boat

IMKATNISSBITCHES: my dadz always on his boat 2. their fishrmen.

ALLISON: but 4 months atta time?

IMKATNISSBITCHES: their fishrmen
ALLISON: [ANGRY FACE EMOJI]
IMKATNISSBITCHES: [FACE WITH STUCK-OUT TONGUE EMOJI]
ALLISON: [FACE THROWING A KISS EMOJI]
IMKATNISSBITCHES: Al—I know u feel different but i dunno . . .
ALLISON: what dont u know?
IMKATNISSBITCHES: i just dont understand whats the big D abt sound? u get along fine without
ALLISON: u were born def i wasnt
IMKATNISSBITCHES: but yer def now
ALLISON: Can't I be both?
IMKATNISSBITCHES: Can a Jedi be both good and bad? No.
ALLISON: this is real.
THEDEAFSTAR99: So is the Force n its strong in u Allison
ALLISON: HA
THEDEAFSTAR99: jus as its strong in her father . . . DARTH GEORGE!!!
ALLISON: [ANGRY FACE EMOJI]
THEDEAFSTAR99: Yasss THE FORCE IS REAL
IMKATNISSBITCHES: so is yer stupidity oscr
THEDEAFSTAR99: what did I say?

Blackout on Allison shutting her laptop.

Scene 7

Lights up on Bell and Mr. Pease. Bell is taking the clay and molding it with his hands. Some deaf islanders watch as Mr. Pease interprets.

BELL: . . . and that's because sound is everywhere. And even though many of you cannot hear it, you can feel it. You can see it. It is vibration. Movement.

MR. PEASE: (*relaying*) Why can't we hear what you hear?

BELL: Sound happens in the cochlea, which is a bony chamber behind each ear. Allow me to show you.

Bell produces a large model of the cochlea, which he has built out of clay.

MR. PEASE: (*relaying*) It looks like a snail shell.

BELL: Yes indeed. It's helpful to think of sound constantly flowing into the cochlea like . . . ocean waves. These waves then brush against thousands of tiny hair cells inside, which amplifies sound. The reason why you cannot hear is because those tiny hair cells inside the cochlea have been badly damaged. Are there any questions?

MR. PEASE: (*relaying*) There are no questions.

BELL: Surely there must be . . . I made a model.

MR. PEASE: They don't have any questions.

BELL: I see. Would you fetch some more clay, then?

MR. PEASE: (*to the islanders*) [He wants more clay.]

> *Mr. Pease dumps a bucket of clay onto a worktable.*
>
> *Bell molds the clay as Pease watches.*
>
> *Mabel enters reading from a book.*

MABEL: Ah! One of the ingredients used to make plasticine sticks is petroleum jelly. I'm quite sure that is what keeps the sticks from drying out and remaining pliable.

BELL: Very busy here.

MABEL: Forgive me. I thought you'd want to know what you got Elsie her for her birthday.

BELL: I'm sorry, Mabel. I . . . there's just so much work to be done. And once you start seeing spots, then my work here won't matter.

MABEL: You'll be happy to know she likes playing with her clay as much as you like playing with yours.

BELL: No one is "playing" here, I assure you.

MABEL: I'm not the one that needs assuring.

BELL: . . .

MABEL: She asks for you. The least you can do is write her a letter.

BELL: You can share with her whatever letters I write to you as you see fit.

MABEL: As I see fit? That is the problem now, isn't it. Soon I will not be able to see fit.

BELL: Which is why I am working day and night, Mabel! Which is why I do not have the time to write letters to my daughter. She'll understand when she grows up.

MABEL: At which point she will resent you. Is that what you want?

BELL: If she's smart, she'll get over her resentment.

MABEL: You're right, she is smart. She understands many things right now. She even understands why you don't dote on her as you did with Edward and Robert—

BELL: DO NOT SPEAK TO ME OF THE TWINS! (*beat*) What use is there bringing them up to me?

MABEL: I'm sorry.

BELL: Had I known how quickly they'd be taken from this world, I would have . . .

MABEL: What? What would you have done?

BELL: Honestly, I think sometimes you'd rather I be home tending to the high bushes instead of doing the important work I'm meant to be doing . . . I am an inventor. I am a teacher of the Deaf. I am your husband. Are these not enough for you? What else would you have me be?

MABEL: A father to your daughter. (*beat*) Only if YOU see fit.

BELL: Mabel. I'm sorry I missed Elsie's birthday.

MABEL: Don't tell me that. Tell her.

> *Mabel disappears.*

Scene 8

> *Very late at night. George is standing on the bow of his boat, staring into the moonlit water. Shift to Barbara in her kitchen, crunching numbers, writing checks, and drinking coffee. Allison enters in pajamas.*

BARBARA: (*speaking/signing*) [It's past midnight.]

ALLISON: [Had a bad dream.]

BARBARA: [Want to talk about it?]

ALLISON: [No. I just want some coffee.]

BARBARA: [You're too young to be drinking coffee.]

ALLISON: [Mark lets me.]

BARBARA: [I'm pretty sure Mark doesn't let you.]

ALLISON: [Yes he does.]

BARBARA: [No.]

ALLISON: [I swear.]

BARBARA: . . .

> *Barbara pours her a cup of coffee and slides it over.*

BARBARA: [Decaf.]

ALLISON: [Mom!]

BARBARA: [Decaf.] (*gesturing*) [Slow down.]

> *She doesn't.*

BARBARA: [Are you nervous? About tomorrow?]

ALLISON: [No. I don't know.]

> *Allison nudges Barbara for more coffee.*

BARBARA: [What was your dream about?]

ALLISON: [Coffee please.]

BARBARA: [Only half a cup.]

ALLISON: [Half?]

BARBARA: [I'll fill up after you tell me your dream. Deal?]

Barbara pours half.

BARBARA: [Tell me about your dream.]

ALLISON: [My BAD dream.]

BARBARA: [Yes, your BAD dream.]

ALLISON: [I was dreaming of pearls.]

BARBARA: [Pearls?]

ALLISON: [I was walking on the beach. My head hurt. Bad. I fell down. Crying. There was a man. The sun was blocking his face. He dropped silver pearls into my ear and the pain went away.]

BARBARA: [That doesn't seem so bad.]

ALLISON: [Then my ears caught fire and my face melted off.]

Barbara gives her the entire pot of coffee.

BARBARA: [Tell me what scares you.]

ALLISON: [I'm scared the CI won't work.]

BARBARA: [There is a chance it won't. We've been over the risks.]

ALLISON: [If the first one doesn't work, the doctors recommend getting a second CI for the other ear.]

BARBARA: [I know.]

ALLISON: [We can hardly afford this one.]

BARBARA: [Let me worry about that. Okay?]

ALLISON: . . .

BARBARA: [Allison, okay?]

ALLISON: [Okay. Is he coming tomorrow?]

BARBARA: [Who?]

ALLISON: [George]

BARBARA: [I don't know. He hasn't gotten back to me.]

ALLISON: [Typical.]

BARBARA: [I know you're mad at him. But he's still your father. He loves you.]

ALLISON: [Doesn't mean I have to love him back.]

BARBARA: [No you don't. But you will not disrespect him. Not in front of me.]

ALLISON: [Why do you always stick up for him? He's the one who left!]

BARBARA: [It was a mutual decision.]

ALLISON: [Not according to Aunt Becky.]

BARBARA: [Remind me to kill your Aunt Becky.]

ALLISON: [Mom.]

BARBARA: [What?]

ALLISON: [Remember to kill Aunt Becky.]

BARBARA: (*laughing*) [Okay, time for bed. You have a long day tomorrow.]

ALLISON: [Goodnight.]

BARBARA: Goodnight.

ALLISON: [Mom?]

BARBARA: [Yes?]

ALLISON: [Thanks]

> *Allison exits.*
>
> *Barbara stares into her coffee cup.*
>
> *George remains staring into the dark water.*

Scene 9

> *Lights up on Bell and Mr. Pease, outside near a shed.*
>
> *Mr. Pease dumps a bucket of clay onto a worktable, next to rows of clay ears, with wires protruding from them.*
>
> *Allison lays in bed, sleeping.*

BELL: Yes. Yes. No.

MR. PEASE: I don't know how you tell them apart. They all look the same to me.

BELL: Remember when I told you the clay was variegated?

MR. PEASE: Yes.

BELL: Come, let's have a look at the different colors.

> *Allison's bed turns into an operating table. She is surrounded by nurses*

NURSE: Injecting local anesthetic along the incision line.

> *Lights up on the waiting room of the clinic. Barbara is seated reading a magazine. George enters. He sits across from her.*

NURSE: Develop the incision.

BELL: I'll just cut along here.

NURSE: Exposing the mastoid.

> *Bell approaches Allison, treating her as the lump of clay.*

BELL: If we develop a pocket in the clay like so . . .

NURSE: Developing the pocket.

BELL: You'll see the clay run almost a blue-green along this canal.

NURSE: Fit is good.

BELL: And then under that layer, we have a pink-red flare along here. See it?

MR. PEASE: Yes, I see it.

BELL: This clay has conductive properties similar to the inside of the ear.

NURSE: Drilling for titanium case.

BELL: If it can carry an electric signal safely across, then it may be possible—

MR. PEASE: To carry sound across.

BELL: Yes.

NURSE: Drilling the mastoid.

BELL: It would work much the same way as my liquid transmitter works for the telephone.

NURSE: Developing facial recess and exposing round window.

BELL: Permitting a small electric current to pass from one point to the next . . .

NURSE: Placing Gelfoam over cochleostomy.

BELL: . . . and recreating exactly the sound it's carrying.

MR. PEASE: You're building a liquid transmitter for the ear.

BELL: Yes.

> *Back in the waiting room . . .*

GEORGE: [Where's your husband? I assumed he'd be here.]

BARBARA: [My husband has a name. M-A-R-K.] (*beat*) [He wasn't sure if you were coming. He didn't want to take the chance.]

GEORGE: [Typical.]

BARBARA: [Can we try not fighting today? For Allison?]

GEORGE: [All my fighting has been for Allison. Can't you see that?]

BARBARA: [I see it. But can't you see she's chasing the world she wants?]

GEORGE: [On land, Allison is a thirteen year old girl who rolls her eyes at me and calls me George. On the water, she's a five year old in overalls jumping up and down on my boat. Tying lures and humming "I love you" right here.]

> (*pointing to his forehead.*) [She may be chasing the world she wants, but it's a world that wants to fundamentally change who she is. It will break her in ways she can't imagine. I'm her father. I'm supposed to keep her from breaking.]

NURSE: Placing implant in patient.

> *With a pair of tweezers, Bell places a shiny pearl-like object into Allison's ear.*

NURSE: Complete closure of periosteal layer.

> *Silence. Silence. Silence.*

MR. PEASE: Now what?

BELL: Now we wait.

> *Black out.*

OPTIONAL INTERMISSION

PART 2

Scene I

Lights up on Barbara and Allison in the Audiologist's office.

AUDIOLOGIST: Okay Allison, it's been six weeks since you've had your operation. We're ready to turn on your implant. Are you excited? Nervous?

ALLISON: [BOTH]

BARBARA: Both.

AUDIOLOGIST: Remember, the moment we activate your implant, it's like you've got brand new ears. So understand, Allison, you may not hear anything right away. Okay?

Allison nods.

Shift to Bell and Mr. Pease at a worktable. Mr. Pease attaches wires to a row of clay ears. Bell stands off to the side, writing a letter.

BELL: Dear Mabel, been up all night making preparations for our trial run. Today we will make a go of it. The entire town has come out to watch.

MR. PEASE: We're ready Mr. Bell.

AUDIOLOGIST: Okay, your implant has been turned on. Let's try the first level. This light will flash every time I send sound to your implant.

A light flashes.

AUDIOLOGIST: Can you hear anything?

Allison shakes her head.

AUDIOLOGIST: That's okay. How about this?

Light flashes. Allison shakes her head.

AUDIOLOGIST: It's okay. We'll try again. How about this?

Allison shakes her head.

AUDIOLOGIST: It's okay if you don't hear anything. Let's try the next level. How about that? Can you hear anything?

Allison shakes her head.

AUDIOLOGIST: And now?

Allison shakes her head.

BARBARA: (*to Allison*) [It's okay. It takes time.]

AUDIOLOGIST: Not everyone hears right away. We'll just keep trying and exploring different frequencies and maps. Give me a minute.

BELL: Connections look good. Give it a crank.

Mr. Pease hand cranks an electric generator. A spark. Then a fire. Mr. Pease quickly puts it out.

AUDIOLOGIST: Okay, how about now?

Allison shakes her head.

AUDIOLOGIST: How about now?

And now?

Now?

Now?

Now?

Now?

The light stops flashing.

AUDIOLOGIST: I'll be right back.

BARBARA: Is everything okay?

AUDIOLOGIST: I'll be right back.

The Audiologist exits.

BARBARA: (*to Allison*) [She's checking something. Everything is fine. She'll be back.]

They sit in uncomfortable silence.

BELL: Try it now.

Mr. Pease cranks the generator.

BELL: More power.

More, Mr. Pease.

Mr. Pease cranks faster until a plume of smoke rises from one of the ears.

BELL: Stop!

Bell yanks the wires out of the clay ear. It shocks him.

BELL: SON-OF-A-BOAT-LICKER-COCK-CHAFER-BALLS!!!

The Audiologist reenters.

AUDIOLOGIST: Okay, let's try this new map. I'm just going to step through different frequencies until you hear something, okay?

The Audiologist makes several attempts as Allison shakes her head "no."

Another attempt.

Another.

Another.

Another.

Another.

Allison jolts. She grabs her head.

BARBARA: [Are you okay?]

Allison points to the top of her head.

ALLISON: [I feel something up here.]

ALLISON: [Why is my ear on the top   BARBARA: She's asking why is my
of my head?]   ear on the top of my head?

AUDIOLOGIST: You remember hearing from your ears. But the implant
bypasses them altogether. You'll learn to relocate where sound happens
in your head. It's normal. Are you okay to continue?

Allison nods.

AUDIOLOGIST: Let's try this setting.

Allison jolts again.

AUDIOLOGIST: Your ears are adjusting. I'll turn it down. How about now.

Allison jolts slightly then recovers.

ALLISON: [It sounds weird]

BARBARA: She says it sounds weird.

AUDIOLOGIST: Allison, that's because your new ear is exactly five minutes
old. You need to give yourself time to readjust. Understand?

Allison nods.

BARBARA: (*carefully*) Allison?

Allison responds to Barbara. She can hear.

Scene 2

Lights up on Allison at George's house. She crinkles tissue paper.

George enters with fishing poles.

Allison opens a door and slams it shut. She repeats.

*Beeping. She looks around trying to figure out where the beeping is coming
from. She realizes it's her laptop and she answers it.*

THEDEAFSTAR99: still feel weird after 6 mos?

ALLISON: very

THEDEAFSTAR99: what does yer mom sound like?

ALLISON: different.

THEDEAFSTAR99: yeah?

ALLISON: yeah. everyone kinda sounds same

IMKATNISSBITCHES: like a robot rt? Thats what i read

ALLISON: i dont know what a robot sounds like

IMKATNISSBITCHES: me neithr. what else u hear?

ALLISON: hmm . . . bubble wrap. itz loud when it popz

THEDEAFSTAR99: rly? but thers nothin innit cept air

THEDEAFSTAR99: . . .

IMKATNISSBITCHES: . . .

THEDEAFSTAR99: going 2 Dougs 2morrow?

IMKATNISSBITCHES: NICE N SUBTLE OSCR!!!

THEDEAFSTAR99: Doug wants u 2 come

ALLISON: rly? did he say something?

IMKATNISSBITCHES: OMG so obv he's INTO U!!!

ALLISON: what did he say?

IMKATNISSBITCHES: he said it would b cool if u came with us.

ALLISON: rly?

IMKATNISSBITCHES: RLY!

THEDEAFSTAR99: but dont wear yer CI. not around him.

IMKATNISSBITCHES: oscr shut yer face hole.

ALLISON: y cant i?

THEDEAFSTAR99: he's Deaf witta big D yo - and so r his 'rents.

ALLISON: . . .

IMKATNISSBITCHES: alli? hello?

ALLISON: gotta go

IMKATNISSBITCHES: dont b mad.

ALLISON: no jus gotta go to speech lesson.

IMKATNISSBITCHES: k

ALLISON: BTW im doing really well with my speech

IMKATNISSBITCHES: . . .

ALLISON: soon i wont need to sign anymore

IMKATNISSBITCHES: ur joking rt?

ALLISON: nt joking. my speech therapist is rly impressed

IMKATNISSBITCHES: ur not going 2 give up asl. u said u wouldnt.

ALLISON: things change i guess.

　　Allison shuts her laptop.

Scene 3

　　Bell sits outside under a tree. He takes in the stillness. Mabel appears by his side reading from a book.

MABEL: It states here British explorer Bartholomew Gosnold named the island of Martha's Vineyard after his daughter. I wonder what we shall name after Elsie?

BELL: . . .

MABEL: The sunrise on the island perhaps? The Elsie sunrise. That has a
nice ring to it.

BELL: . . .

MABEL: Alec, doesn't that have a nice ring?

BELL: . . .

Shift to Allison in the office of a Speech Therapist.

Projection: "AG BELL SPEECH ACADEMY"

SPEECH THERAPIST: So today I really want you to focus on mouth shapes.
It's important to feel it. I think that will help. Okay?

Allison nods.

Note: Allison should have extreme difficulty making these sounds, if any.

SPEECH THERAPIST: Let's start with P sounds. Try to mouth "P. Puh."

ALLISON: P. Puh.

SPEECH THERAPIST: P. Puh.

Allison rests her jaw in her hands.

ALLISON: P. Puh.

SPEECH THERAPIST: Allison, you need to put your hands down.

She does.

SPEECH THERAPIST: P. Puh.

ALLISON: P. Puh.

SPEECH THERAPIST: Pop. Up.

ALLISON: Pop. Up.

SPEECH THERAPIST: Pop. Up.

ALLISON: Pop. Up.

SPEECH THERAPIST: I have a surprise to show you.

The Therapist shows Allison a white egg shaped plush toy.

SPEECH THERAPIST: Pop. Up.

ALLISON: Pop. Up.

A baby chick pops out from the toy egg.

ALLISON: [Do I look like I'm five?]

SPEECH THERAPIST: I know, it's so cute!

MABEL: Elsie made a frog out of the clay sticks you gave her. She named
it Alec.

BELL: . . .

MABEL: Will you draw me something? You used to include such wonderful
sketches in our correspondence. Early in our relationship.

BELL: . . .

MABEL: I would like to see what you see. As if I were standing beside you.

SPEECH THERAPIST: And how about our "D" sounds. Let's say Dad. Duh. Dad. Duh.

ALLISON: . . .

SPEECH THERAPIST: Allison, can you say Dad. Duh. Dad. Duh.

ALLISON: [I don't want to say it.]

SPEECH THERAPIST: Is everything okay?

Allison nods.

SPEECH THERAPIST: Can you say Dad. Duh?

Allison shakes her head.

SPEECH THERAPIST: You don't want to say it? Okay, let's try a different word. How about Sad. Duh. Sad. Duh.

ALLISON: Really?

SPEECH THERAPIST: You don't like that word either?

Allison nods.

SPEECH THERAPIST: Okay, let's move on to "ooo." Remember? We make a little circle when we say "ooo."

ALLISON: Ooo.

SPEECH THERAPIST: Good try. Let's make it really small. Boo.

ALLISON: Boo.

SPEECH THERAPIST: Good try. Boooo.

ALLISON: Booo.

SPEECH THERAPIST: Good for you. You want to look at your mouth in the little turtle mirror?

Allison rolls her eyes. The Therapist hands her the turtle mirror.

SPEECH THERAPIST: I'll going to get your mom.

The Therapist opens the door and Barbara enters.

SPEECH THERAPIST: (*to Barbara*) Have you been working on these exercises with her at home?

BARBARA: Yes of course. Why?

SPEECH THERAPIST: Well, I hoped she'd be further along than this.

Allison looks in the mirror and says . . .

ALLISON: (*slowly*) Boo. Boo. Boo.

Scene 4

Shift to Bell digging through his five steamer trunks, looking for spare parts. Mabel appears.

MABEL: Donkeys only require three hours of sleep each night—

BELL: I am close. Very close. I must get to the ferry before it leaves.

MABEL: —and walruses can go without sleep for up to eighty-four hours.

BELL: Why are you telling me this?

MABEL: I'm wondering if you're a donkey or a walrus? You need to sleep.

BELL: Do not worry, Mabel. I had a slight moment of despair, but I'm fine now.

MABEL: This very early morning I was feeding Elsie.

BELL: Tomorrow I plan to start fresh. I will gather my notes and in the morning—

MABEL: She was making a mess of her soft carrots.

BELL: Mabel, listen to me! Remember the storm waves and how I said the island was the conductor of it? I was only focused on where the waves ended up, not where they began. I should be looking at the other side of the island where the storm waves originated.

MABEL: The soft carrots . . .

BELL: Of course, it's so obvious, right there in front of my face, yet I could not see it—

MABEL: THE SOFT CARROTS ALEC! (*calming down*) I wiped the carrots off Elsie's face and I could not see her dimple anywhere. The one on her right cheek.

BELL: Mabel, I have to get to the other side of the island.

MABEL: So I wiped again, and it reappeared. And each time I blinked it was gone. So I kept my eyes open for as long as I could but I finally had to shut them and when I opened my eyes again, she was gone. My Elsie was gone.

BELL: It was all but a bad dream.

MABEL: My eyes are very tired.

BELL: You must rest them. Shade them from the sun. Retire early in the evenings.

MABEL: I do.

BELL: Then send for the doctor. Get his opinion.

MABEL: Alec.

BELL: The doctor will be able to tell us—

MABEL: The spots, Alec. I'm seeing the spots. That is no dream.

 The ferry horn blows.

Scene 5

The AG Bell Speech Center. Allison, Barbara, and an Interpreter (played by Mr. Pease) are in the Therapist's office. On the wall behind her are framed diplomas, family photos, and a photo of Alexander Graham Bell.

THERAPIST: What I'm saying is everyone learns to hear at a different pace. You're eight months into your CI and there are a lot of adjustments you're dealing with.

ALLISON: [Are you saying I shouldn't be discouraged? Because I'm discouraged. Especially when the speech therapist looks at me like I have something on my face but doesn't want to tell me.]

THERAPIST: I understand. Is it possible you may be misreading her?

ALLISON: [I guess anything is possible.]

THERAPIST: I'll make a note of it and discuss it with her. Okay?

ALLISON: . . .

BARBARA: (*to Allison*) [Okay Allison?]

ALLISON: [Okay.]

THERAPIST: Okay. So any excessive aching? Any tinnitus?

ALLISON: [A little of both. It comes and goes.]

THERAPIST: But not excessive?

ALLISON: [I don't think so.]

THERAPIST: Okay. Will continue to monitor that. Any other issues you want to talk about?

ALLISON: [Those are the only issues I'm having with the CI.]

THERAPIST: Anything else?

ALLISON: [I just said those are the only issues.]

THERAPIST: They don't have to be issues with just the CI. We can talk about anything.

ALLISON: . . .

THERAPIST: Anything.

BARBARA: [Allison?]

ALLISON: [Everything's fine.]

BARBARA: [Really?]

ALLISON: . . .

THERAPIST: How are your friends?

ALLISON: [They're fine.]

THERAPIST: Do they act differently? How do they act in front of you?

ALLISON: [They're still curious about my CI. Most of them are supportive.]

THERAPIST: Most?

ALLISON: [Except Doug.]

THERAPIST: Who's Doug?

ALLISON: [No one important.]

THERAPIST: Okay. Umm . . .

ALLISON: [And George!]

THERAPIST: George is one of your friends?

BARBARA: He's her father.

THERAPIST: Oh, Mr. West. Right.

ALLISON: . . .

THERAPIST: Is your father okay with you calling him by his first name?

ALLISON: [No. But he's not really okay with anything.]

THERAPIST: Do you want to explain that?

BARBARA: [Allison?]

ALLISON: [He's so set in his ways. He's so full of . . .]

THERAPIST: Full of what?

ALLISON: [I was trying to find a negative word to describe it, but all I can think of is the word "pride." But that's not very negative is it? Pride?]

THERAPIST: He's proud of who he is.

ALLISON: [Yes.]

THERAPIST: Do you think he's proud of who you are?

Allison slowly shakes her head.

BARBARA: [Why do you think he's not proud?] (*to the Therapist*) Sorry.

THERAPIST: (*to Barbara*) That's okay.

(*to Allison*) Why do you think he's not proud?

Allison looks at her mom.

THERAPIST: Did he say something to you?

ALLISON: [He doesn't speak. He signs.]

THERAPIST: Right, that's what I meant.

ALLISON: [But sometimes George speaks more with his face.]

THERAPIST: I see. So it was a look he gave you?

ALLISON: [He looks at me differently.]

THERAPIST: Sometimes looks can be misinterpreted.

ALLISON: [I know George's looks.]

THERAPIST: Okay. Thank you for telling me. In this room, you can always talk about how you're feeling. Okay?

ALLISON: [Okay.]

THERAPIST: I think that's enough for today.

(*to Barbara*) Can you bring George to the next session?

BARBARA: Well, George is really busy. He's a fisherman.

THERAPIST: I think it would be best to have you both here next time. I'll be making my final recommendations.

BARBARA: Okay. I'll try.

Barbara and Allison exit.

Scene 6

George's house. Allison is dancing to some extremely loud music. She bounces up and down with the vibrations.

George enters, taps Allison on the shoulder.

GEORGE: [Your uncle Frisner dropped off a batch of fresh oysters.]

Allison continues bouncing.

GEORGE: [I'll teach you how to shuck them. We can have them for dinner.]

Allison continues bouncing.

George waves his hands at her.

ALLISON: [Okay.]

GEORGE: [And maybe some steak?]

ALLISON: [Sure.]

GEORGE: [I think you'll pick it up quickly.]

Allison continues bouncing.

GEORGE: [Shucking oysters. You've always been good with your hands.]

ALLISON: [Ok.]

GEORGE: [Hey.]

ALLISON: [What?]

GEORGE: [Turn off the music for a second.]

She does.

GEORGE: [What's with the one word answers?]

ALLISON: [Nothing.]

GEORGE: [Allison.]

ALLISON: [What?]

GEORGE: . . .

ALLISON: [My speech therapist says I need to limit my signing.]

GEORGE: [Well tell your therapist I said—]

ALLISON: [NO.]

She turns away.

George approaches her and taps her on the shoulder. She turns to him.

GEORGE: [Tell her I said you can do whatever you want but around me you're going to sign.]

ALLISON: [Fine.]

GEORGE: [And not one-word answers. In this house, we talk to each other. Okay?]

ALLISON: [I "hear" you loud and clear.]

GEORGE: (*smelling something*) [What is that?]

(*no response*) [Hey. What is that?]

ALLISON: [What?]

GEORGE: [That smell.]

Allison shrugs her shoulders and buries herself into her phone. George taps her on the shoulder. Allison pulls her shoulder away.

GEORGE: [Is that perfume?]

(*no response*) [Are you wearing perfume?]

ALLISON: [So what?]

GEORGE: [Did your therapist tell you to wear perfume as well?]

ALLISON: [You're being immature.]

GEORGE: [Oh, I can be way more immature than this.]

(*no response*) [Who are you wearing perfume for?]

ALLISON: [Nobody!]

GEORGE: [You're too young to wear perfume.]

ALLISON: [I am not too young.]

GEORGE: [You're a young girl.]

ALLISON: [I'm an independent teenager.]

GEORGE: [Well in this house, you're a girl who doesn't wear perfume. Is it for that boy? Doug?]

ALLISON: [How do you know about Doug?]

GEORGE: [I'm your father. I know about Doug.]

Allison goes back to her phone.

GEORGE: [Put your phone down.]

Allison ignores him.

GEORGE: [Put that phone down!]

Allison throws her phone across the room.

GEORGE: [What's wrong with you?]

ALLISON: . . .

GEORGE: [I said what's wrong with you?]

ALLISON: [I don't know! Why don't you tell me?]

George picks up her phone and hands it to her. She throws it again.

GEORGE: [You can't throw things in this house.]

ALLISON: [Why not? You do all the time.]

Allison turns away.

GEORGE: [Look at me. Allison, look at me.]

She does.

ALLISON: [Yes George?]

GEORGE: [Stop calling me that. I'm your father.]

ALLISON: [Sorry George. I didn't mean to call you by your real name. George! George! George!]

GEORGE: [Did I say something awful to you to hate me?]

ALLISON: [No. You never said anything. Believe me, I'd rather have you say something bad to me than nothing at all. For all my life, you've said nothing. Nothing.]

GEORGE: [We've been over this. I had to work. To support the family. The divorce was messy—]

ALLISON: [Don't blame mom for this.]

GEORGE: [I'm not blaming anyone. The divorce was my fault as much as much your mother's.]

ALLISON: [That's so admirable of you to take part of the blame. Do you feel better about yourself now?]

GEORGE: [Look at me. After realizing how messy the divorce was and how it affected you, I did everything to support your new family. I could have made it very difficult for Mark, but I backed off when he came into the picture.]

ALLISON: [You didn't back off.]

GEORGE: [I did!]

ALLISON: [No, you gave up!]

GEORGE: [That's not true.]

ALLISON: [You didn't stick around. You retreated to your boat and left me when I needed you.]

GEORGE: [It was important for your mother and I to make the transition easy for you.]

ALLISON: [No, you made it easy for YOU. You left me with Mark and I hated you for that. But then I discovered he actually listens to me. He talks to me. He's there for me. More than you ever were.]

GEORGE: [I'm sorry.]

ALLISON: [Aren't you tired of saying sorry all the time?]

GEORGE: [Exhausted.]

Beat.

ALLISON: [Doug invited me to his party last month. He didn't want me to wear my CI because his parents are Deaf. So I decided to go to my AP study group. They were happy to see me. Then my CI battery died, I panicked and ran home. I ran away, like you did.]

GEORGE: [Allison—]

ALLISON: [I bought this perfume so I could smell nice. Not for Doug, not for my friends, not for my classmates. For me. I just want to wear perfume for me. Because there is nothing complicated about it. It's just for me. Okay? Now will you please . . . PLEASE leave me alone?]

GEORGE: [I'll start dinner.]

> *George exits.*

Scene 7

> *The AG Bell Speech Center. A Speech Therapist is briefing Barbara, George, and an Interpreter in her office. Allison sits outside in the waiting area, studying. Bell and Mabel remain visible throughout this scene.*

BARBARA: I'm sorry. Your recommendation is what?

THERAPIST: I know this is difficult to . . . but it is my professional recommendation and I believe we pointed this out initially. Before the preop.

BARBARA: (*to George*) [She's recommending that Allison get a second CI. For her other ear.]

GEORGE: . . .

THERAPIST: Her progress is far below the normative levels.

BARBARA: But she's older than a typical CI candidate. It's to be expected that she take longer to adapt, right?

THERAPIST: It's not just her age. It's . . . well, she's indicated a few issues.

BARBARA: What issues?

THERAPIST: (*opening a file*) According to her CI maintenance reports, right now she can't determine where sound is coming from. Whether it be her friend clapping behind her or someone yelling a block away in front of her. It's all happening in the same place in her head. It's called "head shadow."

> *Barbara looks at George. He says nothing.*

THERAPIST: And you both know about her running out of power in her receiver?

BARBARA: Yes, she forgot to pack an extra battery.

THERAPIST: She left her friends without saying goodbye.

BARBARA: It scared her. I probably would've done the same thing.

THERAPIST: Sure, I probably would too. My point is, if she had a secondary implant in, she'd still be able to hear out the other ear.

BARBARA: I knew this was a possibility. We all did. I just hoped . . . you know?

THERAPIST: I know. We always recommend two implants but we don't push it at the beginning because we want to see if the first one will find her best ear.

BARBARA: (*finds this funny in a sad way.*) Her best ear.

THERAPIST: Yes, the one that has the most neural potential.

BARBARA: With all this technology we have, you would think you should know which is her best ear before the operation.

THERAPIST: We don't know that until we put the implant in. Only then can we test the auditory responsiveness against the cochlea.

BARBARA: I completely understand everything you're saying. I just . . . I . . .

THERAPIST: I know it seems daunting. But a secondary implant will improve her understanding of speech in noise. And it will allow her to localise sound. She'll be hearing in 3D space versus, well, 2D.

BARBARA: The head shadow?

THERAPIST: Yes. And like I said before, it will guarantee continuous sound in case one of the receivers fail. She won't have to run away from her friends.

BARBARA: (*to George*) [I'm sorry. We knew this was a possibility. I hoped she would just need one.]

THERAPIST: There's one more thing.

BARBARA: Of course there is.

THERAPIST: She also needs to reduce her signing. We've talked about this.

BARBARA: I know. It's just that, that's how she communicates with her father.

THERAPIST: I know. But her over-reliance on her hands is not helping.

GEORGE: . . .

THERAPIST: Mr. West, you've been quiet. I would love to hear your thoughts on this?

BARBARA: George?

GEORGE: [I've been staring at that photo.]

THERAPIST: Oh, that's my family.

GEORGE: [No the other one. Of AG Bell.]

THERAPIST: Oh, yes. Well, this speech center is part of the Alexander Graham Bell association. Are you a history buff?

GEORGE: [Not really. But I know a lot about Bell.]

THERAPIST: My son wants to be an inventor, just like him.

> *Allison gets impatient and goes to the door and tries to listen.*

GEORGE: [Inventor? He always thought of himself as a teacher of the deaf.]

THERAPIST: I understand.

GEORGE: [No I don't think you do. You see, I've been sitting here this entire time half watching what you're saying because AG Bell is staring right at me and it's . . . pissing me off. This man . . . .no, this monster who . . .]

George stands up. Which causes Barbara to stand up.

BARBARA: George.

GEORGE: (*to the Therapist*) [Do you know why we, the Deaf community, hate Bell?]

The Therapist shakes her head.

GEORGE: [He hated us. So we hate him. He hates us just because we're Deaf.]

THERAPIST: His wife and mother were both deaf.

GEORGE: [And he was ashamed of that. I'm sure he thought he was helping us but he wasn't. He thought we weren't normal. He failed at "curing" our deafness, so he decided to destroy us.]

THERAPIST: I don't think any of us are in a position to really know what was going on in his mind.

GEORGE: [He thought he could get rid of us by telling the country, in fact the entire world, that the deaf should not marry each other for fear of passing on the "deaf gene" to our children. But ninety-percent of Deaf children are born to hearing parents.]

THERAPIST: I don't think I really want to get into all of this.

Allison knocks on the door. George does not hear this.

BARBARA: (*to the Therapist*) I think that's Allison. Let's take a break.

Barbara fetches Allison. The Interpreter sits.

George remains focused on the Therapist.

GEORGE: [Does any of this bother you at all?]

THERAPIST: I'm sorry I don't know what he's saying.

GEORGE: [Talk to me, not him.]

THERAPIST: I'm sorry Mr. West.

GEORGE: [Right, because God forbid you learn to sign. It's not like you ever deal with any deaf people on a daily basis.]

THERAPIST: I'm sorry, I don't . . .

GEORGE: [Does it bother you to work for a company built by a man that believes we are . . . inferior.]

THERAPIST: Mr. West, I know you have very strong opinions on—

GEORGE: [Bell wanted us to stop signing. The way you want my daughter to stop signing. He wanted us to sit on our hands and speak with our mouths because that's the only way we would be normal to him. And to you.]

THERAPIST: . . .

GEORGE: [There was a time on Martha's Vineyard when there were so many deaf islanders, the hearing LEARNED how to sign in order to communicate. Not the other way around.]

THERAPIST: Mr. West—

GEORGE: [Would you like me to speak to you instead of signing? Is that it? Will that make the entire hearing world happy?]

Barbara reenters with Allison. Allison stays behind George.

GEORGE: [Before the operation, before all the speech therapy, you thought Allison was someone who needed to be "corrected."

I don't care what anyone says, my daughter inherited her deafness. Do you know what that means? To inherit something? It means it was always meant to be a part of her. It's handed down from generations before her. It is the past reaching forward into the future and tapping her on the shoulder to remind her that in our family, deafness is not a disability, but an inevitability. That's what she is to me. Inevitable. And before any of this happened, to me, my daughter was—]

He waves the Interpreter to stop interpreting.

GEORGE: [Perfect! Perfect! She is perfect!]

George turns around and sees Allison.

Scene 8

Shift to Bell and Mabel.

MABEL: They come and go. The spots.

BELL: How far apart?

MABEL: It used to be once a day. Now it's every hour.

BELL: Mabel. You didn't tell me they were getting that bad.

MABEL: I tried. Sometimes you don't . . .

BELL: Forgive me.

MABEL: There is no need to ask for forgiveness.

BELL: . . .

MABEL: Alec? What are you thinking?

Beat.

BELL: I'm thinking about when we first met.

MABEL: I was fifteen. My father hired you to teach me to lip read.

BELL: Yes. I remember the night I officially called upon you. We had a thorough conversation in the greenhouse. I went home elated and the next morning received a note from you. All it said was "I do not dislike you."

They share a laugh.

MABEL: I've been rereading all of my books. Before everything goes dark on me.

BELL: Mabel—

MABEL: No, it's all right. The books comfort me. The words, the texture of the pages. Last night I combed through the dictionaries. I looked up the word sound. Not sound that you can hear. But the other sound. As in water.

BELL: Like the Vineyard Sound.

MABEL: Yes. I always thought sound was a strange word for water. So I did some digging of my own. It originates from the old Norse word Sund.

BELL: I knew that.

MABEL: It means "gap."

George appears. He is sitting on a pier.

BELL: It makes sense, since the Vineyard Sound runs between the two islands.

Allison appears.

MABEL: I dug a little deeper and I discovered another meaning for Sund. It can also mean "swimming." I like that better.

BELL: Why, you don't swim?

MABEL: I guess because even though there is a gap in between the two lands . . . a Sound is narrow enough for anyone, if he or she is willing, to swim across.

BELL: I would like to have made more progress.

MABEL: Perhaps it's not meant to be, Alec.

BELL: Perhaps not in my lifetime. But at some point in the future, the deaf will hear again. And when they do . . . I can only imagine what it will be like for them.

Mabel extends her hand.

MABEL: Come home dear Alec. Come home to me and Elsie. Your daughter does not dislike you.

Bell reaches out for her. They disappear. George and Allison remain.

EPILOGUE: sound

George is on the pier, tying a lure to a fishing pole.

Allison taps George on the shoulder.

ALLISON: [Did you wet the fishing line? You don't want it to snap on you.]

GEORGE: [I don't expect any big fish to bite near the pier.]

ALLISON: [You never know what's down there.]

GEORGE: [I actually kinda do.]

She sees George his having trouble tying his lure.

ALLISON: [Here, let me.]

She sits next to him and helps.

GEORGE: [A double jam knot? When did I teach you that?]

ALLISON: [You didn't. But I watched you tie this knot over and over again. Then I taught myself.]

GEORGE: [How old were you?]

ALLISON: [I think I was ten.]

GEORGE: [I'm impressed.]

ALLISON: [That was the point.]

Long silence.

ALLISON: [Dad?] *(beat)* [I'm sorry.]

GEORGE: [Me too]

George hands Allison a fishing pole.

They cast their lines out to sea.

ALLISON: [Do you know what I love most about fishing?]

GEORGE: [What?]

Allison turns off her receiver and removes it from her ear.

ALLISON: [The quiet.]

They both stare out and take in the silence of the Vineyard Sound. Lights slowly fade to black.

END OF PLAY

REFERENCES:

Inside Deaf Culture
By Carol Padden and Tom Huphries 2005

Everyone Here Spoke Sign Language
by Nora Groce

The Bell Family Papers—Library of Congress
http://memory.loc.gov/ammem/bellhtml/bellhome.html

Upon the Formation of a Deaf Variety of the Human Race
By Alexander Graham Bell

"True Love and Sympathy" The Deaf-Deaf Marriages Debate in Transatlantic Perspective
By Joseph J. Murray

Genetics, Disability, and Deafness
By John Vickrey Van Cleve 2004

Bell's Work on the Vineyard
Martha's Vineyard Gazette, July 10, 1992

Pages of History: The Martha's Vineyard Deaf Community
by Donna Scaglione—Martha's Vineyard Life 2006

Never the Twain Shall Meet: Bell, Gallaudet, and the Communications Debate
By Richard Winefield

SEAYOUNG YIM is a Seattle-based playwright. Her play, *Do It For Umma*, won both the People's Choice Award for Outstanding New Play at the Gregory Awards and Seattle's Gypsy Rose Lee Award for Excellence in Local Playwriting in 2016. Her work has been featured at Annex Theatre, Theatre Off Jackson, Mirror Stage, Theatre Battery, Live Girls! Theater, Pony World, SIS Productions, Pork Filled Productions, and 14/48 Projects. She is a member of the SIS Writers Group, a collective of Asian American playwrights. In addition to theater, Seayoung has been involved with various social and racial justice organizations in Washington State.

Seayoung Yim

Do It For Umma

CHARACTERS:

UMMA   Korean, 60-something mother to Hannah and Jason. Ghost and owner of the convenience store. Intense, terrifying, with a hidden sense of humor.

HANNAH   Korean, 20-something daughter of Umma. Jaded and vulnerable, trying to get her shit together.

JASON   Korean, 30-something son of Umma. Handsome and charming with some douchebag tendencies.

MRS. YI   Korean, 50-something owner of a dry cleaner next door to the convenience store. Outwardly serene and open, inwardly calculating.

DREA   20-something strip mall security guard. Law student. Earnest and principled. In love with Hannah.

THREE CHORUS MEMBERS   The chorus members tell the parts of the story that may be unsaid and help transitions between scenes and worlds. They may move together as a unit of ajummas (middle aged or older Korean women who stereotypically may wear visors, floral or patterned button shirts, and voluminous pants.) CHORUS 1 and 3 play Korean Drama characters: Mrs. Hwang and Mrs. Jo, and CHORUS 2 plays the Korean drama narrator.

SETTING:

An American strip mall with a dry cleaner and a convenience store

TIME:

Present day or a few years earlier

ACT I

Prologue

At the convenience store in a ghostly realm. Umma's shadow is seen walking. Lights up on Chorus.

CHORUS ALL: Things you may buy in a Korean-owned convenience store.

CHORUS 2: Six-packs of beer kept at 38 degrees.

CHORUS 3: Deep-fried burritos.

CHORUS 1: "Oriental items," such as nunchucks and ninja stars and Buddha.

CHORUS 2: Patriotic items, such as American eagle figurines, $19.99.

CHORUS 3: Cans of pop: all kinds, regular and diet.

CHORUS 1: Cigarettes and chewing tobacco.

CHORUS 2: Gummy worms, 10 cents.

CHORUS 3: Random t-shirts.

CHORUS 1: Cardboard cut outs of beer mascots.

CHORUS 2: Packs of herbal supplements for penis enlargement.

CHORUS ALL: $6.99.

CHORUS 3: Lotto and scratch tickets.

CHORUS ALL: MAYBE YOU WON!

An ominous sound is heard.

CHORUS ALL: And all these things make up the bee-jee-ness of comfort.

Doorbell sounds. Umma enters and talks to an unseen customer.

UMMA: Very nice. You like t-shirt? Only $6.99. 100 percent cotton. You try? Don't like? OK. Thank you!

Chorus and Umma wave to the customer sweetly.

UMMA: (*To Chorus, who listen to her raptly.*) Asshole always come in and mess up t-shirts. Unfold every t-shirt. Like dis, make biiig mess. But they never ever buy nothing. Makes my blood pressure so high! Always say, "How muchee?" "How muchee?" How muchee, my ass. Eh, you know when you inside a store don't ask the clerk, "What time you close? I come back later." That's bullshit. You never come back. I know. So many times, I heat up my food in microwave cuz sooo hungry. Bastards come in, then I have to stop. Don't buy nothing and my food is cold. So, I heat it up gain. Then another bastard comes in!

Store doorbell sounds.

UMMA: So yeah, this my store. You look. Look, we got nice stuff. Look, aaall this kind of candy we sell. Oh, you know, when I was kid, we soooo hungry we ate army base garbage and make kkool kkool ee jook. You know, kkool kkool?

(*Makes pig noises.*) You take whatever shit, dis and dat, and boil it down: kkool kkool. Get it? My family, we took turn eating, different days. One time, American G.I. feel sorry for me and gave me candy bar. Woo-WAH. I put it in mouth, and it was most delicious thing I taste. I was so selpish, didn't share with nobody. But I eat dis, and all my pain go away. I thought: "This how America tastes, everyday?" But you know, you have too much just one thing—it all tastes like shit. Now I own all kind of American candy! Can you beliebe?

    Doorbell sounds.

UMMA: I don't like candy with hard caramel. My teeth not so good. No time going to dentist. Hard candy make your tooth loose if you chew too muchee. You know, very bad if you dream like your tooth falling out. Be carepul you never dream bad dream. Or your Umma gonna die.

CHORUS 1: This was the kingdom of UMMA, owner of THIS convenience store.

CHORUS 2: Every day, she wore the lipstick color: magenta crush.

CHORUS 3: Her poufy hair was always on point.

CHORUS 1: And lightly scented by deep-fried corndogs.

CHORUS 3: She worked standing seven days a week.

CHORUS 1: Her only respite was found watching VHS tapes of Korean Dramas in between customers.

CHORUS 2: She never had to pee because her bladder could hold all the water in the Yellow Sea.

CHORUS 1: Yes, all of this was her small fiefdom, until her untimely death this week.

CHORUS 3: She leaves behind a son, Jason.

    Chorus reacts giddily to the mention of Jason's name.

CHORUS 2: And a younger daughter, Hannah.

Scene I

    At night. Hannah is cleaning up the convenience store. She suddenly notices dead Umma in the store. Hannah screams and falls backward.

UMMA: Oh, you not happy to see Umma? OK, I go. You never gonna see me again.

HANNAH: You just died. I—I—I haven't even had a chance to talk to my therapist about grief.

UMMA: You go to therapist? You want people think you crazy? What matter with you?

HANNAH: Oh, my god. YOU! You're what's the matter with me!

UMMA: Don't be so sensitive. So weak.

HANNAH: I haven't even had time to process your death and you've already come back to harass me.

UMMA: Stupid. I saw my classmates executed before my eyes with machine gun. (*Makes machine gun motion.*) POW POW POW POW. You think I have time to talk therapy, process war? NO. Too busy working 7 day a week. You think Umma do nothing for you. But look: I took good care of you, gave you so much food, look how fat you got. Aigoo. You think this look good? Hanging out like dis? (*Beat.*) Yah, anyway we talk serious bee-jee-ness now.

HANNAH: What serious business? Oh, you're here to punish me because I've been procrastinating on funeral arrangements. Oh god. The funeral. Fuck, do I have a card that's not maxed out?

UMMA: I told you save money. Stupid. You know, church lady said her daughter bought her cruise trip to Europe AND Acura. She come over to store to brag. Of course, I have nothing to say cuz you buy me nothing when I live.

HANNAH: That's right. I suck! Why doesn't Jason get yelled at too? Shouldn't he do more since he's the oldest?

UMMA: Ah, my Jason. My son. How is he?

HANNAH: Fine, I guess. (*Beat.*) You know what? I'll take care of the funeral. That's the least I can do, since I suck so bad.

UMMA: No. Don't waste your money on puneral.

HANNAH: Umma, you sure? Costco has some nice caskets. Affordable.

UMMA: You save your money. Sign up for Weight Watchers. And you, lazy ass, can't even keep your room clean, and you kill all the houseplants. How you gonna take care of my grave, lazy? Shameful. No. You just do simple cremation; scatter my ashes somewhere pretty like water fountain at Nordstrom.

HANNAH: Oh, I think I saw a Groupon for a cremation that looks—

UMMA: OK, you shut up now. I want to talk you serious. About boke soo. You know what boke soo is?

HANNAH: Um. No.

UMMA: Aissh! Why you no pay attention during Korean school?

HANNAH: I don't know. Maybe because I preferred to watch cartoons on Saturdays instead of hanging around sanctimonious bitchez.

UMMA: AISSH! Don't say bad word: "Bitchee." You be lady. Lady don't say word like bitchee. You want people to think I do bad job cuz I am single mom? (*Beat.*) Anyway, stupid. Boke soo means revenge.

HANNAH: Bahk soo.

UMMA: Why you say it like white person? BOKE SOO. BOKE SOO.

HANNAH: Bahk soo. Bo-Boke soo.

UMMA: Ung. You need to do boke soo for me. Do it for Umma.

HANNAH: For what?

UMMA: My murder. Next door lady kill me, Mrs. Yi.

HANNAH: Mrs. Yi at the dry cleaners?

UMMA: Yeah, she is real bitchee.

HANNAH: She seems so nice though. Wow. Cold-blooded. So cold-blooded.

UMMA: You give me boke soo. You kill her for me.

HANNAH: Gosh, Umma. I really want you to be avenged and all, but damn. This interaction could be a hallucination or the result of all the drugs I took in high school.

UMMA: Oh my jee-jus! You did drug? I can't breathe. Oh, my blood pressure. I feel faint! You're going to kill me with your wickedness.

Umma begins fanning herself. Hannah looks at her unmoved.

HANNAH: Nice try. I was about to feel hella guilty, but then I remembered that you're already dead. Nope, can't pull that shit on me anymore. And now, nothing fazes me when I'm on Prozac.

UMMA: You do revenge! I am your Umma. I won't leave you until you do it. Listen to me. Look at my eyes. What do you see?

HANNAH: Please don't make me count your wrinkles again. You still have great skin. Even as a dead person.

UMMA: No, you bah-boh-ya! My eyes! My NOON! Look at my eyeballs. What do you see?

HANNAH: They're bloodshot?

UMMA: See? Sign of powl play.

HANNAH: OHHH. Foul play. Really though? You're always staying up late working. That's why.

UMMA: YAH! Eeh nyun-ah! You spending all the time watching Law and Order, no studying. Still you learn NOTHING. Blood vessel breaking in noon is sign of powl play.

HANNAH: FOUL, UMMA. FFFFOUL!

UMMA: OK, you little shit. "FOUL PLAY!" You know what the Mrs. Yi did to me? She come in here after we closed. She bring me blouse I asked her to dry clean. I gib her Diet Coke. You know, she never pay cuz she bitchee. She eat all potato chip like dis. And the Kit Kat. She eat all my food and she neber gib me discount for dry cleaning. Yam chay jee? So, she keep talking and talking about boring dis and dat. Talking and eating, mouth open like a farmer. Won't shut up, like she nerbis.

HANNAH: Nervous?

UMMA: That's what I said. Why you so stupid?

HANNAH: Because you didn't breastfeed me. I didn't get the colostrum to make me smart. All I got was that shitty formula.

UMMA: They told me all American thing is best, they say. American pormula better than my milk, they say. SO, I want to give you best.

HANNAH: But you breastfed Jason.

UMMA: That's because we had no money to buy pormula when he baby. We didn't have store. Then when you born, we have store, but your shitty appah was gone drinking all time. I was so stressed running store myself. And you look like him. That's why you stress me out so much! You have his shitty blood! And what? You want me to take out boob while helping customers? Disgusting!

HANNAH: I need to lie down. Sleep or wake up from this.

UMMA: No rest until you give me boke soo.

HANNAH: Ask Jason for help! I bet when you visit his 30-something-year-old ass, you'll be offering to clip his toenails and cook him ghost food. But me? You come here and ask me to commit murder and clean up shit! Is it cuz I'm a girl? Why do I always have to wipe everyone ELSE'S ass? What about me?

UMMA: Yah! You think I don't wipe your ass? I wipe so many ass. I am ass champion!

HANNAH: I don't even know what to say. God! Don't all your emotional needs get met in the underworld? Do you still need me to fulfill your hopes and dreams?

UMMA: No rest until you give me BOKE SOO.

The front door opens and door buzzes. Sound of footsteps.

HANNAH: Umma, who is that? Oh my god? Is it her? UMMA?

Umma is gone. Hannah closes her eyes in fear. Drea enters wearing her security guard uniform.

DREA: Hannah?

Hannah screams.

DREA: Hannah, it's just me. Sheesh.

HANNAH: DREA! You scared the shit out of me!

DREA: Sorry, Hannah! I came as soon as I could. How are you doing?

HANNAH: I'm doing terrible. I'm not sure what's reality anymore.

DREA: That feeling is natural. Grief can really shake up your nervous system. Your energy seems very frenetic. Would you like a hug? Let me hold you.

Hannah accepts the hug.

HANNAH: What would I do without you?

DREA: Ah . . . well. It's nice to be needed. I just want to be there for you.

HANNAH: Are you hungry? I can microwave a pizza for you. Or you can have some onion dip in a jar—it's a new kind we just got in the store.

DREA: Well, it's like I'm booed up with a celebrity chef.

HANNAH: Ummm, except we're not together. I'm not your boo.

DREA: Oh, yeah, I know. It just feels like it cuz you're always spoiling me with food.

HANNAH: I get it from Umma. She was always shoving impossible amounts of food down my throat before the enemy could get it.

DREA: Who's the enemy?

HANNAH: Who knows? I think she was just traumatized from being starved as a kid. She'd always make more than one family could eat—then watch me eat it with such intensity, take it away from me mid-bite and call me fat, like a sacred ritual, repeated over the decades.

DREA: Well, it sure sounds like a complicated relationship. I'll pass on the food. Thank you. Trying to stay away from processed things. Have you tried the Whole 30 diet? My poops have been amazing since I—

HANNAH: DREA, do you think there's a way my Umma could have—Hey, have you noticed anything strange around here in the mall lately?

DREA: Oh, there's always strange stuff happening around here.

HANNAH: Like what?

DREA: Well, the other day, I had to regulate on two people dressed up as furries, who decided to have a picnic right inside the middle of the take-and-bake pizza shop. Another time, I saw a man peeing into one of the public garbage cans. This was when I worked day shift, so all the little kids could see and there were a lot of 'em cuz it was during the sidewalk sale. So, you can imagine how awkward that was.

HANNAH: No, something more serious.

DREA: What could be more serious than whipping out your hoo-ha in the middle of the day and peeing in plain view of the general public?

HANNAH: Like violence. Murder. Foul play.

DREA: Aww, honey. You've been watching too many BBC murder mysteries. You see me as some kind of detective chief inspector. But I'm just a security guard by night, law student by day.

HANNAH: Fine, OK. But just keep your eyes out for me, though. Keep an eye out for Mrs. Yi.

DREA: Mrs. Yi at the dry cleaners? I thought you were cool with her.

HANNAH: Yeah, no. I hear she's a real bitch.

DREA: Well, I'm not just going to spy on her cuz you think she's a b-word.

HANNAH: I think she did my Umma wrong. Just keep an eye out on her. Please. Could you?

DREA: I suppose. But you know I won't go above the law. It wouldn't be right.

HANNAH: I know. I know. Just check on her and tell me if you see anything fishy. I'm just asking you to do what you normally do: keep an eyeball out.

DREA: You mean detect. This is the first step in security guard methodology. Detect any suspicious activity or issues.

HANNAH: That's all you do? You just detect shit? Well, you can't, like, arrest anybody though, right?

DREA: Well, we also try to deter. Like stop or try to stop a crime from occurring. If it got that serious, I would have to observe and report the crime to authorities.

HANNAH: It gets me all hot when you talk all official security lingo. Sooo, I want you to tell me if you detect any suspicious activity with Mrs. Yi, promise?

DREA: All right, I promise.

HANNAH: I love it when you're in uniform. It's so cute and dorky.

DREA: Hey, I need you to take me seriously right now.

HANNAH: I do, boo. I do.

DREA: Oh, now I'm your boo.

HANNAH: Oh, shut up.

DREA: It's OK. I can wait.

They exit with Drea chasing Hannah flirtatiously.

Scene 2

The next day. In the back room of the convenience store, Jason and a woman are talking. Their voices are heard but they are not visible, perhaps only their shadows.

JASON: I know it's been a minute, but you know my Umma just died. No, you're the one for me. I never felt this way before. You make me feel royal. It feels like it feels like the Shilla Dynasty up in here. You bringing me persimmons and rice wine. I feel free flowing some pansori right now.

Jason may sing or lip-sync a line of pansori.

MRS. YI: That was so nice, Jason. Now, how much longer do I have to wait for you? I don't like being in the shadows like a servant. If I am your queen, I want to be in the light. Up high on a throne. Next to you. I want to wear my braids high above my head.

JASON: For sure. For sure. You're my woman, you know?

MRS. YI: Jason, how do I know?

JASON: Fine. Done. You got it. From this moment, you are my queen, my wang-bee.

MRS. YI: Call me your majesty.

JASON: Your majesty.

MRS. YI: Say it in Korean.

JASON: Dae wang ma-ma!

MRS. YI: Now say your divine favor shines greatly upon me.

JASON: Shit, I don't know how to say that. That's too hard.

MRS. YI: Aisssh. Why didn't you study Korean harder? Sung-oon ee mahng kup hah nai dah. IS that so hard?

JASON: Umma always gave me shit for that too.

> Footsteps of Hannah are heard.

JASON: Sssh!

HANNAH: (Yells from offstage.) Jason? Jason, you asshole! Are you back here?

> Jason scrambles and motions for the woman to exit after a rushed kiss. She exits. Hannah enters the back room.

HANNAH: Jason! JASON SUNG KIM!

JASON: DAMN. Why you gotta put my government out there like that? First, middle, last name. Now anybody could have my personal info and could be stealing my identity.

HANNAH: Nobody gives a fuck about your name, Jason. God. Paranoid. What are you doing here anyways?

JASON: You my little sis. Trying to be brotherly. You should call me Oppah. Why don't you call me Oppah? Show some respect.

HANNAH: I will never call you Oppah. Gross. You don't show me any respect—making me run the store by myself when you're in the back doing the nasty in Umma's store. I heard a girl's voice back there. The SHAME.

JASON: Damn, why you always ear hustling my convos? Look, I was gonna help. I just had a situation. I'm here now. Present.

HANNAH: Yo, I was googling Korean funerals and it looks like you have a shit ton to do for Umma's funeral.

JASON: Why me?

HANNAH: Cuz you're the "jang nam?"

JASON: Huh? What's that?

HANNAH: God, why don't you know Korean? Jang nam is the eldest son.

JASON: Oh shut the fuck up. You don't even know that much more Korean than I do, besides what little you learned from the stupid Korean dramas you and Umma watch.

HANNAH: Whatever. I've been reading up on this and no wonder she was nicer to you than me. Always getting fed first. I know there was at least one time you were fatter than me, and she called you, "handsome and sturdy," but called me fat. HEY. Are you listening? You have to organize a bunch of shit for the funeral.

HANNAH: Like what?

Chorus and Umma enter solemnly. Umma is inside a large picture frame wrapped in black ribbon as if she is a still portrait. Chorus becomes Google search results.

CHORUS 1: The eldest son should wear a black suit with a hemp armband.

CHORUS 2: Carefully collect the nail clippings of toes and fingers from your Uh-Mo-Nee and place them into a pouch with the burial.

CHORUS 3: Feed three spoonfuls of rice to your Umma via a willow spoon.

CHORUS 1: Add coins. Rice and money for a safe journey to the other place.

CHORUS 2: Wrap a framed photo of your Umma in black ribbon.

CHORUS 3: Offer to guests, simple foods: rice cakes, beef soup, fruits.

CHORUS 1: Don't forget to also offer: alcohol, a symbol of happiness. Very important.

CHORUS 2: Prepare a grief room, where your wail must be the loudest.

CHORUS 3: Beat your chest—Pound and wail.

CHORUS 2 AND 3: Pound and wail.

CHORUS ALL: Pound and wail til bruises form. Bow 90 degrees to your mother. BOW TO YOUR MOTHER!

UMMA: Hey lazy. Why you taking so long? WHY MRS. YI NOT DEAD YET?

Umma motions a throat-slitting motion to get Hannah's attention. Hannah frantically motions for her to go away. The funeral procession disappears.

JASON: All these funeral instructions seem so mystical. There must have been some practical reasons why our people did this shit. I miss her. It sounds so quiet in the store without her yelling. At us. At customers or the beer delivery guy. The quiet is just so weird.

HANNAH: Funny, I can still hear her pretty clearly. (*Beat.*) Hey. So . . . why do you think Umma died?

JASON: It was a heart attack.

HANNAH: You don't think there was something fishy? Like "powl play?"

JASON: What the H is powl play?

HANNAH: Sorry, I mean foul play. You know, suspicious activity. Because she died too soon. She should've outlived us all, since you know she was always eating those special beans and health powders. And getting stronger every day, like a shaman wizard.

JASON: Yeah, her and those powdered tiger testicles and shit. She would be like:

Umma appears or her voice is heard to say the next lines as Jason mouths them.

UMMA: "Jason-Ah, come here. I make you smoothie. Very expensive, I order from Korea, OK? Dis make your future wife very happy, Jason. Put in some epport, understand?"

JASON: I think that was the closest thing to a sex talk we ever had. Hey, maybe she'd be glad that I'm getting some now.

HANNAH: No, she hates sex. Probably because nobody ever went down on her.

JASON: WHAT? Who says shit like that? You don't know that. Never mind. Change the subject.

HANNAH: So back to her death. Could it be possible that someone killed her?

JASON: Get the fuck out of here. Who would want to kill our Umma? She was just an adorable little AJUMMA.

Lights shift. Chorus appears.

CHORUS 1: Ajumma: originally a respectful term for a married woman.

CHORUS 2: As a stereotype, ajumma can mean an older woman with a low social status.

CHORUS 3: One who is pushy and aggressive.

CHORUS 1: One who often wears mismatched prints.

CHORUS 2: And golf accessories. (*Pronounced: gol-poo ahk sae sah ree.*) Like a visor.

CHORUS 3: And sports a short poufy perm for volume. (*Pronounced: BOLE YUME.*)

Chorus disappears.

JASON: She was just an adorable little AJUMMA. And she'd curb stomp you if you fucked with her, so trust: anybody, who tried, would be the one dead. Not her. And I can't really imagine anyone wanting to kill her.

HANNAH: What about a neighbor? Like Mrs. Yi, for example.

JASON: OK, maybe you need to rest up cuz the grief is taking its toll. Wait, why are you bringing up Mrs. Yi?

HANNAH: Jason, I think I'm having visions. Please don't minimize what I'm about to say. Jason, I saw Umma. Right here in midst of the cases of Rainier and Schlitz.

JASON: Nah. Nah. Nah! This is what happens when you watch too many Ghost Hunting shows.

HANNAH: No, she came to me. Jason, it was terrible. She was yelling at me, "BOKE SOO! BOKE SOO!" She said: Mrs. Yi killed her.

JASON: I need you to get a grip. Take a nap cuz there is no way Umma was murdered. She had a heart attack. Sit down. You have no proof of this at all.

HANNAH: You're right. How do I get Umma to stop bothering me? HELP ME, JASON! You're my only family now. God. That's depressing. BOKE SOO, Jason! BOKE SOO!

JASON: There's no need for fucking boke soo. Like Biggie said, "It was all a dream!" Take a nap. Want me to roll you a blunt? No, wait, that makes your hallucinations worse. Yeah, no. Here, have some beer. Beer makes everyone happy.

Jason sits Hannah down with a can of beer. He joins her.

JASON: Dude, isn't this, like, nice? Brother and sister hanging out, chilling, having a beer together. Admittedly, it's been a minute.

HANNAH: Seriously though, why are you here? You hate the store. You never come here. Don't you have to work?

JASON: I got laid off, maybe fired. So, I got time for some family bonding and shit. So, I'll be here more.

HANNAH: (*Hannah can barely hide her glee.*) I'm sorry. YOU got fired from your fancy engineering job? Oh, the disgrace.

JASON: Don't seem so happy about it. I was supportive of you when you finished community college and got a retail job.

HANNAH: Fuck you, Jason. Classist.

JASON: Hey, I got feelings too. Stop being a dick to me. Our mom just died. Let's just try to bond and shit. Or at least get drunk together. OK?

They cheers their beers and then have a contest to see who can shotgun their beer the fastest. Jason cheats by blocking her from drinking, so he can win. He exits victoriously. Hannah might flip him off.

Scene 3

Later that evening. Umma sits over Hannah, who opens a can of beer and shotguns it.

UMMA: YAH! Stop drinking so much. Oh-mo. Oh-mo. Look at this girl. Oh-mo.

HANNAH: OK. I'm ready. Tell me. How did she kill you?

UMMA: So, she came in. Drinking two can of my Diet Coke and she ate my potato—

HANNAH: Yeah, you already said that!

UMMA: Don't snap at your dead mother, you little shit.

HANNAH: Sorry, but you're repeating yourself.

UMMA: It's Alzheimer! You make me so crazy I get Alzheimer. Uh yoo, neh hyeol ap ohl lah! (*Beat.*) So, Mrs. Yi, she come in. Bring in dry clean blouse, but do very bad job. Still ketchup stain on front like dis. That night she act more weird. She try to be extra nice, she bring me her terrible cooking—some disgusting soup, tastes like dog shit. She just sit there in pront of me, waiting so she can watch me eat, like stalker. I want her to leave so I can finish watching my Korean bideo but she stay. Her big face staring at me, like dis: like a biiiiiig ugly watermelon. Then, finally she say she want to buy my store.

HANNAH: Why the hell does she want to buy our convenience store?

UMMA: That's what I said. But she said no. She want to expand her dry cleaners. Tear out wall make one big green eco-friendly cleaner.

HANNAH: Huh. Why didn't you just sell it to her? You were always bitching about the long hours and crappy profit margin.

UMMA: Yes, bee-jee-ness very bad. Look, I start selling porno bideos to make more money even though I feel so bad to Jesus.

HANNAH: Then, I don't understand why you didn't just sell.

UMMA: But she offer me soooo little money for sale. She think I am stupid, desperate. Plus, I sell, what I do? Buy a new bee-jee-ness, start same bullshit all over again in different mall? I can't get job. Nobody gonna hire old lady with bad English. But here, my store. I am Queen. Nobody gonna tell me what to do.

Two chorus members enter to reenact Umma's murder as she describes it, using shadow play or pantomime. The mood should evoke an over-the-top Korean drama.

UMMA: That night, you know, Mrs. Yi hold my hand. So weird, yeah? I tell her stop being weird. But she gets on her knees and she begging, cry and cry. I tell her, I can't help her by being MINUS! I ask her please go, I closing store. She follow me to the door crying: waa wahh waahh. I slap her cuz I feel weird. We get to door. She put plastic dry cleaning bag, you know, big one like dis, and she put over my face. I try screaming but the bag hold my scream! Nobody gonna hear! Like dis! (*Umma lets out silent scream.*) My eyes explode in the bag. Pop! And then that's it. I die. I fall over cases of Pabst, Schimdt, and Rainier. Make biiiiig mess.

Chorus vanishes.

UMMA: (*Beat.*) You like this, huh? You like Umma dead. So, I don't bother you no more. You don't have to take care Umma when she old. You happy, huh?

HANNAH: To be honest, I'm kind of relieved. You always made me feel so heavy. Not just because you always called me fat. But because you always said I ruined your life. Why couldn't you be a little softer to me? I remember other kids got notes in their lunches from their moms with hearts and stuff. You never wrote me any. I used to write my own notes, and have you sign them like they were permission slips. "Have a good day at school. Love, Mrs. S. H. Kim." I know I had it way better than you did, compared to what you've been through. And that's what makes you so strong. But fuck, it's so hard being around you.

UMMA: I only say hard things because I care. You think your prends, friends care? They just say oh you be lazy. It's OK, smoke the dope, work in art supply store porever. No problem. But you know who care more than anybody? Your UMMA! Your Umma cares! And nobody gonna tell you be better cuz nobody care except your Umma. Everything I did: good, bad—all for you. Because Umma loves you! Why I have to say out loud? Make it cheap. You know already. Don't have to say.

HANNAH: It's so sad that I have to be drunk to hear you say that you love me. Why is that?

UMMA: This is dwipuri. You know dwipuri? You work hard all day. You have to be strong because enemy, like your neighbor, might take everything. But it is hard being strong all of time, understand? Sometime we drinking so we can be soft. You know, when you born it feel my heart now outside my body walking around, I get smash anytime. Hannah-yah, wait if you ever have child, you will know. You suppering never end till you die. But, I am dead and still I supper! Now, make Umma peaceful in heart. I raise you. Now make Umma proud.

HANNAH: I tried my whole life. I don't know how.

UMMA: Now you know. Kill Mrs. Yi.

HANNAH: How do I even know she's guilty? I can't just take your word for it!

UMMA: Make her supper how she make your Umma supper. She needs to be stomped to death! She left me here to die, your Umma. You can't let me wander my store with the HAN boiling in my chest. You must release it for me before I explode and make black hole.

Door knocking is heard.

HANNAH: Fuck, who is that? Can't they see we're closed?

More knocking.

MRS. YI: (*Offstage*) Hannah? Hannah-yah! You there? I saw your car in the parking lot.

HANNAH: Mrs. Yi? I can't breathe. I can't breathe! Umma, I don't know what to do.

UMMA: You know: KILL HER.

HANNAH: Umma, I'm, I can't. I'm not ready! I don't believe you yet!

MRS. YI: (*Offstage*) Hannah-yah. I have something for you. I brought you some soup.

UMMA: See? She's always bring her shit soup. (*Beat.*) Oh, my god. What if she want to kill you? Kill her before she kill you. Kill her, Hannah. Self-depense!

Umma exits.

MRS. YI: Where is this child? Hannah-yah! You sleeping?

HANNAH: Mrs. Yi? I'm here. I'm awake. I'm coming.

Mrs. Yi enters holding a big pot of soup. Chorus enters.

CHORUS 2: (*As narrator*) For a minute, Hannah's brain was jumbled and burnt up like some dol sot bi bim bap, forehead sweating like condensation off of a chigae pot. But she collected herself. And she had a thought. She would invite Mrs. Yi to watch a Korean drama to determine her guilt. She decided the best way to get into the psyche of this woman was to observe her reaction to melodrama on screen that mirrored real life. SHEE-JAK!

HANNAH: (*Hannah bows.*) Ahn young hah sae yo, Mrs. Yi. Please come in. Sit. Sit. Would you like to chew on some dried octopus? Or sip on water, beer, or your favorite: Diet Coke! How about some Kit Kats or potato chips?! Whatever you feel . . .

MRS. YI: Oh, you poor motherless child. Let me look at you. Oh. Ee lee wah. You'll never be as beautiful like your mother, but you have nice strong legs like an ox. Here, have some soup.

HANNAH: Maybe in a little bit. Please don't trouble yourself. Say, would you like to watch with me the latest and greatest of Korean dramas?

Mrs. Yi and Hannah watch a drama. Dramatic, emotionally wrenching Korean drama music plays. Chorus become Mrs. Hwang and Mrs. Jo.

CHORUS 2: (*As narrator*) "Love's Flower Crushed by the Cruel Heel of Time" or "Kkote Sah-rang" in Korean. Picture this! 1970s, Republic of Korea— the country in the throes of yet another US-backed military dictatorship. Episode 57. The beautiful and formidable Mrs. Hwang is finally now the CEO of a heating pad dynasty. You know, the kind for heating up your booty at night in bed. It's a very lucrative way to build a business empire, really, given Koreans never turn on the house heat.

Mrs. Hwang is seated at a desk. She is played by Chorus 1. Mrs. Jo stands before Mrs. Hwang, head bowed, eye contact avoided in a deferential manner, and hands folded. She is played by Chorus 3.

MRS. JO: So, Sah-jang-nim, what do you think of the new heating pad designs?

Mrs. Hwang flings papers in Mrs. Jo's face.

MRS. HWANG: Yah, when you go to sleep tonight, why don't you close all the windows and leave the fan on? So, you can die . . . of fan death!

MRS. JO: (*Mrs. Jo is fake crying.*) That's so cruel. I don't understand, Sah-jang-nim.

MRS. HWANG: Oh, you don't, do you? I know you've been plotting against me, Mrs. Jo.

MRS. JO: No. NO! I've only been a faithful servant to you.

MRS. HWANG: You think I don't know? You've seduced my only son because you covet my kingdom. Treacherous bitch!

> *Cue dramatic music. Mrs. Hwang dramatically slaps Mrs. Jo to the ground. She then looks defiantly and directly at the audience, as if it is a camera.*

MRS. JO: Well, so now you know. Your reign is over, hag. Time for a new queen.

MRS. HWANG: Moh? Guh-lae gat un nyun! You'll get nothing from me!

> *Mrs. Hwang moves to strike her. Mrs. Jo overpowers her and takes a heating pad cord to choke Mrs. Hwang to death. Mrs. Jo stands over her dead body and laughs. Focus shifts back to Hannah and Mrs. Yi.*

HANNAH: Mrs. Yi? Are you alright?

MRS. YI: Oh mo. This is just so violent. I—I didn't know this was gonna be so violent. Oh dear. I, um.

HANNAH: Mrs. Yi. Are you unwell?

MRS. YI: No. Just a little stomachache.

HANNAH: Oh yes, the sight of murder gets my stomach flipping too. Do you have diarrhea? I got meds for that, you want some—

MRS. YI: I should get back to the store.

HANNAH: But this is just the prologue. Don't you want to know what happens to the MURDEROUS Mrs. Jo?

MRS. YI: I'll come by later and maybe we can finish it.

> *Frazzled, Mrs. Yi exits. Umma enters.*

HANNAH: You want to know what I think?

UMMA: What do you think, my daughter?

HANNAH: The bitch is guilty.

UMMA: I KNOW.

HANNAH: It's fucking ON NOW.

UMMA: Now, she is your won soo, too.

HANNAH: Won soo?

UMMA: Mortal ENEMY. WON SOO UHL GAHP UH RAH!!!!!

UMMA AND HANNAH: WON SOO UHL GAHP UH RAH!!!!

Scene 4

At the convenience store. Hannah is putting plastic six-pack rings on cans of beer and or stickering items with price gun. Drea enters.

DREA: Hey, Hannah.

Hannah shrieks in surprise.

DREA: Whoa. Whoa. It's just me. You really need to stop screaming every time I come a-courtin'.

HANNAH: Sorry. I'm so jumpy lately.

DREA: I think you've always been a little jumpy. Like you have PTSD or something. *(Beat.)* Ah, Hannah. We should like, give it a go. We could be so good together. There's so much sexual tension between us. I can feel it, can't you?

HANNAH: Oh, DREA. Why do you put up with me?

DREA: Uh-oh. This kind of sounds like a rejection.

HANNAH: Like you keep hanging around, like this dust on the cases of beer. And I am over there like a feather duster, to brush you away. But you always come back. Always. Why?

DREA: Dust? Well, that's not very flattering.

HANNAH: And yet, if you don't come back, I sort of miss you. But, I'm sorry. I'm not sure if I'm ready for a healthy relationship with appropriate boundaries. Maybe later?

DREA: All right. It's no problem. Really. I will wait. There's a strange sort of allure in your emotional distance.

HANNAH: DREA. Intermission. Mrs. Yi killed my mom. I KNOW NOW.

DREA: Urrr, what?

HANNAH: Yes, she fucking killed my mom.

DREA: But urrr, how do you know this?

HANNAH: I just have a feeling. Trust me, I have a way of reading people. Come on, let's go detect some shit. I want to spy on her.

DREA: OH, I just came over cuz it's my 15-minute break. I was hoping we could just fool around a little before I had to go back on my shift.

HANNAH: There ain't no time for fooling around, you fool! Don't you see, my mother's honor is at stake!?

DREA: What is it that you plan to do exactly?

HANNAH: I want to gather more evidence of her villainy.

DREA: I thought "YOU KNEW" already.

HANNAH: Come on. If you go with me, I can prove to you that she's a bitchface.

DREA: Well, I gotta go now. My time's about up. I got to get back to guarding the sex shop. Lots of people stealing vibrators these days.

HANNAH: OK, after your shift.

DREA: I got finish my law school paper. It's due tomorrow. I gotta stay up all night.

HANNAH: I have a feeling you're putting me on the bottom shelf. You used to treat me like Dom Pérignon and now I'm just some half-drunken box wine.

DREA: Wow, I know you keep saying we're not together. But with your guilt tripping me this hard, it sure feels like we're together. THIS is what monogamy feels like.

HANNAH: Fine, whatever. I don't have time for you either.

DREA: Hannah, don't be like that. (*Beat.*) Oh hey. I was thinking about what you asked me about seeing anything strange around the mall. I don't want you to freak out. What I saw is technically a crime, given the back lot is a public space visible to the general public.

HANNAH: Yeah, ok, what did you see?

DREA: Well, I saw two people in a car during one of my late shifts last week. A car parked in the back parking lot and they were . . . they were . . . um—

HANNAH: Well what? What? Spit it out!

Drea pantomimes various sex acts.

HANNAH: WHAT?!

Scene 5

At Mrs. Yi's dry cleaners. A chorus of abandoned clothes enters and cascades down stage as if they are on a garment conveyer circling in a loop.

Mrs. Yi controls the conveyer belt, delighting in her power to make them move and stop at will. She marvels at how many customers she has. Perhaps she dances with the clothes and stops the conveyer belt when Umma appears on the belt, suspended, and dead. She awakens.

UMMA: You killed me. I don't po-get, BITCHEE! I neber PO-GET!

Mrs. Yi screams, escaping, and runs into Jason's arms.

Scene 6

Lights are dim. Jason and Mrs. Yi are making out passionately at the dry cleaners. Then they stop.

MRS. YI: What's the matter?

UMMA: My mother is dead. I'm bummed out. I wish she was still here.

MRS. YI: Oh, my darling. I'm here. Let me hold you. You must be strong because sadness is a weakness, Jason.

JASON: And I got laid off.

MRS. YI: You what? Oh, that's OK. You'll get another job. You're smart and young.

JASON: Most of all I'm stressed cuz Hannah says there's all this funeral shit I gotta do cuz I'm the eldest son. Is that true?

MRS. YI: Yes. You're the jang nam.

JASON: See, I knew you would know. What else do I need to do? Food, right? Ah, could you help me get the good food cuz me and Hannah only knows how to microwave Hot Pockets. And like, I got to get a picture of Umma and frame it with a black ribbon, right? Oh, and I also got to bow to it in front of everyone, huh?

MRS. YI: Can we not talk about this now?! WHY IS EVERYTHING ABOUT YOUR UMMA? I'M SICK OF IT! YOU ARE SELFISH FOR WISHING SHE WAS STILL HERE.

JASON: What the fuck? Fine.

Jason moves to exit.

MRS. YI: Oh, god. I'm sorry, honey. Don't leave. I guess it just hurt me to see you in such pain. It was overwhelming. I'm sorry. Forgive me. I said the wrong things.

JASON: Umm, did you have anything against my Umma? Or Hannah?

MRS. YI: Ha, why would you ask that?

JASON: Hannah is maybe having a breakdown. She is convinced that that you killed our Umma. I know it sounds super out there. But she is serious about it.

MRS. YI: Grief takes shape in many forms. It spurs some to blame mere humans for what is in God's plan. I had nothing against your Umma. Truth be told, I had hoped we would become close like sisters—we being neighbors and all. And that she would become like an Unni to me. And maybe, we could rely on each other. But she never warmed up to me. She never invited me over. Never asked me for a favor. I always had to go to her. She never, ever, melted her heart. But Jason, I never took it personally. Never. Because I eventually understood she liked doing things her own way and that was OK.

JASON: I understand. I didn't mean to insinuate anything, OK, ajumma?

MRS. YI: JASON! DON'T call me AJUMMA. Anything but AJUMMA.

JASON: But I've called you AJUMMA since I was a kid.

MRS. YI: But, I'm not that old, am I? Don't I look young still?

JASON: Oh yeah. You definitely look good.

MRS. YI: I've gotten so much done on my face. Flew three times to Korea. That's why my face is smooth as a baby's ass. Not like other women my age that look like baloney is peeling off their faces. So anyway, don't spoil my good feelings. Stop calling me AJUMMA and call me Candy.

JASON: Candy? Candy? Really? That's hilarious. Huh. Candy.

MRS. YI: This is my American name.

JASON: But why Candy? You don't look like a "Candy."

MRS. YI: It's a cute name. Cute, like me.

JASON: But that'll be so weird calling you Candy. You've always been ajum—

MRS. YI: STOP! STOP! That makes me feel OLD! I don't want to feel OLD! And don't you want to be closer to me, Jason? AJUMMA is such an ugly, old word. It puts distance between us. It puts years and years between us. Why is it that once you are married you are automatically AJUMMA? There is so much pressure to get married. "MARRY! MARRY MARRY!" they say. But once you do BOOM! You are AJUMMA. Even Mr. Yi has been dead long time—I am still AJUMMA. Seen as unfashionable. Old. BASIC. I try really hard to look like this. I only eat one meal per day. And wear corset to stay slim. I grow my hair long, you know—fashionable, like young girls do, not the short poufy perm like AJUMMA style. I wear all the cute clothes, and heels—even though I stand all day long washing clothes. I try to learn how you young people talk, like "that's so phat!" Eh? Dry cleaning on fleek! I try so hard—AND YOU STILL THINK I AM AN AJUMMA. I wish I was dead. I don't want to live as an AJUMMA. Why doesn't somebody just kill me? Just kill me!

Jason abruptly kisses Mrs. Yi.

JASON: Hey. You're the hottest AJUMMA I've ever known.

Mrs. Yi punches Jason.

MRS. YI: Little asshole. If you want to be with some young girl your age, that's fine. You're done playing with an old meatball like me. That's fine. Go ahead. I don't—

Jason abruptly kisses Mrs. Yi again.

MRS. YI: Call me Candy.

JASON: This seems so wrong. So disrespectful. C—aaaaa-ndy. And kind of hot, actually. The day I rear-ended you with my Lexus was the best day of my life.

MRS. YI: You were so apologetic. You came to get your dry cleaning done twice a week.

JASON: You finally warmed up to me. And even started packing food for me when I'd pick up the cleaning. And then that spring day—

MRS. YI: When I was reaching for the wire hangers on the top shelf—

JASON: You fell into my arms.

MRS. YI: Yes.

JASON: And we made out like we were sucking the marrow out of some beef bones.

MRS. YI: No, don't be so vulgar.

JASON: CANDY!

MRS. YI: JASON!

Jason and Mrs. Yi make out passionately. Clothes start coming off their bodies when suddenly a flashlight held by Hannah turns out to expose Jason and Mrs. Yi in mid-embrace. Hannah makes a retching noise.

JASON: Hannah?

HANNAH: OH, my fucking . . . DISGUSTING!

JASON: Hey Hannah.

HANNAH: UGGGGH! Ew! Ew! Ew! How could you? She's like Umma's age.

MRS. YI: No. I am at least 10 years younger than your Umma.

HANNAH: I can't. So, you two are just screwing everywhere and anywhere you can, huh? Screwing here, at the store, screwing in cars in the parking lot!

JASON: How did you know about the parking lot?

HANNAH: I have my eyes and ears out in the street, you nasty-ass.

JASON: Are you, like, spying on us? Spying on your own brother like a government informant!

MRS. YI: I thought you would be more open-minded, being a modern woman. Why is ok for an older man to be with a younger woman but not the way around? You are not a true feminist.

JASON: *(consigning with Mrs. Yi.)* DAAAMN.

HANNAH: Maybe I wouldn't mind so much if YOU DIDN'T KILL OUR UMMA. *(Hannah talks directly to Jason.)* Jason, listen to me. You can't trust this AJUMMA. She's full of treachery.

JASON: Hey. Don't call her AJUMMA. Call her Candy now.

HANNAH: Candy? Candy?

MRS. YI: Hannah, what's gotten into you? I didn't hurt your Umma! You sound so wild right now.

HANNAH: This is part of your plot, isn't it? Seducing Jason to take the store! I'm onto you, bitch. Jason, come with me. We need to talk.

JASON: You don't tell me what to do. I'm your Oppah. You listen to ME.

MRS. YI: Hannah-yah, I know it's hard for you but . . . Jason is my bae.

HANNAH: YOUR BAE?! Uh-uh. No. Come on, Jason. Let's go.

Hannah struggles to pull Jason away from Mrs. Yi. Jason pushes Hannah away.

JASON: I'm staying.

MRS. YI: See? He wants to stay with me.

HANNAH: I see you have Stockholm syndrome, Jason. Why is it that the only time you listen to women is when they are Umma's age?! Well, you let me know when you're really ready to be set free. Can't help those who don't want to be helped. UGH.

Hannah begins to exit but stops and looks through Mrs. Yi's trash. She pulls out a plastic dry cleaning bag with a magenta crush lipstick stain. She holds a flashlight to illuminate the lipstick. She takes it and exits

ACT II

Scene 7

Back at the convenience store with Hannah and Umma.

HANNAH: Can you believe it, UMMA? Jason and Mrs. Yi! So fucking nasty. (*Silence.*)

For how long do you think? And what's, like, the attraction? He can't be that good in bed. Bet he doesn't know how to caress anything but his video game controls and his Lexus—he's so selfish. Ugh. Why am I ruminating over something so disturbing? I guess he just wants to have an older Korean lady take care of him for the rest of his life. Oh, my god, he's replaced you with her. Do you think that's what's up? (*Pause.*) Are you in shock? Dude, did you KNOW?

UMMA: That night she tell me. Old bitchee!

HANNAH: UMMA, Damn! (*Beat.*) Why didn't you tell me?

UMMA: I thought I save you from bad thing. What I tell you? World is nasty place. TRUST NO ONE. Not even other Koreans. Especially other Koreans.

HANNAH: Do you think she's just using him to get our store?

UMMA: Ung.

HANNAH: Such an elaborate plot for a dry cleaning business expansion.

UMMA: You must stop her from taking our store. Convince Jason. I thought he smart cuz he go to college but he don't have no common sense.

HANNAH: What did Mrs. Yi say to you that night about Jason?

Mrs. Yi appears as a flashback.

MRS. YI: I love Jason. Please give us your blessing!

UMMA: EEh guh-lae gat un nyun! I kill you with my sharpest box cutter before I let you be with my only son. The balls on this cow, so enormous!

MRS. YI: Unni, please.

UMMA: Don't call me Unni, you COW!

MRS. YI: UNNI—you have so much—children that care for you. I'm all alone in the world! With nobody, no family—no children. Husband gone. Have pity on me. Let me have somebody to love. I'll take good care of him. Give him to me.

UMMA: You want my store. You want my son. YOU WANT EVERYTHING THAT'S MINE! NO WAY!

Umma slaps Mrs. Yi.

MRS. YI: (*Coldly.*) You know, we are not so different. You and me. You could have been me. Alone. If your path had been different. Maybe, you don't deserve what you have because you treat your gifts like burdens. If I had what you had, I'd feel such gratitude, as if I had plucked the stars from the firmament.

UMMA: YAH! SHUT UP WITH YOUR BAD POETRY. AND GET OUT OF MY PUCKING STORE! PUCK YOU! PUCK YOU ONE HUNDRED TIMES!!

Umma chases Mrs. Yi out, preferably with a weapon like a broom or a pepperoni stick. Umma is exhausted from the exertion and takes a moment to recover and then speaks to Hannah.

UMMA: I have terrible enemy. That's why I need your help. I know you complain Umma only cares about Jason. Not true. Umma loves you, too.

HANNAH: But you baby him! You're sweet on him. I'm the BABY! I'M THE BABY! Why did you always clip his toenails but not mine?

UMMA: Oh, you want me to clip your toenail? OK, no problem. I do now.

Umma bends over to clip Hannah's toes.

HANNAH: No, I don't really want you to. I just wanted the offer! Why were you always coddling him but not me?

UMMA: I don't know. Custom. You son has to be treated like king in house. Custom. Long time ago, family have to be good to son because they take care parents when old, like pension plan. Daughter, get married to other family and don't make no money. Oh, you know, Jason take care of Umma with money. Pay many bill. He is good son but a little helpless because he has no common sense.

HANNAH: And you just think I'm a stupid, broke loser with no common sense.

UMMA: Hannah-yah. OK, you don't like when I tell you truth so I try to talk to you softer. Not loser, just no ambition.

HANNAH: I wanted to get so far away from you and this shitty place. But I stayed. You know why? I was fucking worried about you being alone.

UMMA: Yeah, I know this. Umma rely on you with f-feelings. You listen with Umma, you help Umma with store. If you don't come help me, I don't pee or eat for 12 hours. Umma don't say but Umma is grateful to have strong daughter like you. Understand, stupid?

HANNAH: You almost said it. You almost said it. Say it.

UMMA: Say what?

HANNAH: Tell me I'm your favorite!

UMMA: Get out of here. You are my favorite daughter.

HANNAH: That's bullshit. Tell me I'm your FAVORITE CHILD.

UMMA: I can't say that. That is terrible.

HANNAH: Fine, forget about BOKE SOO then. You can float here by the cartons of cigs and cases of beer forever. I don't care. I changed my mind. Your love is so conditional. It's gross. I'm not killing Mrs. Yi anymore.

UMMA: Hannah-yah. Listen to me. Please. If you do not do this, I will never rest. I will toil porever in this in hell because my Han will be stuck in my chest. Here. Here. Here. Please, please I beg you. KILL HER FOR ME.

Hannah begins to exit.

UMMA: I didn't leave the store to Jason.

HANNAH: What?

UMMA: I left the store to you in my will. You could run it how you want. You can throw away porno, too, if you want. Since you peminist. But you know, they sell very good. Those ones bestseller. (*Umma gives a thumbs up.*) And you could have a picture of me by the register. Right there. And think of me when you get a hundred-dollar bill. Wait, that is not often. When you get $5 bill.

HANNAH: I thought you'd give the store to Jason. I thought he'd get everything.

UMMA: Jason don't want store. I think you should have it.

HANNAH: Really, Umma? You left me your life's work? Did you leave me the store because I'm your favorite?

UMMA: Aigoo. You stop this now.

HANNAH: I'm your favorite! I'm your favorite! Suck it, Jason!

UMMA: Now you have the store. You need to fight for store. Or Mrs. Yi try to take it. You need to be strong, not stupid weakling. This ALLLLLL yours. Boke soo, Hannah-yah.

HANNAH: But, Umma, I don't know how to kill her.

UMMA: Why you say, "Don't know." It's not so hard. You can take cash register like dis. Over head. Like dis.

HANNAH: Ugh. What about the blood?

UMMA: We have Windex. Oh, what if you shoved her head in deep fryer?! Her face will be crispy like pork belly. Bah-sak bah-sak. HAHA.

HANNAH: Ummm, the police will come, and I'll go to jail.

UMMA: Asian people don't go to jail.

HANNAH: OH, YES, THEY DO.

UMMA: OK. If you go to jail, this is sacrifice you make for your Umma. Raising you was like jail, you know. It's now your turn to do time for your Umma. You young people don't know how to supper enough. (*Beat.*) OK. So, you do dis for Umma?

    Pause.

HANNAH: Fine. OK. I'll do it for you.

    Black out. Sound of alarms sounding.

Scene 8

    Back at the convenience store. Hannah is cutting boxes with a box cutter or cleaning up. Drea enters.

HANNAH: Hey, boo. See? I'm getting better. I didn't scream when you entered. (*Beat.*) What's the matter, dude?

DREA: HANNAH. Seriously. How could you?

HANNAH: COULD WHAT?

DREA: Vandalize Mrs. Yi's shop?

HANNAH: Her shit got vandalized? Good. Wait, you think I did it? I wish I thought of it.

DREA: Hannah, I can't. Do you understand that I am learning the law to be a prosecutor? I don't want to have to prosecute you some day.

HANNAH: God, you sound like a square. DREA. LISTEN. She killed my UMMA. I have evidence. Once a murder happens, what are you supposed to look for in an investigation?

DREA: The weapon.

HANNAH: Yes!

DREA: I thought your mom died of a heart attack. Are we looking for a bacon burger?

HANNAH: NO. Dude, she was murdered.

DREA: But, how do you know this? What is your evidence?

HANNAH: (*Hannah pulls out a dry cleaning bag.*) That's just it. See? It's all stretched out and gross. My mom died in here. That's her lipstick color: Magenta Crush! See?

DREA: Hannah. I really want to be supportive, but this is sounding . . . um. I don't know. Out there.

HANNAH: She told me. My Umma. She came to me.

DREA: She what?

HANNAH: She said Mrs. Yi killed her. With this!

DREA: I don't know, Hannah. I don't know if I should be involved with you in this. This is just too much. I can't.

HANNAH: Wait. Let me show you something. Something I've never shown anybody. When I have a bad day, I bring it out and look at it.

DREA: No. I really don't have time.

HANNAH: Please. Wait. (*Hannah shows Drea a Twix bar hidden in a box.*) Cookies n Crème Twix. Discontinued in 1991. May be the last one left in this state.

DREA: OH SHIT! NO WAY! I remember those! And whatever happened to Crystal Pepsi?

HANNAH: This was totally the BEST FLAVOR EVER. After I ate these— I could face anything. And now is another time of great adversity. I think we should open this and eat it. I want to share my most prized possession with you.

DREA: Gross. It's like over twenty years old. (*Beat.*) God. You're so bad for me. Why can't I resist you?

Drea and Hannah eat the Twix together and kiss.

Scene 9

Later, in the convenience beer cooler. Jason and Mrs. Yi sit together after some lovemaking.

JASON: Do you know, as a kid, this beer cooler was my favorite place in the whole world? I was always such a sweaty kid, so I loved coming in here. I could get away from everybody and just sit here with the malt liquor. Play my Gameboy. And I liked messing with the customers. I could see their big adult hands reaching for a case of beer and I'd be like, "NO! Not that one. THIS ONE'S ON SALE!" I'd shove different cans of beer towards people. And I'd try to stick my little hand out and shake their hands. It was like the other side was a different world and I was in a frozen fortress where no one could touch me. And now, I'm with you, right here in my favorite place. And, damn, Candy. It's 38 degrees up in this cooler, but with you here, it feels like I'm in a mouth of a volcano.

MRS. YI: Oh, stop being so vulgar. I feel you don't treat me respectfully. Is it because you are finished with me, finally? Be honest.

JASON: OH Mrs. YI—We've only just begun—

MRS. YI: Candy. I told you. Candy. How many times do I have to tell you?

JASON: Candy, my sah-rang. What's the matter? We just made sweet love. Why are you upset? I tried that thing you asked me to do. I looked up. I thought it was better this time.

MRS. YI: Don't touch me. I hate this place!

JASON: Well, let's go. You hungry? Shall I buy my baby a cheesesteak?

MRS. YI: No. You know, someone vandalized my store? Broke my window!

JASON: Yeah, I saw that. Probably some dumbass kids. Sorry, Candy.

MRS. YI: Glass everywhere. I cut myself cleaning it up. Jason, I think it was Hannah.

JASON: Hannah couldn't do that! She's a little weird and high strung but she isn't, like, violent.

MRS. YI: (*Crying.*) Why does she hate me? I only try to be good to her. She is so cruel! She tries to crush our happiness like a trash compactor.

JASON: Give her time. I just think she's just weirded out that we're, like, dating.

MRS. YI: DATING. Oh, is that what this is?

JASON: Yeah, you're my ladyyyyyyyy. And I'm your maaaaaannnnn. What more do you want?

MRS. YI: You know what I want: a guarantee.

JASON: What kind of guarantee?

MRS. YI: That you care about me.

JASON: Once you taste this bomb-ass cheesesteak I'm gonna buy you, you'll KNOW I love you. Much SAH-RANG HAE, CANDY! Aww, come on. You know I care.

MRS. YI: You do?

JASON: Mos def.

MRS. YI: How do I know?

JASON: Feel here.

Jason places Mrs. Yi's hand on his heart.

MRS. YI: What?

JASON: DO you feel my love?

MRS. YI: No, I don't.

Jason slides Mrs. Yi's hand lower, closer towards his crotch.

MRS. YI: Now, I definitely feel nothing.

JASON: Now that hurts my feelings. As an Asian man, I feel like you are just perpetuating harmful stereotypes.

MRS. YI: Stop Jason! Stop with the jokes! I don't care if this is your favorite place. I don't want to do it here. Or the parking lot. Or on my new steam ironing board. I want to be in a nice bed, nice place. Like Holiday Inn. Or in a bedroom. Any bedroom. You know, you treat me like an old meatball that you toss around in an alleyway! And I know you're just going to throw me away when you're done. And I will feel the pain of being alone, YET AGAIN.

Mrs. Yi begins to cry loudly.

JASON: Oh, Candy, baby. I love you.

MRS. YI: You do?

JASON: Believe me. I want to be emotionally available to you. Not like my appah who didn't know how to give hugs and bounced when shit got hard. I want to be like the noo roong jee on your rice pot. I, like, want to be up on you, like, forever.

MRS. YI: You do?

JASON: No lie. I do. Wait here.

Jason comes back with a Twinkie with a lit candle stuck in it or a can of Diet Coke.

JASON: Candy-shee. Will you marry me? Be my yobo?

MRS. YI: Ask me in Korean.

JASON: Um. OK. Candy-shee, HA JA!

MRS. YI: You just said let's do it.

JASON: Yeah, let's get married.

MRS. YI: This doesn't feel very proper. Why don't you kids learn Korean properly? It's a shame.

JASON: Damn, not again. Look, when I first came to the states I kept getting beat up in school for being in ESL. So, I studied my ass off, so I could be in regular classes. But now I catch hell from Koreans for not being able to speak. Hey, why don't you teach me? Teach me how to say it.

MRS. YI: 저랑 결혼해 주시겠어요? Chuh rang kyol-hone hae joo shee geh suh yo?

JASON: What?

MRS. YI: 저랑 결혼해 주시겠어요? Chuh rang kyol-hone hae joo shee geh suh yo?

JASON: One more time.

MRS. YI: Aissh! Never mind. This will take forever. I'll pretend you did it properly. (*Beat.*) This is wonderful. Now finally, I have the son I always wanted.

JASON: WOAH! Son? I'm not your son! Um . . . you mean husband!

MRS. YI: Son, husband. What's the difference? Both require you to cook, clean, and fetch remote controls. HA! Let's get married!

A fantasy wedding commences. Chorus enters to assist with the ceremony. They enter and bring wedding clothes, such as a jokduri, made of convenience store materials and candy. They place red dots on Mrs. Yi's cheeks and forehead as part of the wedding make-up, and the dots can be price stickers instead of the traditional paint.

CHORUS 1: We welcome you to the joyous wedding of Jason-ah and Mrs. Yi-slash-Candy. Jason-ah, do you take Mrs. Yi-slash-Candy to be your lawfully wedded wife?

JASON: I do.

CHORUS 1: And do you, Mrs. Yi-slash-Candy take Jason to be your lawfully wedded husband?

MRS. YI: I do. But where are the rings?

Jason pulls a soda ring out of his pocket. Jason puts it on Mrs. Yi's finger.

MRS. YI: Aigoooo. Is this a pop can ring?

JASON: Umm, yes? But diamond later.

MRS. YI: You mean diamondssssssss. I expect diamondssssss later. Diamondssssssss.

JASON: Yeah, when I get another job. Hey, does this mean you're an ajumma again?

She hits his arm playfully. They kiss like you do in western style weddings. Then take a moment before they bow to each other, in the manner of a traditional Korean wedding ceremony. The Chorus bows at the same time. Mrs. Yi and Jason may drink box wine or cheap wine out a gourd or Diet Coke ceremoniously.

CHORUS 1: And so, Jason-ah and Mrs. Yi-slash-Candy were wed.

In place of rice, the Chorus unenthusiastically throws corn nuts or other convenience food in the air and exits.

MRS. YI: Now you have the store. We can combine the properties to create one large green dry cleaner. You know, like the reunification of Korea— TONG-IL! Our hearts were divided like this land, and now we will have TONG-IL.

JASON: Huh, how interesting. Combining lands . . .

MRS. YI: You don't mind, do you? I know you are embarrassed by the store. And you know they are getting rid of the discount grocery and they gonna put in a Whole Foods in a few years. Just wait. The neighborhood is going to change, you know? Having green-eco-friendly business will be good for the environment and your health. And since being green is so popular now, maybe we sell it for more profit later. Who knows? Isn't it a beautiful idea? A plan for greatness?

JASON: Only, I don't get the store. Hannah gets the store.

MRS. YI: Uh, what did you say?

Scene 10

At the dry cleaners. Mrs. Yi is closing. Hannah sneaks up on her. Mrs. Yi sees her, and Hannah sprays Windex in her face. Mrs. Yi screams and covers her face. Hannah takes a bottle of 40 and poises it over Mrs. Yi's head. Suddenly, police lights flash across their faces.

Scene 11

Sound of jail doors slamming. Lights up on Hannah talking on a jail payphone to Drea, who is on her cell at the store.

HANNAH: I've been calling and calling. Why didn't you pick up?

DREA: My phone died. It's charged now.

HANNAH: Where are you?

DREA: At your mom's store, checking up on things.

HANNAH: I get the sense you're avoiding me.

DREA: Well, umm, no. But now maybe you've come to your senses.

HANNAH: What do you mean?

DREA: Well, now you can stop with this revenge plot.

HANNAH: Are you kidding? No way. This was just a hiccup. That bitch, YI, was just one step ahead of me somehow. How did she get the cops to come? But she won't see me strike next time. I'm gonna boke soo so hard. (*Beat.*) Well, on the upside, at least I didn't get charged. God. When they brought me in, one cop fucking laughed at me. He was like: "What did you do little girl? Cheat on your math test?" I'll show those MOFOs what a nice Korean girl is capable of.

DREA: Hannah. Please I'll do whatever it takes. I'll quit school. We can move in together, start our life now. We don't have to wait. Please just let this revenge business go.

HANNAH: Stop being so fucking clingy and patronizing. I know what I am doing!

DREA: What's left if I don't cling on?

HANNAH: We're not like official or anything. And besides, I need to focus right now. I'm sorry that sounds harsh. (*Beat.*) Hey, please just come and get me. And can you bring me a cheeseburger? There is like no food at jail.

DREA: What do you need to focus on, exactly?

HANNAH: What's really important: family.

DREA: As in, not me? Aren't we like a family?

HANNAH: No. Not really. We aren't blood.

DREA: OWWW.

HANNAH: Ugh.

DREA: Pain here. It feels like I'm dying—

HANNAH: Don't.

DREA: Inside.

HANNAH: Stop. Please just come get me.

DREA: Love is a fucking degradation.

HANNAH: What's that supposed to mean?

DREA: You can only see that I love you when I degrade myself. I'm just your servant. Your donkey. Go here. Pick me up. Do this. Spy on my neighbor. Bring me a cheeseburger.

HANNAH: That's not true. Drea, get it together. I need you to be on my side now. I know I've been difficult, but I'm under a lot of stress: physical and metaphysical stress. PLEASE, stand by my side while I defend my family honor.

DREA: I called the cops on you.

HANNAH: You fucking did what?

DREA: That's why you went to jail overnight. I told cops to check out the dry cleaners when I saw you go over there.

HANNAH: What? WHY?

DREA: I was doing my job, Hannah. Detect. Deter. Observe. And then, it got so bad I had to report. Report you: the love my life. Mrs. Yi told me you busted her window and she's scared of you. And then, when I saw you go over there again, I was forced to report you.

HANNAH: But I didn't bust her fucking window. How many times do I have to tell you? It was her. Wait, you were spying on me? You spied on me and not her? It's true, we live a police state!

DREA: You have to believe I felt so sick after I did it. I threw up in class. But I couldn't have you go to prison for something much worse. Like murder. What if you killed an innocent person?

HANNAH: Mrs. Yi is not INNOCENT

DREA: You need help. You need a lot of help.

HANNAH: She killed Umma. She needs to die. And now I can't fucking trust you. Umma was right. You can't trust anyone but family.

DREA: Hannah, don't do this!

HANNAH: I don't need you anymore. Don't ever talk to me again. I see now loving you means hating myself. And no more of that now. K BYE.

DREA: Stop it! Hannah, you're all I have. I can't concentrate because of you. You're all I can think about. I worry about you so much that I can't study or pass my tests. I'm flunking law school! I love you.

HANNAH: I don't care. Goodbye.

DREA: If you leave, I'll have to drown myself in this nasty ass mop bucket.

HANNAH: GO AHEAD! I DON'T CARE! I NEED YOU LIKE I NEED ECZEMA!

She hangs up. Drea gets a mop bucket and sticks her head in it. She dies.

Scene 12

Hannah and Jason are back at the convenience store. Umma is present but not immediately noticed.

HANNAH: Thanks again for getting me out of jail, bro.

JASON: Oh, you know, we family. I hope now we can begin to mend this shit between us.

HANNAH: I realized I really had no one else to call except you, Oppah. Hey, I really appreciate you being there for me, like this.

They hug. Jason breaks away suddenly.

JASON: Fuck! I forgot. You're supposed to eat this raw tofu.

Jason carefully unwraps tofu wrapped in fabric and offers it to her.

HANNAH: What the hell for?

JASON: Dummy, you're supposed to eat raw tofu when you get out jail.

HANNAH: I don't understand the correlations between soybeans and the criminal IN-justice system.

JASON: Shut up and take a bite.

HANNAH: No!

JASON: Do what your Oppah tells you to do for once. I just picked your ass up from jail.

HANNAH: No, I want to know why.

JASON: Fine. Let me look it up. OK.

Chorus enters as Google Search Results.

CHORUS ALL: Here are some theories:

CHORUS 2: ONE: feeding tofu is correlated with Japanese colonization of Korea when Korean prisoners were starved terribly. Family members wanted to give ex-prisoners something nutritious, like tofu, as soon as they got out.

CHORUS 1: The color of tofu—white—represents purity.

CHORUS 3: OK, from AskaKorean.blogspot: "In her essay titled Tofu (Doo boo) famed novelist Park Wan-Seo wrote that eating tofu represents a transformation. As tofu is the liberated spirit of beans, one also wishes one's criminal spirit is likewise . . ."[1]

CHORUS ALL: "TRANSFORMED." FORMED-FORMED-FORMED-FORMED.

HANNAH: But, I don't want to be transformed. I'm making my own fucking justice.

JASON: I need you to stop being um, unhinged. I need you to start being hinged. I didn't want to get you. I thought you should stay in jail for what you did. You really could have hurt Candy, my wife. And she convinced me to pick you up because she considers you a sister now and she—

HANNAH: WOAH. That murderous, treacherous bitch is your wife?! Oh god. What's the matter with you? Don't you know you she's trying to steal everything from us? Wait, she told you to get me? Why would she do that?

JASON: (*Jason is eating some tofu.*) This is not so bad. Kind of refreshing, really.

Jason goes to town on the tofu, eating at least half of it. He sets it down. Mrs. Yi enters.

HANNAH: And the murderess enters. Hello, murderess.

MRS. YI: Hannah-yah. I didn't kill your Umma. I swear.

HANNAH: I'm gonna cut you up like a seafood pancake. I'll skewer you like a squid for grilling.

Hannah pulls out the dry cleaning bag.

HANNAH: Recognize this? You killed mom with this. See the lipstick stains? Nobody wears this color except my Umma. She died in here and now, I'm going to use it on you.

JASON: What's going on, Candy?

MRS. YI: I didn't want—I—I. I didn't really kill her!

JASON: What did you say?

HANNAH: Yeah, what did you say?

MRS. YI: She really had a heart attack.

HANNAH: Don't talk about my mother's heart, you whale. You endangered whale. Admit that you did it and maybe I'll make it hurt less when I kill you.

---

1. "Tofu after Prison," Ask a Korean! (blog). March 8, 2014, http://askakorean.blogspot.com/2014/03/tofu-after-prison.html

MRS. YI: She died in front of me. But I didn't actually kill her!

JASON: What do you mean? What the fuck do you mean?!

HANNAH: How do you explain the bag then? (*Beat.*) Whatever, I don't need to know the minutiae. You die now.

MRS. YI: Alright! Alright! You have to believe me when I say I only came over to talk to her. But she couldn't be reasoned with. She called me a—

MRS. YI AND UMMA: A WHORE BITCHEE.

MRS. YI: I got so angry. I don't know how, but I put the bag over her face. I was killing her. Then I realized what I was doing. I took the bag off. But, by then, she was so worked up. She got a heart attack. Maybe from high blood pressure. Anyway, I just froze. I didn't help her. I couldn't. So, I just watched her face turn pale like ash. And die.

JASON: But why? Why would you do that? I don't understand. Was it some kind of sick voyeuristic thing? My god, she must have been suffering and you just stood there? Did you enjoy it?

MRS. YI: No. But.

JASON: But what?

MRS. YI: My love, don't you see? This is a sacrifice that I made so that we could be together. She didn't want us to be together.

JASON: Umma knew about us?

MRS. YI: She said she would turn you against me, Jason. She said you would never be with me if she opposed it because you were such a hyo jah— you always did what she wanted.

UMMA: Look at her ugly face—like a pork bun left in the steamer too long. Can't stand looking at it.

MRS. YI: Jason. Jason. Look at me.

JASON: I can't. I can't look at you.

MRS. YI: Not too long ago, you said you loved me. What's changed?

JASON: You killed my fucking Umma.

MRS. YI: Maybe I wanted too much. I wanted the kingdom and you. Please tell me one thing.

HANNAH: God, this is SO BORING! Jason, let me kill her.

JASON: Tell you what?

MRS. YI: Would you have defied your Umma to be with me? If she told you to cast me aside?

JASON: I feel kind of dizzy. Hannah, I don't feel so good.

MRS. YI: Oh, Jason. You bah-boh-ya, Jason! Why?! Why did you eat the doo boo? It wasn't for you!

JASON: Candyyyyyy . . .

> *Jason dies.*

HANNAH: Now you have killed my whole family.

UMMA: MY JASON! KILL HER, HANNAH-YAH!

MRS. YI: He wasn't supposed to die! YOU were supposed to die!

UMMA: DO IT FOR UMMA!

UMMA AND CHORUS: DO IT!

Quickly, Hannah and Mrs. Yi fight as Umma and Chorus watch. Hannah and Mrs. Yi force-feed the tofu to each other. Hannah uses the dry cleaning bag to suffocate Mrs. Yi. In any case, Mrs. Yi dies. Umma comes down to the floor and cradles Hannah's head in her lap.

UMMA: Good job. Now we got boke soo. I can take some vacation. Remember, Hannah-yah, Umma loves you like you are most precious jewel in her heart. Understand, bah-boh-ya?

CHORUS 1: Then . . .

CHORUS 2: The whole strip mall

CHORUS 3: Bursts into giant flames

CHORUS ALL: (*Unenthusiastically*) Everyone dies.

Lights shift. Chorus exits.

UMMA: There was biiiiig fire. All dis, gone. Because of you know, Han. No English word is same. Is like, suppering, angry, sad peeling STUCK in your ma-uhm. No way out. When too much my han, buried in da mall make everything blow up, go BOOM. Burn everything. Anyway. So bitchee Mrs. Yi was right: Whole Poods coming in here. And you know, this spot where store burn? Whole Poods put in cold case and they sell bullshit organic kimchee in bullshit recycled jar. You know how muchee they sell dis? $25! Can you beliebe this? Before I was so scared white people customers get angry if they smell my kimchee in my store so I wrap in two plastic bags very, very tight. Like dis. Now berry popular. Before, people ask me "Why is Korean food so spicy?" I say, because we know pain. Then they ask, "Why is Korean food so salty?" Because da salt preserve our pain. We all die, but you know, now we together again.

END OF PLAY

GLOSSARY OF KOREAN TERMS

-Ah 아	Informal suffix added to a name, never should be used for an elder or your boss. Usually used to call someone—i.e. "Jason-ah! Come here."
Ahn young hah sae yo 안녕하세요	"Hello, how are you." A greeting that's formal and respectful.
Ahn young 안녕	"Hi." Less formal, only said to people you're close to.
Aigoo 아이고	"Oh my," some times with a tinge of frustrated dissatisfaction or irritation.
Aissh! 아이씨	An interjection used to display frustration or anger, perceived as swearing by some.
Ajumma 아줌마	Term to describe a woman who is grown, sometimes with some pejorative connotations about age. Contextually, it can also be used as a term of endearment. For example, you may call your friend's mother ajumma, as a sign of respect and closeness.
Appah 아빠	Dad
Bap 밥	Rice, or could mean any meal (informal usage)
Bah-boh 바보	Dummy
Bah-sak Bah-sak 빠싹빠싹	Onomatopoeic word to convey a crispy sound
Boke soo 복수	Revenge
Bole-yume 볼륨	Korean pronunciation of "volume"
Chigae 찌개	Korean stew
Dae wang ma-mah 대왕마마	Your great majesty
Dae 대	Big or great
Dol sot bi bim bap 돌솥비빔밥	A type of rice dish with mixed vegetables and beef served in a heated stone bowl.
Doo boo 두부	Tofu

Dwipuri 뒤풀이	A party or celebration usually involving drinking to mark a victory or survival.
Ee lee wah 이리와	"Come here."
Golp ooh ahk sah raee 골프악세사리	Korean pronunciation of "golf accessories"
Go seng 고생	Suffering
Guh-lae gat un nyun 걸레같은 년	Extra bad cursing, literally meaning rag-like whore or bitch.
Guh-lae 걸레	Rag; when used to describe someone, it is a very bad word, usually toward women, like whore.
Ha ja! 하자	"Let's do it!"
Han 한	Unresolved grief or rage
Hyo jah 효자	Filial respectful son, word rooted in Confucianism
Hyo nyo 효녀	Filial respectful daughter
Jang nam 장남	Eldest son
Jokduri 족두리	Korean bridal crown
Junk food, eeh jee? 이지	"It's junk food, huh?"
Chuh rang kyol-hone hae joo shee geh suh yo? 저랑 결혼해 주시겠어요	"Would you marry me," said respectfully, with formality.
Kyol-hone ha ja 결혼하자	"Let's get married." (informal usage)
Kkool kkool ee juk 꿀꿀이죽	Porridge made from army base garbage
Kkool kkool 꿀꿀	Onomatopoeic word to convey a sound that a pig makes
Ma-uhm 마음	Heart, feelings, or one's will
Moh? 뭐	"What?"

Muk jee ma lah 먹지마라	"Don't eat it!" (In the play's context, it's more like: "FINE! DON'T EAT IT, THEN!")
Neber 네버	Korean pronunciation of "never"
Noon 눈	Eye(s)
Noo roong jee 누룽지	The crispy browned layer of rice stuck on the bottom of a rice pot.
Nuh moo jae soo up suh 너무새수없어	Literally means having "no luck" or "no fortune." It can also be used as a curse (욕) towards another person— So saying someone has no 새수 means that interacting with that person is unpleasant to the point where it is comparable to any "unlucky" situation, like stepping on dog shit.
Nyun 년	Bitch
Oh-Mo 어머	"Oh my," or, "Oh no," to show some surprise. Usually seen as a feminine phrase.
Oppah 오빠	Older brother, usually said by females
Pansori 판소리	Type of traditional Korean folk music, with some elements that sound like spoken word.
Porever 포애버	Korean pronunciation of "forever"
Sah-jang-nim 사장님	President of a company or boss
Sah-rang 사랑	Love
-shee -씨	Suffix added to name to show respect
Shee-jak 시작	Start
Sung-oon ee mahng kup ha nai dah 성은이 망극하나이다	"Your divine favor shines greatly upon me." This is usually said as a form of formal address to royalty.
Suppering 서퍼링	Korean pronunciation of "suffering"
Tong-il 통일	Reunification of the Korean peninsula

Uh-suh 어서	"Come on, do it!" only said to your equals, subordinates, or to people beneath you, like your children as a command of sorts. Never to people who are you are elders or in higher status.
Umma 엄마	Mom (pronounced UM-mah) (NOT pronounced: OOH-MAH or Uma Thurman)
Uh-moh-nee 어머니	Mother (more deferential than mom or umma)
Uh yoo, neh hyeol ee ap ohl lah! 어유,내혈앞이올아!	"Oh, my blood pressure is rising!"
Ung or Mm 응	Like "yeah" or a grunt in the affirmative, like "Mm-hmm, yes."
Unni 언니	Older sister, usually only said by females.
Wang bee 왕비	Queen
Wang 왕	King
Wen soo 웬수	Mortal enemy in dialect variation of won soo (원수). It is often used with individuals your closer with. i.e. your wife, husband, partner, and children.
Wen soo bah gah jee 웬수 바가지	Mortal enemy in dialect variation of won soo (원수) often used with individuals you're closer with. i.e. your wife, husband, partner, and children. Bah gah jee (바가지) is a bucket or scoop, usually made out of a gourd. The two words together "Wen soo bah gah jee" (웬수 바가지) means "full of enemy," and or "You are so annoying" or "You are such a problem that it's like you're my enemy."
Won soo 원수	Mortal enemy
Won soo uhl gahp uh rah! 원수을갚아라	"Make your enemy suffer!" or "Pay back your enemy!"
-Yah -야	Suffix added to someone you feel close to, who is younger than you or your equal. Like "-shee" but much more informal.
Yah! 아!	Can also mean "Hey!" or "Yo!" But used very informally—never say "yah" to address a superior or elder unless you're trying to start a fight.
Yam chay jee? 얌체 지	"Aren't they a shameless, shady person, huh?" A yam chay is a shady person.

APPENDIX: PRODUCTION INFORMATION

TERRA INCOGNITA premiered at Annex Theatre in Seattle, Washington, July 29 – August 20, 2016. Directed by Pilar O'Connell, dramaturgy by Gavin Reub, choreography by Alyza DelPan-Monley, costume design by Wanda Rodriguez, lighting design by Ranleigh Starling, scenic design by Mary Ann Keeney, sound design by Chris Leher and Shane Regan, projection design by Leo Mayberry, props by Brendan Mack, puppet design by Ben Burris, stage management by Andrew Hunter.

Angel – Eva Estrada Campos
Nadia – Lillian Afful-Straton
Sheila – Gretchen Douma
X. / Simon – Jordan-Michael Whidbey

NADESHIKO was produced by Sound Theatre Company and premiered at the Center Theatre in Seattle, Washington, April 13 – May 7, 2017. Directed by Kaytlin McIntyre, assistant directed by Francesca Betancourt, costume design by Hannah Larson, lighting design by Richard Schaefer, set design by Catherine Cornell, sound design by Dana Amromin, projection design by MJ Sieber and Luke Walker, props design by Brandon Estrella, Wendy Hansen, dialect coaching by Marianna deFazio, stage management by Laura Owens, assisted by Malie Fujii.

Risa – Maile Wong
White-Haired Man – Greg Lyle-Newton
Nadeshiko – Ina Chang
Sue / Shoko – Mi Kang
Toshio – Josh Kenji

NADESHIKO was developed within the Seattle Repertory Theatre Writers Group, with additional developmental assistance from the Umbrella Project.

ROZ AND RAY premiered at Seattle Repertory Theatre, Braden Abraham, Artistic Director, Jeffrey Herrmann, Managing Director, October 14 – November 13, 2016. Directed by Chay Yew, set design by Tim Mackabee, costume design by Rose Pederson, lighting design by Geoff Korf, original music and sound design by Christopher Kriz , dramaturgy by Kristin Leahy, Ph.D, stage management by Erin B. Zatlotka, assistant direction by Lia Fakhouri.

Dr. Roz Kagan - Ellen McLaughlin
Ray Leon - Teagle F. Bougere

ROZ AND RAY co-premiered at Victory Gardens Theater in Chicago, Illinois, Chay Yew, Artistic Director, November 11 – December 11, 2016. The direction and design team were the same, with the following exceptions: costume design by Christine Pascual, lighting design by Diane D. Fairchild, dramaturgy by Isaac Gomez, stage management by Amanda J. Davis, assistant direction by Arianna Soloway.

Dr. Roz Kagan - Mary Beth Fisher
Ray Leon - James Vincent Meredith

ROZ AND RAY was commissioned and developed with support from The Playwrights' Center's McKnight Commission and Residency Program, Minneapolis, MN, and was also supported by Hedgebrook, The Alley All New Festival, the Seattle Repertory Theatre Writers Group, and an Edgerton Foundation New Play Award.

BO-NITA premiered at the Seattle Repertory Theatre in Seattle, Washington, October 18 – November 17, 2013. Directed by Paul Budraitis, scenic design by Jennifer Zeyl, costume design by Harmony Arnold, lighting design by Robert J. Aguilar, sound design by Matt Starritt, video design by Leo Mayberry, dialect/vocal coach: Judith Shahn, stage management by Cristine Anne Reynolds.

Bo-Nita – Hannah Mootz
Understudy to Bo-Nita – Kayla Lian

SOUND premiered at Azeotrope/ACT Lab in Seattle, Washington, September 11 – October 4, 2015. Directed by Desdemona Chiang and Howie Seago, assistant directed by Jessica Kiely, costume design by Christine Tschirgi, lighting design by Jessica Trundy, set design by Adam Zopfi-Hulse, sound design by Mariah Brougher, video design by AJ Epstein, stage management by Sarah Dale Lewis.

George – Ryan Schlecht
Barbara – Lindsay D. Evans
Allison – Cheyenna Clearbrook
Alexander Graham Bell – Richard Nguyen Sloniker
Mabel / Ensemble Liz Gibson – Mabel / Ensemble
Mr. Pease / Voice of George / Ensemble – Andrew Wilkes
Therapist / Voice of Barbara / Ensemble – Jessica Kiely
Audiologist / Voice of Allison / Ensemble – Stephanie Kim

DO IT FOR UMMA premiered at Annex Theatre in Seattle, Washington, February 2 – 17, 2016. Directed by Sara Porkalob, costume design by Corinne Magin, lighting design by Emily Leong, set design by Emily Sershon, sound design by Erin Bednarz, stage management by Haley Kellogg.

Hannah – Skye Stephenson
Umma – Ina Chang
Jason – Christian Ver
Mrs. Yi – Maggie Lee
Drea – Katie Driscoll
Chorus – Laura Dux
Chorus – Anna Saephan
Chorus – Corinne Magin

Lauren Yee

Lauren Yee's recent plays include *Cambodian Rock Band* (South Coast Rep), *The Great Leap* (Denver Center, Seattle Rep, and Atlantic Theatre Company), *King of the Yees* (Goodman Theatre, Center Theatre Group, ACT Theatre, Canada's National Arts Centre/Gateway Theatre). Other plays include *Ching Chong Chinaman* (Pan Asian, Mu Performing Arts), *The Hatmaker's Wife* (Playwrights Realm, Moxie, PlayPenn), *Hookman* (Encore, Company One), *In a Word* (SF Playhouse, Cleveland Public, Strawdog), *Samsara* (Victory Gardens, O'Neill Conference, Bay Area Playwrights Festival), and *The Tiger Among Us* (MAP Fund, Mu). Recent awards: Kesselring Prize, Francesca Primus Prize. Member of the Ma-Yi Writers' Lab, Playwrights Realm alumni playwright. Current commissions: Geffen Playhouse, La Jolla Playhouse, Lincoln Center/LCT3, Mixed Blood, Portland Center Stage, and Trinity Rep. BA: Yale. MFA: UCSD. www.laurenyee.com.

27828399R00167

Made in the USA
Columbia, SC
03 October 2018